JACK
THE RIPPER'S
BLACK MAGIC
RITUALS

'The most intelligent of people
are not necessarily the wisest.'

In memory of George and Olwyn Edwards
and Kevin Edwards.

Dedicated to Emily Edwards.

JACK THE RIPPER'S

BLACK MAGIC RITUALS

IVOR EDWARDS

JOHN BLAKE

Published by John Blake Publishing Ltd, 3 Bramber Court,
2 Bramber Road, London W14 9PB, England

First published in hardback in 2002

ISBN 1 904034 27 6

British Library Cataloguing-in-Publication Data: A catalogue record for this book is
available from the British Library.

Design by ENVY

Printed and bound in Great Britain by CPD (Wales)

1 3 5 7 9 10 8 6 4 2

Papers used by John Blake Publishing Ltd are natural, recyclable products made from
wood grown in sustainable forests. The manufacturing processes conform to the
environmental regulations of the country of origin.

Every attempt has been made to contact the relevant copyright-holders, but some
were unobtainable. We would be grateful if the appropriate people could contact us.

The publisher acknowledges the claim of Mr Melvin Harris to be a primary source of certain
material contained in this book. Mr Harris is the author of *Jack the Ripper: The Bloody Truth,
The Ripper File* and *The True Face of Jack the Ripper*.

CONTENTS

INTRODUCTION 7

CHAPTER 1

HOW IT ALL STARTED 11

CHAPTER 2

A BRIEF HISTORY OF LONDON 15

CHAPTER 3

THE FIRST VICTIM 25

CHAPTER 4

THE SECOND VICTIM 35

CHAPTER 5

THE THIRD VICTIM 45

CHAPTER 6

THE FOURTH VICTIM 67

CHAPTER 7

THE FIFTH VICTIM 103

CHAPTER 8

ANALYSIS OF THE DEATH SITES 123

CHAPTER 9

JACK THE RIPPER'S OCCULT PLANS
FOR THE WHITECHAPEL MURDERS 137

CHAPTER 10

RIPPER MYTH AND INACCURACY 151

CHAPTER 11

WHO WAS JACK THE RIPPER 161

CHAPTER 12

A CLASSIC CASE OF MISHANDLING
BY POLICE AND PRESS 197

CHAPTER 13

THE REAL STORY OF JACK THE RIPPER 205

APPENDICES

APPENDIX 1

D'ONSTON'S CHRONOLOGY AND
OFFICIAL RECORDS 245

APPENDIX 2

MAP-READING MADMAN 251

APPENDIX 3

GENERAL INFORMATION ON
SACRED GEOMETRY AND VESICA PISCIS 255

APPENDIX 4

THE ORIGINS OF OCCULT INTIMIDATION
AND TERROR TACTICS 263

APPENDIX 5

PRESENT DAY OCCULT
RITUAL MURDER 267

INTRODUCTION

UNTIL IVOR EMAILED me about his discoveries relating to the Jack the Ripper murders, it had never occured to me that these events might be occult in nature. Ivor referred me to his publisher's website, which briefly described his work and its relationship to sacred geometry. He wrote to me in response to seeing my website, which relates sacred geometry to the human form.

My work grew out of an analysis of the Vesica Piscis, an ancient geometric symbol which has been used to express both natural principles and notions of Christian theology. Ivor also pointed out a reference to 'The Bubble Universe', a concept recently developed as a result of observations in astronomy. The Bubble Universe refers to the formation of galaxies within structures common to intersecting spherical energy wavefronts (which have a diameter of millions of light years).

The Vesica Piscis is formed by two intersecting circles that share a common radius, and it is perhaps the primary two-dimensional image of sacred geometry (the branch of numerology and geometry that describes the distribution of elements in three dimensions). The Golden Mean, Pi and other mathematical constants are a natural consequence of the properties of three-dimensional space, and these constants are an integral part of the lexicon of sacred geometry. This geometry is sacred by virtue of the way the deity constructed three dimensions, thereby generating a set of geometric and numerical ratios and constants.

When I read that Ivor discovered the Vesica Piscis as the geometric pattern overlying the location of the victims of Jack the Ripper, I realised that this symbol could be used to express both the good and evil in humans – a true reflection of human nature. The fact that these locations drew not only a Vesica Piscis and nested Vesicas (including a cross oriented to the cardinal directions), but also the profile of the Great Pyramid and other occult symbols is evidence that the murders were rooted in black magic ritual. As the facts relating to the five murders are now presented by Ivor Edwards, it becomes evident that the occult connection must have been the prime motive, and this dramatically narrows the search for the identity of the killer.

This book is the result of nine years of full-time research. It focuses on the motive, planning and execution of the murders, and concludes with the naming of a suspect that had escaped serious scrutiny by the London Police due to their less comprehensive investigation. The evidence that Ivor Edwards has collected and presented reveals an astonishing confluence of facts supporting a most convincing case about the possible motive behind Jack the Ripper's murders.

The locations of the murders comprise key points forming a cross, a Nazi symbol and a parallelogram on the map of London. These points orientate towards the cardinal directions and fall on positions that define that most ancient of geometric mystical symbols – the Vesica Piscis. Such symbols have been used throughout the history of the occult by secret societies, for good as well as evil purposes.

Included in this book as part of the investigation into the murders are:

POLICE RECORDS

NEWSPAPER ARTICLES

KNOWN RECORDS OF VICTIMS AND SUSPECTS INVOLVED

INTRODUCTION

METHODS OF THE MURDERS

WEAPONS USED

NATURE OF THE MUTILATIONS

BODY PARTS TAKEN FROM THE VICTIMS

MARKINGS ON THE BODIES

NATURE OF OCCULT RITUALS

HISTORY OF OCCULT MURDERS

NATURE OF OCCULT MURDERS

NATURE OF OCCULT SYMBOLS

MESSAGES AND MATERIALS LEFT BY THE MURDERER

LINGUISTIC CLUES

NATURE OF THE VICTIM'S LOCATIONS AND THE ENVIRONMENT
OF EACH MURDER SITE

POSITIONS OF THE CORPSES

THE SURGICAL SKILL OF THE MURDERER AS NOTED IN THE
POST-MORTEM EXAM

OTHER MEDICAL EVIDENCE

THE TIMEFRAME OF OPPORTUNITY FOR THE MURDERS

WALKING TIMES OF PROBABLE ROUTES TO AND FROM THE
CRIME SCENES

THE MEASURED DISTANCES BETWEEN THE VICTIMS

HISTORY OF SERIAL KILLERS

On the basis of these investigations, Ivor has identified the most probable suspect, who was questioned twice by the police and released due to lack of evidence. The additional information and evidence documented here leaves little doubt in my mind that this case has at last been solved. The evidence and other facts that relate to this one particular suspect include:

HIS PERSONAL HISTORY AND CHRONOLOGY

HIS SURGICAL EXPERIENCE AND KNOWLEDGE

HIS INTELLIGENCE AND STEALTH

HIS KNOWLEDGE OF THE OCCULT AS REVEALED IN WRITINGS
AND ASSOCIATIONS

HIS ANALYSIS OF THE MESSAGE LEFT BY THE KILLER TO TAUNT
  THE POLICE

HIS HISTORY OF ASSOCIATIONS WITH PROSTITUTES

HIS WRITINGS FOR OCCULT PUBLICATIONS

HIS TRAVEL TO THE WEST COAST OF AFRICA TO STUDY
  MAGICAL CULTS

HIS LOCATION IN THE WHITECHAPEL AREA DURING
  THE TIME OF THE MURDERS

HIS ABILITY TO LEAVE AND RETURN WITHOUT DETECTION
  DURING THE MURDERS

HIS SIZE, AGE AND GENERAL DESCRIPTION AS
  REPORTED BY POSSIBLE WITNESSES

THE STATEMENTS BY THOSE WHO KNEW THE SUSPECT

THE MOTIVE OF REVENGE OF AN INFECTION PASSED TO
  HIM BY A PROSTITUTE

THE ADDITIONAL MOTIVE OF REVENGE FOR LOSING
  HIS JOB AS A RESULT OF THE INFECTION

By trying to understand the motivation behind the planning and execution of these murders, as revealed by evidence comprising police reports, newspaper accounts and other public records, Ivor has found new evidence of a motive relating to the occult. He has then compared these findings to the background and personal information of the one 'closest fit' suspect in order, finally, to identify Jack the Ripper.

Prof Charles R. Henry,

Virginia Commonwealth University, Richmond, VA, USA

How it all Started

MY INTEREST IN the Whitechapel murders was aroused during 1963, after reading my first book on the subject. However, my curiosity did not lie with who the killer may have been, but rather with why he committed the crimes. Serious research commenced during 1993 after viewing a Thames Television programme entitled *Crime Monthly*. The programme laid the blame for the murders at the feet of a poor Polish Jew named Kosminski. When this man was placed in the frame I thought of the old verse:

Oh, it's the same the whole world over,
And isn't it a shame,
It's the rich that get the pleasure,
And the poor that get the blame.

I did not know at the time how true these words were to ring. For the very idea of the killer being a lone, poor, mad Jew stalking his victims down fog-enshrouded alleyways could not be any further from the truth. Kosminski was aged 24 at the time of the murders. Many experts would agree that the killer was in the same age group as his victims. The programme did not let this point interfere with the story.

My first objective was to forget about all the myths and untruths which had ever arisen from the subject. The second objective was to obtain Ordnance Survey maps of the period from the British Museum map room in London. The same type was also obtained from Ordnance Survey at Southampton. My third objective was to locate the exact spots at which the killings took place. The area was checked out by day and by night. A book as the end result could not have been any further from my mind. If anyone had informed me then that my work would involve spending over nine years of my time and, thousands of pounds, and attending computer courses, I would have thought them quite mad!

The first myth about the killer to be placed on the rubbish heap was the one about him being a local man. The most efficient way to move from A to B is in a straight line. The killer moved in a straight line and on the main roads of the area. One can walk from the main crossroad which connects Commercial Road, Commercial Street, Whitechapel High Street and Leman Street to reach four of the five side streets in which a murder took place by simply walking in a straight line on the main roads.

From the main crossroads in Whitechapel one can walk in a straight line to:

Court Street, which leads into Bucks Row (site 1)
Hanbury Street, which leads into the yard at No. 29 (site 2)
Berner Street, which leads into Dutfield's Yard (site 3)
Dukes Street, which leads into Mitre Square (site 4)
Dorset Street, which leads into room 13, at 26, Dorset Street (site 5)
(See plan section with the routes marked.)

It is very clear that the killer was using the four main roads to move about, Whitechapel High Street and Whitechapel Road in particular. Once all the sites were located, the exact locations were then placed on my map. It was at this point that sites 1, 2, 3 and 4 appeared to form a parallelogram and that sites 3-4 were located at the two ends of a straight, horizontal line when measured from the bottom of the map.

Believing this fact was more than coincidence, my next task was to do what, to my knowledge, no other person has ever done before me, and measure the distances from victim to victim, as the crow flies, on a map. They were also measured in the field with a surveyor's wheel. The following facts emerged:

The distance from site 1 to site 2 was 930 yards.
The distance from site 2 to site 4 was 930 yards.
The distance from site 3 to site 4 was 950 yards.
The distance from site 3 to site 5 was 950 yards.

Other measurements that were taken proved just as conclusive. When compass bearings were taken in the field it was found that sites 1, 2, 3 and 4 were located due east, south, north and west! Facts such as these spoke for themselves. The solution was now forming, and it was not necessary to be an academic to realise the significance of what it all meant.

The next task was to locate the start of the plan and the end of it. This took three years to complete. At this stage the true motive for the murders became very apparent. Jack the Ripper was, it emerged, a 'one off'.

There is no public record that the police or any person investigating these crimes has ever bothered to measure the distances from victim to victim. Neither had they worked out that victims three, four and five all lie on a 500-yard radius, nor numerous facts uncovered during my research. Many measurements shown in my research are unique.

This book has been compiled and illustrated to give a true picture of events. Photos are used in conjunction with plans, maps and diagrams to give the reader a true feel for the exact layout and nature of each site.

For the first time since 1888, the routes travelled by the killer are shown, including the distances and times involved. Therefore, the reader is in a far better position to judge the facts without the need to rely on imagination. Reconstructions were also taken in the field. All five sites were surveyed together with the general areas of Spitalfields, Aldgate and Whitechapel.

Most Ripper authors give a short breakdown of each murder without surveying any site in depth. The suspects list is next on the agenda, from which the author picks a likely suspect. A story is then woven around the chosen suspect until it fits. Unlike most other Ripper books this one does not contain a suspects list.

It is the first time since 1888 that such a comprehensive study of the sites and general area has taken place. An entirely different approach has been undertaken; no other work has ever been produced on the subject which dealt solely in such detail with the planning and execution of the Whitechapel murders. This is precisely why this unique work stands out from all the rest.

Melvyn Harris, world-renowned Ripper author, investigator, debunker of hoaxes and consultant to Arthur C. Clarke on 38 programmes, informed me, 'You have taken this case further than me.'

A Brief History of London, the East End and Crime in the Capital
(AD 73–1888)

THE EAST END of London is the area on the north bank of Old Father Thames, and runs east from the Tower of London. The area takes in Tower Bridge approach, Aldgate, Houndsditch (so called because a Roman ditch was found in which lay the remains of many hounds), Spitalfields, Whitechapel (so named because the chapel was painted white), Bethnal Green, Shoreditch, Mile End, Wapping, Limehouse, Shadwell, Stepney, Poplar and the Isle of Dogs. Today the area is known as Tower Hamlets.

The centre of the Roman Empire, which covered at its widest extent 2 million square miles and housed 100 million people, grew out of a small settlement by the River Tiber. Another small settlement, this time by the Thames, would be destined to become the centre of the greatest empire the world had ever seen. Whoever controlled the Thames at this point also controlled the town and whoever controlled the town also controlled the country. This is why the Celts, Romans, Saxons and Normans built on the same site.

The Celts were trading on the banks of the Thames prior to the Roman invasion, which began in AD 43. The Romans named the area Londinium and used it as a military storage depot. In AD 61 it was burned to the ground by Boudica, Queen of the Iceni who revolted against Roman rule. It was rebuilt again by AD 100. A bridge was built on the site of London Bridge by the Romans and the area soon became the centre of Roman activity. It developed into a trading centre with the continent and was used as a port. By AD 400, its population numbered nearly 60,000.

When the Romans left in AD 410, London was plunged into the Dark Ages. From 460–600 it became a Saxon trading town. A church dedicated to St Paul – London's patron saint – was located on Ludgate Hill as early as 604. It was here that the City developed, and grew in size and stature.

The Danes sacked the town in the 9th century and settled in the area. In 883 Alfred the Great defeated the Danes and drove them out. The town was then named Lunduntown. At the Battle of Hastings in 1066 (which took place at Battle in Sussex) the Normans won the day and Saxon rule came to an end with the death of King Harold. William the Bastard was crowned King of the English at Westminster after marching on London. He built the Tower of London to consolidate his position.

Tower Bridge is situated east of London Bridge. It crosses the river at the approach to the Tower. William built a stone bridge to replace the old Roman wooden structure. It was the only bridge to cross the Thames until 1750. William's stone bridge was to last until 1832.

The first bomb ever dropped on British soil (from a Zeppelin) fell in Coopers Row (130 yards north of the Tower of London, which may have been the target), 630 yards from the main junction on the Whitechapel High Street, which is situated at the heart of the

Ripper's killing ground. The same general area was bombed in the Blitz during the Second World War.

Between 1176 and 1209 the area within the old Roman city grew rich and more powerful as the years passed and the outlying areas were eventually included. The Black Death of 1348–49 killed at least 60,000 people which accounted for about two-thirds of the population. During the Middle Ages the population never exceeded that of Roman London.

Three cases of Bubonic Plague took place between 1603 and 1636. While in 1665 another outbreak of plague accounted for another 65,000–70,000 lives. In September 1666 the Great Fire of London destroyed a very large area of the city. By 1700 the population had grown to 300,000 and was sustained, in spite of the high death rate.

Much of London was violent and filthy. The streets were filled with mud, offal, excrement and rubbish, and the stench was overwhelming. It was a breeding ground for rats. The Thames was little more than a filthy, sluggish and polluted stretch of water. Housing built for the workers, warehouses, factories, prisons, slums and all other manner of buildings were needed to support London. The expansion of the docks combined with the demand for entertainment by sailors, dockworkers and the masses gave rise to development of the outlying areas, hence the birth of the East End.

As the docks grew in size and importance, the crime rate grew with it. Half of the country's shipping passed through London's docks. So much trade attracted a vast array of specialist criminals. Gangs plundered entire cargoes and insurance frauds were commonplace. So massive were the thefts that the 'fences' established themselves in stores and warehouses.

London became the largest city in Europe by the end of the 17th century and contained a tenth of England's population. Its growth reflected the emergence of England as a major trading nation. The government did what it could to make matters worse for the working classes. The Enclosure Act, which recurred in 1750-1870, was another blow to the poor. Common land was taken over by local landowners, and the loss of rights to common land caused severe hardship to the peasantry. The wealthy grew richer while the poor lost what little they had.

> They hang the fellow that steals the goose
> From off the common.
> But let the larger villain loose who steals
> The common from the goose.

The land-owning classes were producing more corn than the people could eat (and people were still starving), but they came up with a solution to the problem by turning the surplus into gin.

By the early 18th century, gin had become the everyday drink of the working classes. The death rate became twice the birth rate by 1720, and the average lifespan of a male was 29. By 1742, there was one gin shop for every 70 inhabitants and over a quarter of the houses in many parts of London were gin shops. Between 7 and 8 million gallons of gin were consumed by the population. It was reported that one in eight Londoners died due to excessive drinking.

For many of London's poor, life became a short and squalid journey through alcoholism to destitution and a pauper's grave. The docks bred a lot of the crime and when the docks were closed in the 1960s the crime that was associated with them died out. The infamous Ratcliffe Highway ran east from the Tower, parallel to the docks. It was considered to be one of the worst roads in London in the 18th and 19th centuries. The Highway was notorious for crime and was a very dangerous area in which to live. It was lined with dope dens and shops which bought and sold many exotic items brought ashore by sailors and travellers.

Brothels, pubs, ratting dens and cock-fighting dens were only a sample of the entertainment available. Crime-fighting in the capital was totally corrupt. It provoked and encouraged crime. Charles Hitchin, the Under City Marshal, worked hand in glove with the notorious master criminal Jonathan Wild. When the Marshal was later imprisoned, Wild took over the business of crime-fighting, naming himself 'Thief-taker General of Great Britain and Ireland'.

He organised gangs in areas to steal goods, which would be returned to the owners for a fee. Goods not collected would be sold on. Wild sent an estimated 67 criminals to the gallows because they either failed to share their loot with him or tried to cheat him. He received 40 pounds for every criminal convicted.

Wild made 2,680 pounds from those 67 lives. This was only one of the many scams he perpetrated. He became the most detested man in London. Wild was eventually hanged on 25 May 1725, for receiving stolen property.

Mr Egan and Mr Salmon were thief-takers who prompted young men to commit crime, only to give false evidence against them. The purpose of this was to gain the reward when the victims were hanged. When their crimes were exposed they could only face imprisonment or the pillory. They were placed in Smithfield pillory where an enraged mob stoned Egan to death, maiming Salmon.

We have all heard of the Bow Street Runners, forerunners to the modern day police force. Thomas De Veil became a Middlesex magistrate who openly admitted that he only accepted the job because he knew that magistrates could line their own pockets and extort sexual favours from prostitutes. De Veil learned a considerable amount from the illegal activities of Jonathan Wild.

He took a house in Bow Street in 1740 that became his office and the court. He carried out most of his business from a dubious pub in Bow Street called the Brown Bear. He was well known as one who prompted crime which could then be solved, in order to receive reward money. It was De Veil and his successor, Henry Fielding, who made Bow Street the centre of London crime-fighting. Many of their methods were illegal, regardless of accounts to the contrary.

The Bow Street Runners used the tactics of the old thief-takers to obtain their results. Their legacy lives on. In the 1960s I personally knew police officers who encouraged crime – burglary in particular. One such individual was promoted over the years and was placed in charge of the CID department in a large provincial town near London. Some police officers today still refer to catching criminals as thief-taking. Thief-taking was thief-making.

A typical street scene showing how the Crown and government cared for its young subjects

During the 19th century the population in London rose to over 2 million, and the crime rate soared. Pimps, pirates, murderers, whores, muggers and thieves all worked the area. In and around Ratcliffe Highway, warehouses were filled to the brim with every item needed to run the base of the British Empire. Booty and trade goods from every country in the Empire found its way to the docks.

Near to the river and the docks stood the houses of the dockworkers, doss houses, poor houses, pubs, churches, slaughterhouses and stores. Suffice to say that the locals had a very hard time of it. Many children were dressed in rags and wore no footwear. This, then, was how the British Crown and government looked after the welfare of its population. A minority of leeches motivated by power and greed grew rich on the pain, suffering and misery which they inflicted on the many they exploited.

Throughout London's history, executions were considered by the masses to be mere entertainment. A mentality prevailed which was no different from that of the Romans at the Coliseum in Rome. Scenes of sheer brutality and barbarity occurred in the name of justice, in which the hapless victims were hanged, drawn and quartered. The intestines would be ripped from the victim and burned on a brazier. People were boiled and burned alive at Smithfield. The methods of torture utilised were endless. At the end of the day what was left of the victims would be placed on public display as a warning to others.

The appliance of terror was used to manipulate and control the masses. In the 700-year history of one execution site at Tyburn tree (now Marble Arch) over 50,000 men, women and children were publicly hanged. A girl of 14 was hanged in 1782 for keeping company with gypsies. In 1833, a nine-year-old boy was publicly hanged for stealing printer's ink valued at a penny. That was one of the more serious cases. Public executions were not abolished in Britain until 1868.

Conditions in the East End were comparable to those in the Warsaw Ghetto. Baby farming was practised throughout London; it was not illegal. Many children not yet in their teens were involved in prostitution. Children were also expected to work to survive. Many of these children were homeless and went on the streets. They had to join up with others to survive, hence the birth of many street gangs.

Children had no choice in the matter. Such poor, grief-stricken areas could be found the length and breadth of the country.

One of the greatest pieces of hypocrisy ever to be placed on a public building was written over the entrance to the Central Criminal Court (known as the Old Bailey). It read: *Defend the children of the poor and punish the wrongdoer.* The East End was only one such area in existence in Britain. One could not be any poorer than these people. It was from such a context that Jack the Ripper was to take five individuals and rob them of the only things they possessed of any value, their lives.

Contemporary police records indicate that about 1,200 prostitutes worked the Whitechapel district in 1888. The five victims of Jack the Ripper resided in the district of Spitalfields and two were murdered there. Two were murdered in Whitechapel and one in Aldgate in the City. The area of Spitalfields, in the East End of Jack's London in 1888, was filled with many Jewish and Irish immigrants with a smattering of other nationalities. It was considered to be one of the worst areas in London for poverty.

Crime was rife, with many gangs in competition. Murder, mugging, rape, child abuse, skinning (stripping children of their clothes which were then sold) and robbery were just a few of the most frequent of crimes. The cry of 'Murder' was so commonplace it was simply ignored. This, then, was Spitalfields; the neighbourhood the five victims of the killer known as Jack the Ripper inhabited.

Enter Jack the Ripper

In the annals of murder, one name reigns supreme, towering above all others. We are all familiar with the unknown killer dubbed Jack the Ripper who murdered five prostitutes in the East End of London in 1888. However, Jack's reputation and legacy have been blown out of proportion by irresponsible and unscrupulous journalists working for a media lacking in integrity and motivated by greed, power and sensationalism. Jack the Ripper, considered by some as the forerunner to the modern serial killer, has become the victim of overkill.

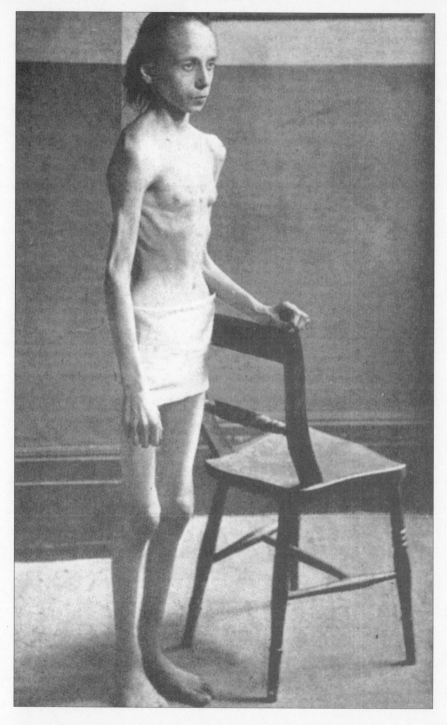

This young girl (photograph taken in 1896) could quite easily be mistaken for a concentration camp victim

Mention the name Jack the Ripper to most people and their romantic imagination will conjure a cloaked figure, presumed to be a surgeon, with top hat and Gladstone bag gliding down fog-enshrouded alleyways. His victims are pictured as young, buxom, beauties decked out in fine Victorian satin dresses with under-garments of lace and silk.

There was nothing romantic about Jack the Ripper's East End. It was cold and wet when three of the five murders were committed. The main roads were utilised by the killer and not the labyrinth of alleyways in the area. The killer did not wear a top hat or carry a Gladstone bag. Four out of five victims were anything but young and buxom, and the attire of this class of prostitute usually consisted of dirty dresses. Many prostitutes wore men's boots, which were laced up the front. Underwear was not worn, for quick sex was the order of the day.

The only correct general suppositions ever made about the killer are that he was middle class and a surgeon. So much rubbish has been accumulated over the years and so many untruths have been written that the true situation has been grossly misinterpreted. This state of affairs will be dealt with later. Also, many works on the subject have been undertaken by those with little or no experience in criminology.

THE FIRST VICTIM

FRIDAY, 31 AUGUST 1888, WHITECHAPEL

Age: 45
Profession or calling: Prostitute
Hair: Dark (turning grey)
Eyes: Brown
Face: Discoloration of face
Complexion: Dark
Marks or peculiarities: On person a piece of looking glass, a comb and handkerchief

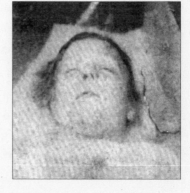

Dress: Brown ulster, seven large buttons, horse and man standing by side thereon, linsey frock, brown stays, blue ribbed woollen stockings, straw bonnet

MARY ANN NICHOLS, also known as Polly, worked in the Whitechapel Road, plying her trade as a prostitute during the dark hours. She was the wife of William Nichols, a printer's machinist of 37, Coburg Road, Old Kent Road, London. The above description was sent with a summary report, dated 19 October 1888, written by Chief Inspector DS Swanson, CID, Scotland Yard.

Her marriage had failed in 1880 and, due to her habits, she lost custody of her two children. She spent most of the time in the Lambeth area until 1888. She absconded from her employers, Mr and Mrs Cowdry, in Wandsworth in July 1888 after stealing clothes.

From 2 to 24 August, she shared a bed with Ellen Holland at 18, Thrawl Street. From 24 to 30 August, she resided in Flower and Dean Street. At 11.30pm on 30 August she was seen walking her patch (territory) along the Whitechapel Road.

Polly was seen leaving a pub named the Frying Pan at 12.30am in Brick Lane. She went to 18, Thrawl Street drunk and wearing a new bonnet, but was refused a bed for the night since she did not possess the price required (4d). On leaving she stated to the deputy, 'See what a jolly bonnet I've got now.'

At 2.30am, she was met by Ellen Holland on the corner of Osborne Street and the Whitechapel Road. She was drunk and staggering and informed Ellen Holland that she had earned her doss money three times over during the day and had spent it. She refused to go back to Thrawl Street with Ellen Holland and was seen to walk up the Whitechapel Road in the direction of Bucks Row and the London Hospital.

It is my contention that, while in the locality of the London Hospital in the Whitechapel Road, she was approached by a man after 3.20am. She was then taken to Bucks Row, possibly via Woods Dwellings, which is located on the busy Whitechapel Road and opposite the London Hospital. Woods Dwellings gives far greater privacy for access into Bucks Row.

The entry into Woods Dwellings from the Whitechapel Road consists of a small archway, which can be overlooked from the Whitechapel Road. From this entrance to Woods Dwellings, for a distance of about 10 yards, the passage is narrow and covered. The exit from the passage in Winthrop Street, at the side of the Board School, is stepped and slightly wider.

It is worth noting at this point that sites 1, 2, 4 and 5 all consisted of a covered passage. The most efficient way to travel from the London Hospital to the Bucks Row site is via Woods Dwellings. The

Woods Dwellings, the probable route taken by the killer and Chapman to Bucks Row from the Whitechapel Road. Whitechapel Road market can be seen at the entrance to the passage. The passage is unchanged (smells included) since Jack the Ripper's day in 1888

Ripper's priorities were always cover and time, in that order, an important consideration when examining how he worked.

By 3.30am, which is midway between the stable beat times of 3.15am and 3.45am, the man had led his victim to an alcove at the entrance to a stables, the doors of which were closed. He positioned his victim in the corner of the alcove, placing himself directly behind her. She was now trapped.

He placed his left hand over her nose and mouth, rendering her unconscious. The victim was then placed down on her left side and her throat was cut twice, left to right. The killer was right handed. He was positioned behind her and the flow of blood from her throat was directed away from him.

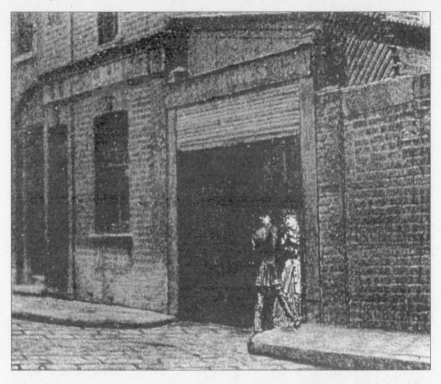

Brown's stable as it appeared at the time of the murder. The killer is depicted manoeuvring his victim into the corner of the alcove from which there is no escape

The victim was then turned on her back for better access when the killer proceeded to perform the mutilations. He was either standing or leaning over the victim in the cover of the alcove or on her right. The depth of the alcove in 1888 was deeper than in later years.

Ripperologist Martin Fido reiterated this on 12 May 2001 by making the following statement: 'It's my impression that the 20th-century garage building which incorporated the old gateway pushed the frontage forward a little and there would seem to have been a little more depth shown in the 1888 illustrations of the finding of the body.'

The murderer would not have been seen by anyone walking in either direction on his side of the road until they were level with him. These events were reconstructed and he would definitely not have been seen at 3.30am. The mutilations on this victim took less than one minute. The killer had experience in working quickly in adverse conditions. The 3.30am train, passing only yards away, drowned out any noise made by the victim and the killer.

In an unconfirmed report, Mrs Harriet Lilley, living at 7, Bucks Row, claimed to have heard whispering in Bucks Row moments prior to the 3.30am train. She then heard gasps and moans. She went so far as to awaken her husband William, a carman. She then stated that a train went by, drowning any further sounds. (I have checked at the public records office and Mrs Harriet Lilley did live in Bucks Row.) The killer was unconcerned with how long it took to find the body, for he knew he would be back in his lair in less than two minutes.

At 3.40am the body was found by Charles Cross (a carman), who resided at 22, Doveton Street, Bethnal Green. Cross was on his way to work at Pickfords in Broad Street when he found the victim. Cross was joined by Robert Paul (a carter), resident of 30, Foster Street, Whitechapel, who was also on his way to work. After checking for signs of life, they went in the direction of Hanbury Street to seek police help.

At 3.45am PC Neil found the body (unaware that it had already been seen by Cross and Paul at 3.40am). Neil signalled PC Thain with his lamp. Thain happened to be passing Bucks Row at the Brady Street end. PC Mizen arrived after being informed by Cross and Paul in Hanbury Street of their find. PC Thain left the scene to fetch Dr Llewellyn, who was called from his surgery at 152, Whitechapel Road at 4.00am.

When he arrived at Bucks Row he found the victim on her back, legs drawn up, her throat cut twice. She also had bruising to her face. He noticed that there was only a wineglass and a half of blood beside the body. After a preliminary examination the body was removed by PC Thain, who took the body on an ambulance to Montague Street infirmary workhouse.

Inspector Spratling went to the mortuary to take a description of the body. It was here that the abdominal mutilations were discovered. Dr Llewellyn was called out again to examine these newly discovered injuries. On his arrival he found that the cadaver had been stripped and cleaned by the two mortuary attendants,

Robert Mann and James Hatfield. Dr Llewellyn made a full examination of the body at the mortuary. The original autopsy report has been lost but *The Times* reported:

Doctor Llewellyn stated that, 'Five of the teeth were missing and there was a slight laceration of the tongue. There was a bruise running along the lower part of the jaw on the right side of the face. That might have been caused by a blow from a fist or pressure from a thumb. There was a circular bruise on the left side of the face, which also might have been inflicted by the pressure of the fingers. On the left side of the neck, about 1in. below the jaw, there was an incision about 4in. in length, [which] ran from a point immediately below the ear. On the same side, but an inch below, and commencing about 1in. in front of it, was a circular incision, which terminated at a point about 3in. below the right jaw. The incision completely severed all the tissues down to the vertebrae. The large vessels of the neck on both sides were severed. The incision was about 8in. in length.

'The cuts must have been caused by a long-bladed knife, moderately sharp, and used with a great deal of violence. No blood was found on the breast, either on the body or clothes. There were no injuries about the body until just about the lower part of the abdomen. Two or 3in. from the left side was a wound running in a jagged manner. The wound was a very deep one, and the tissues were cut through. There were several incisions running across the abdomen. There were also three or four similar cuts running downwards, on the right side, all of which had been caused by a knife which had been used violently and downwards. The injuries were from left to right, and might have been done by a left handed person. The same instrument had caused all the injuries.'

The swollen face and lack of blood indicate asphyxiation. Vital organs were attacked indicating that the killer knew exactly where they were located. Polly Nichols was identified by Ellen Holland. She was buried at Ilford Cemetery on 6 September 1888.

At 3.15am, PC Neil had walked past the spot where Nichols was to be found at 3.40am and all was clear. At 3.30am, Mrs Lilley apparently heard the murder. At 3.45am PC Neil found the body. Nichols was killed 15 minutes after the beat PC passed the spot at 3.15am, and 15 minutes before the spot was checked again by the beat PC at 3.45am, thus leaving her time of death at 3.30am, exactly in the middle of the beat times.

Three slaughtermen, named Britton, Mumford and Tomkins, employed on the nightshift by Messrs. Harrison Barber & Coy in Winthrop Street gave a satisfactory account for their time. This was partly corroborated by a policeman on night duty. A night watchman named Patrick Mulshaw was employed by Whitechapel board of works in Winthrop Street. He saw nothing suspicious and heard no one. With all the police activity in the area why was the killer not seen?

The killer simply checked the police beat times. He was one step ahead. He picked the time and he also picked the place. If Mrs Lilley had put her head out of her window and had looked into Bucks Row, she would have seen nothing, for the murder took place in the stable alcove, which was not visible from the cottages.

The sites were checked many times from Monday, 16 August 1993 to Friday, 6 February 1998.

Bucks Row Revisited

The board school building has been converted to apartments, but the wall from the school to the old stable is still intact with its original pier. In 1888 the stable entrance was narrower and deeper than in later years. Two cottages next to the stable were demolished and a wall with two small windows replaced them. The East Pier was knocked down but the West Pier where the murder took place was not moved.

The row of cottages are gone, replaced by new flats which reach from the site of the old stable to the Brady Street end. The old pub and several cottages in Brady Street still existed in 1993, but are now gone. The road is very narrow at the Brady Street end. The complete length of Winthrop Street is only wide enough for a horse and cart.

The victim on this site was found with her head facing east and her feet in the corner of the alcove facing west. Her left arm was touching the stable door and it was in line with her body. The body was found in the alcove and not in the gutter, neither was it found on the pavement in full view.

I stood a person in the corner of the pier in this alcove. From the board school end of Bucks Row this person could not be seen from the pavement. Neither would he have been seen from the Brady Street end on the same side of the road. Walking towards the alcove on the pavement where the old cottages once stood I could not see the person in the alcove.

If a man and a woman were in the alcove I would not have seen them. This experiment was conducted during daylight hours. Knowing the exact position in which the body was found, it would have been impossible to see the killer at work from either end of the approach to the stables (on the same side as the stable). The alcove was not in sight of the cottages as many have stated to be the case.

Plan of Bucks Row

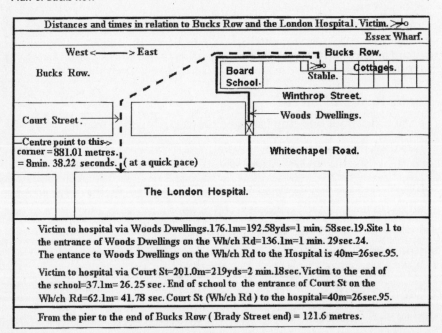

Bucks Row 1998. 'X' marks the murder location from the old Essex Wharf. The depth from the outer edge of the brick pillar shown to the stable door was about 19–20 inches, which gave good cover for a couple standing in the corner. 'W' marks the entrance to Winthrop Street from Bucks Row. 'F' marks the footbridge leading from Woods Dwellings into Winthrop Street

The man who found the body was walking in the direction of Court Street from Brady Street. He stated that he did not see anything until he was level with the alcove and he was on the opposite side of the road, a distance of 10 yards. He also stated that he thought the body was a tarpaulin. At the time of the killing, 3.30am, any person looking down the road from either end or looking out of any window in the row of cottages would have seen nothing.

Bucks Row, now Durward Street, Hanbury Street, Berner Street, now Henriques Street, Mitre Square and Dorset Street (now without a name) were all filmed, photographed and measured with a surveyor's wheel, and distances were timed.

To give an indication of how close this site is to the London Hospital, via Woods Dwellings, it takes about 1 minute and 58 seconds to walk the 176.1m. I have walked all the distances and measured them. Brady Street is located east of the board school at the end of Bucks Row. From the end of Bucks Row (at the Brady Street end) to the murder spot it is 121.6m.

THE SECOND VICTIM

SATURDAY, 8 SEPTEMBER 1888, SPITALFIELDS

Alias: Annie Sivvey

Age: 45

Profession or calling: Prostitute

Height: 5 feet

Hair: (wavy) dark brown

Eyes: Blue

Nose: Thick nose

Mouth: Two teeth deficient in lower jaw

Complexion: Fair

Marks or Peculiarities: On person portion of an envelope stamped 'Sussex Regiment' dated 23 August 1888

Dress: Black skirt and jacket, striped petticoat, crepe bonnet

BORN ELIZA ANNE SMITH, Annie Chapman was a prostitute who plied her trade at night in Spitalfields. This victim was a carbon copy of Polly Nichols (victim one) in terms of their backgrounds. Both were turned out on to the streets for having no money. For want of a bed (4d) they both lost their lives.

Chapman was also wearing a brown bodice and lace-up boots. This victim lived in west London until moving to Windsor in 1881. She had two daughters and a crippled son.

One daughter died in 1882. Chapman had left her family and moved back to London, because her habits, as with Nichols, broke up her marriage. In 1886 she was living at No. 30, Dorset Street, then she moved to Crossinghams lodging house at 35, Dorset Street (opposite Mary Kelly, victim five, who lived in the rear of No. 26). It was at this address that she was living with a man named Jack Sivvey. Medical evidence shows that she was dying of diseases to the brain membranes and of the lungs.

On 7 September, at 11.30pm, she was seen in the kitchen at Crossinghams by the lodging house deputy, Timothy Donovan. At 12.12am on 8 September, William Stevens, a lodger at Crossinghams, saw her in the kitchen. Later, between 1.30am and 1.45am, Donovan asked for her rent money. She replied, 'I haven't got it, I am weak and ill and have been to the infirmary.' She then left, asking that a bed be kept for her.

John Evans, the night watchman at Crossinghams, saw her go into Paternoster Row towards Brushfield Street. At 4.45am John Richardson went to 29, Hanbury Street to check on security. He sat on the steps leading to the back yard and trimmed a piece of leather off his boot, and he observed no sign of the body of Chapman. He left at about 4.48am. At around 5.30am a woman named Mrs Darrell, also referred to as Long, saw Annie with a man aged in his 40s standing on the pavement near No. 29, Hanbury Street.

The man was taller than Chapman and he was wearing dark clothes and a deerstalker hat. He was heard to say to Chapman, 'Will you?' to which she replied, 'Yes'. Mr Cadosch, a young carpenter resident of No. 27, Hanbury Street (next door to No. 29), stated that about 5.30am, he went into the yard of his house when he heard a woman's voice cry out, 'No!' Shortly afterwards he heard a bump against the fence dividing No. 27 and No. 29 where the victim was later found. Mr Cadosch heard no more and left for work.

If Mrs Cadosch had spawned a more inquisitive child and he had

A print from the Illustrated Police News *showing John Richardson trimming leather from his boot at the scene of crime prior to the murder*

looked over the fence, the killer's greatest fear would have been realised – he would have been caught on the job, and you would not be reading this book. No one would have heard of Jack the Ripper. No. 29, Hanbury Street had 17 people living in it. The passage and the yard were both used as a haunt by local prostitutes and their clients.

John Davis, carman, a resident of No. 29 went into the yard just before 6.00am and found the victim. The body was lying on its back, level with the fence, with the head near to the back steps of the house. Her intestines were placed over her left shoulder. Dr George Bagster Phillips was called at 6.20am and arrived at 6.30am. The

Hanbury Street looking east towards Brick Lane. No. 29, Hanbury Street is located at the point marked 'A'

The scene of crime in the rear yard of 29, Hanbury Street.

inquest was held on 14 September 1888. Dr Phillips, describing the scene of crime, wrote:

> The left arm was placed across the left breast. The legs were drawn up, the feet resting on the ground, and the knees turned outwards. The face was swollen and turned on the right side. The tongue protruded between the front teeth, but not beyond the lips. The tongue was evidently much swollen. The front teeth were perfect as far as the first molar, top and bottom, and very fine teeth they were. The body was terribly mutilated. The stiffness of the limbs was not marked, but was evidently commencing. The throat was dissevered deeply; that the incisions through the skin were jagged, and reached right round the neck. On the wooden paling between the yard in question and the next, smears of blood, corresponding to where the head of the deceased lay, were to be seen. These were about 14 inches from the ground, and immediately above the part where the blood lay that had flowed from the neck.

Dr Phillips was of the opinion that there were indications of anatomical knowledge which were only less indicated in consequence of haste. He believed the murder weapon to be such an instrument as a medical man used for post-mortem purposes. 'The whole of the body was not present, the absent portions being from the abdomen. The mode in which these portions were extracted showed some anatomical knowledge.'

The post-mortem examination was made by Dr Phillips at Whitechapel Workhouse Infirmary Mortuary in Eagle Street on Saturday. The post-mortem stated:

Protrusion of the tongue. There was a bruise over the right temple. On the upper eyelid there was a bruise, and there were two distinct bruises, each the size of a man's thumb, on the forepart of the top of the chest. The stiffness of the limbs were now well marked. There was a bruise over the middle part of the bone of the right hand. There was an old scar on the left of the frontal bone. The stiffness was more noticeable on the left side, especially in the fingers, which were partly closed. There was an abrasion over the ring finger, with distinct markings of a ring or rings. The incisions into the skin indicated that they had been made from the left side of the neck. There were two distinct clean cuts on the left side of the spine. They were parallel with each other and separated by about half an inch. The muscular structures appeared as though an attempt had been made to separate the bones of the neck.

Dr Phillips was of the opinion that the breathing of the deceased had been interfered with prior to the cause of death. He omitted further details of the mutilations, which would distress the jury and public alike.

Cause of death was due to syncope, or failure of the heart's action due to loss of blood, caused by severance of the throat. A Metropolitan Police report from CID, Scotland Yard, dated 19 September 1888, by Inspector F. G. Abberline, included the following: 'The deceased was in the habit of wearing two brass rings (a wedding and a keeper) these were missing when the body was found and the finger bore marks of their having been removed by force.'

A print from the Illustrated Police News showing Dr Phillips pronouncing life extinct on Chapman.

On 19 September, Dr Phillips was recalled to give evidence in relation to the after-death mutilations omitted from his evidence on 14 September. Phillips and coroner Wynne Baxter were both of the opinion that the court should be cleared of women and boys, due to the nature of the evidence.

Reporting restrictions were placed on the press for the same reasons. In essence the evidence noted that the victim's intestines had been partially removed and placed on Chapman's shoulder, and that her uterus, the upper portion of her vagina and most of the bladder were entirely removed. He noted that the work was probably completed by an expert (no adjacent organs were damaged during the attack) and the knife must have been 5–6in in length. In closing this portion of his evidence he noted that the way the knife had been wielded pointed to knowledge of anatomy.

It is quite obvious from the medical evidence on this victim that she was asphyxiated before death. Also, the evidence points to the perpetrator being a medical man. As with Nichols, this victim was also killed in a corner, the only difference here being that her head was in the corner, the opposite placement of Nichols. We know by Cadosch's evidence that the killer did not surprise Chapman as he had wished to do. Before he had a chance to get her into a corner and get behind her, she became fearful and shouted 'No!'

Cadosch stated that he heard a bump against the fence after he heard her cry out. I don't believe the killer had sexual relations with this victim on site, or any other. There is no medical evidence to show that sex took place. Firstly, Chapman was attacked and rendered unconscious; bruising to her face, a protruding tongue and a lack of blood at the scene all indicate that she was unconscious before her throat was cut.

She was then placed down on her left side with her head by the back door steps. The killer placed himself behind the victim and cut her throat twice, left to right. The blood flowed away from the killer. Splashes of blood were found on the fence near the ground, which would seem to confirm this. The appearance of the muscular structures was due to the excessive force used to cut the throat and not by any attempt at decapitation.

It took no more than two minutes for the killer to perform the mutilations. If anyone believes this to be nonsense, I'll simply state that many years ago I was employed by FMC (Fresh Meat Company) and I have gutted thousands of pigs, sheep and cattle. I have timed myself when gutting a cow with the suet and certain vital organs removed and achieved the task in four minutes. That includes sorting out the items, emptying the stomach contents, cleaning the tripe, cutting away the pancreas, then washing it in cold water, folding it in a neat and deliberate fashion to await freezing.

The slaughter gang in which I worked was on piece work. We learned to work very quickly for great speed was of the essence. It is easy to tell if a worker is experienced or not. If done correctly there is no damage to items taken or remaining. The doctor's report on Chapman mentioned no damage done to the remaining parts.

A surgeon is trained to feel for symptoms on a patient. To some extent he could work by touch alone, therefore a surgeon could work in poor light but a slaughterman would not be trained in the same manner and would not be able to work at speed in the dark. It was said by one of the doctors working on the case that a slaughterman would have no difficulty in locating the organs in such circumstances. Talking from experience in such matters, the man who committed these murders was certainly no slaughterman.

Dr Phillips stated that the weapon used by the killer was such as used by surgeons in post-mortems, which is not surprising. It would be expected of the killer to use the correct tool for the job. After all it was the tool of his trade. I would not use a surgeon's knife for gutting a cow any more than I would expect a surgeon to use a gutman's knife on a corpse.

No. 29, Hanbury Street has been demolished to make way for a brewery.

All measurements are from victim to victim and **not** from any surrounding area.

O/S MAPS 1873,1880,1894,

Victim No. 2. +-------------930 yards----------------+ Victim No. 1.

Corner of yard   Corner of alcove,

29, Hanbury Street   Bucks Row

THE THIRD VICTIM

SUNDAY, 30 SEPTEMBER 1888, WHITECHAPEL

Alias: Known as Long Liz
Age: 45
Height: 5ft 2in
Profession or calling: Prostitute
Hair: Dark brown and curly
Eyes: Light grey
Nose: Thin
Complexion: Pale
Mouth: Upper teeth missing in front
Dress: Old black skirt, black crepe bonnet, old long black jacket trimmed with fur, small bunch of flowers on right side, consisting of maidenhair fern and a red rose. Two light serge petticoats, white stockings, white chemise with insertion in front, side-spring boots, coloured striped silk handkerchief worn around the neck

ELIZABETH (SOMETIMES ELISABETH) STRIDE was born in Torslanda, near Gothenberg, Sweden in November 1843. Her maiden name was Elisabeth Gustafsdotter. In 1865 she was registered as a prostitute in Sweden but moved to London in 1866. She married John Thomas Stride in 1869, giving her maiden name as Gustifson of 67, Gower Street.

From 1885 to 1888 she lived with Michael Kidney. Press reports relating to Kidney's inquest testimony placed him as living in Dorset Street. Most authors have given his address as 33, Dorset Street. In a statement to the Central News Agency his address was down as 35, Devonshire Street, Commercial Road. In 1886 Stride applied for aid from the Swedish Church and gave her address as Devonshire Street.

What is known with certainty is that Stride was living at 32, Flower and Dean Street in September at the time of her murder. The coroner, in his summing up at the inquest, mentioned that she had stayed in Devonshire Street, Commercial Road, supporting herself by sewing and cleaning. She had stayed at 32, Flower and Dean Street at varying intervals since 1882. Long Liz, as she was known, spoke English without a Swedish accent.

On 29 September 1888, she was cleaning at 32, Flower and Dean Street. At 6.30pm she left for the Queen's Head Pub, returning at 7.00pm. At 11.00pm two men, J. Best and John Gardner saw her in the Bricklayers Arms Pub in Settle Street. She was in the company of an Englishman, 5ft 5in tall with weak, sandy eyelashes and a black moustache, wearing a morning suit and a billycock (bowler) hat. The man with Stride was of 'clerkly' appearance and well dressed. This man was not her killer. Jack the Ripper would not wish to be seen in a public house with any victim prior to murdering them.

Best and Gardner began to lark about, saying to Stride, 'That is Leather Apron getting around you.' Leather Apron was the nickname for Ripper suspect John Pizer. The couple left the pub in the pouring rain after being jibed by Best and Gardner. They were seen walking down Settle Street towards Commercial Road in the direction of Berner Street.

Stride was next seen by William Marshal in Lower Berner Street at 11.45pm. This witness stated that he was standing in his doorway at No. 64 for 10 minutes around 11.45pm. He saw a lady he later identified as Stride on the pavement opposite No. 58 talking to a man. The man was 5ft 6in tall, stout, middle-aged, educated, decently dressed in a small black coat, dark trousers and a 'peaked sailor's cap'. His voice was mild and English; he was heard to say to Stride, 'You would say anything but your prayers.'

The pair were then seen to walk in the direction of Matthew Packer's shop at 44, Berner Street. The *Evening News*, 4 October, reported Packer selling fruit from his house and that Stride was in company with a man who stopped at his premises at 11.45pm. Packer stated that the man was 5ft 7in tall, wearing a wide-awake hat, dark clothes, a long black coat and that he had a sharp commanding manner being rather quick in speaking. He was of 'clerkly' appearance.

Packer's statement (considered to be suspect by police) asserted that he sold the man half a pound of black grapes for 3d. The couple then crossed over the road opposite the International Working Men's Educational Club and Dutfield's Yard. According to Packer they stood there eating grapes for about half an hour.

The entrance to the yard was flanked by two gates, which stood open. Inside the entrance to Dutfield's Yard a narrow court led to the printing offices of the Yiddish journal *Der Arbeter Fraint*. To the right of the court stood the club which was a two-storey building at 40, Berner Street. To the left of the court was No. 42 and, behind that, a row of cottages.

At 12.30am PC Smith saw Stride and a male companion standing on the spot where Packer alleged he saw Stride with a man. PC Smith had instructions to stop and question any male in company with a female after midnight. PC Smith chose to ignore this order. Why? Maybe he thought that the man with Stride looked too respectable to fit in with his idea of what Jack the Ripper looked like.

PC Smith stated that the man was 5ft 7in tall, aged about 28 and respectable looking. He was wearing dark clothes and a deerstalker hat. He later identified the woman as Stride. Joseph Lave, a printer visiting London from America, had temporary lodgings at the club. He came out of the club at 12.30am to get some fresh air. He passed into the street, remaining outside until 12.40am. He did not see anything unusual and all was quiet.

Mrs Fanny Mortimer who lived at 36, Berner Street, several houses from the crime scene, was standing in her doorway for 10 minutes between 12.30am and 1.00am. She neither saw nor heard anything to arouse her suspicions and all appeared normal until the body was found. However, she stated that she did see a young man carrying a black shiny bag, walking very fast down the street from Commercial Road. He looked up at the club, then went round the corner by the board school.

This man was Leon Goldstein of 22, Christian Street, a member of the International Working Men's Club. After Mrs Mortimer had made her original statement, on the day of the murder, Goldstein went to Leman Street Police Station to eliminate himself from the enquiries. His black shiny bag contained nothing more than empty cigarette boxes. However, this incident, widely publicised, was partly responsible for the birth of yet another Ripper myth. This time it involved the fairy tale about Jack the Ripper carrying a black, shiny Gladstone bag.

At 12.45am James Brown saw Stride with a man in Fairclough Street. Stride had her back to the board school and was talking to a stout man, about 5ft 7in tall, wearing an overcoat that almost reached his heels. He had his arm on the wall as if to stop her from leaving. Brown heard her say, 'No, not tonight, maybe some other night.' Why did Stride turn down a client, if he was a client? Did she have more important business to attend to or was she just very wary of this character? About 15 minutes later Brown heard a cry of 'Murder' while indoors at No. 35, Fairclough Street.

Israel Schwartz, a resident of 22, Ellen Street, stated that he turned into Berner Street from Commercial Road at about 12.45am. The *Star* published an interview with Schwartz on 1 October 1888 which stated:

Information which may be important was given to the Leman Street police yesterday by an Hungarian concerning the murder. The foreigner was well dressed, and had the appearance of being in the theatrical line. He could not speak a word of English, but came to the police station accompanied by a friend, who acted as interpreter. He gave his name and address, but the police have not disclosed them. A Star man, however, got wind of his call and ran him to earth in Backchurch Lane. The reporter's Hungarian was quite as imperfect as the foreigner's English, but an interpreter was at hand, and the man's story was retold just as he had given it to the police. It is to the effect that he saw the whole thing.

It seems that Schwartz had gone out for the day and his wife had expected to move, during his absence, from their lodgings in Berner Street to others in Backchurch Lane. When he first came homewards about 12.45am, he walked down Berner Street to see if his wife had moved. As he turned the corner from Commercial Road he noticed, some distance in front of him, a man walking as if partially intoxicated.

He walked on behind him and presently he noticed a woman standing in the entrance to the alleyway where the victim was later found. The half-tipsy man halted and spoke to her. Schwartz saw him put his hand on her shoulder and push her back into the passage, but feeling rather timid of getting mixed up in quarrels, he crossed to the other side of the street.

Before he had gone many yards, however, he heard the sound of a quarrel, and turned back to learn what was the matter, but just as he stepped from the kerb a second man came out of the doorway of a public house a few doors off and, shouting out some sort of warning to the man who was with the woman, rushed forward as if to attack the intruder. Schwartz stated positively that he saw a knife in the second man's hand, but he waited to see no more. He fled incontinently to his new lodgings.

Schwartz gave information to police on 30 September 1888, taken down by Chief Inspector Swanson. This statement read:

12.45am. 30th. Israel Schwartz of 22, Helen Street, Backchurch Lane, stated that at this hour, on turning into

Berner Street from Commercial Street (sic Road), and having got as far as the gateway where the murder was committed, he saw a man stop and speak to a woman, who was standing in the gateway. The man tried to pull the woman into the street, but he turned her round and threw her down on the footway and the woman screamed three times, but not very loudly. On crossing to the opposite side of the street, he saw a second man standing lighting his pipe.

The man who threw the woman down called out, apparently to the man on the opposite side of the road, 'Lipski,' and then Schwartz walked away, but finding that he was followed by the second man, he ran so far as the railway arch, but the man did not follow so far. Schwartz cannot say whether the two men were together or were known to each other.

Israel Lipski (1865-88) was an alleged murderer whose name was used in 1888 as an anti-Semitic insult. He lodged at 16, Batty Street

Below is a reconstruction of the situation in Berner Street as it appeared just prior to the murder of Elizabeth Stride. One suspect is lurking in the doorway of the Nelson Beer Shop. The attacker has thrown Stride to the ground. Schwartz has turned to view the scene

(adjacent to Berner Street) and worked as an umbrella-maker. During June 1887 he was alleged to have poisoned Miriam Angel, a fellow lodger. He was hanged in 1888.

Chief Inspector Donald S. Swanson sent a report to the Home Office dated 19 October 1888, in which he stated: I respectfully submit it is not clearly proved that the man that Schwartz saw is the murderer.

Because the witness Schwartz was at hand when Stride was attacked the events which took place should be simple to clarify. However, Schwartz's contradictory statements, one to the press and the other to the police, further confuse the issue because they differ in content on several crucial points.

- The press report stated that the suspect tried to push Stride into the passage
- The police report stated that the suspect tried to pull her into the street and then threw her down on the pavement
- The press report does not mention any screaming from the victim
- The police report stated Stride 'screamed three times but not very loudly'
- The press report stated that the man in the doorway shouted a warning to the man who was seen to attack Stride
- The police report stated that the attacker who threw the woman down called out, 'Lipski', apparently to the man on the opposite side of the road
- The press report stated that the second man had a knife in his hand

Perhaps the man in the doorway initially stood lighting a pipe. After the attack on Stride commenced he may well have produced a knife, going for Schwartz simply to scare him away from the scene before dealing with the attacker and scaring him away. He is then alone with Stride and she is at his mercy.

The police report stated that the second man stood lighting a pipe.

The Attacker: Age 30, 5ft 5in, complexion fair, dark hair, small brown moustache, full face, wearing a dark jacket and trousers and a black cap with a peak.

The man in the doorway: Age 35, 5ft 11in, complexion fresh, hair light brown, dark overcoat, old black hard felt hat with a wide brim.

We can be certain that it has been incorrectly assumed that the killer was disturbed by Diemschutz at 1.00am and that the former left the scene (going in search of another victim to satisfy his bloodlust!) when the latter went into the club. Diemschutz did not see anyone apart from the victim, neither did he hear anyone and Jack the Ripper did not rush around killing on sheer speculation due to bloodlust.

Two reasons are given for such an ill-founded conclusion. The first being that the horse shied (implying that the killer was present) and refused to move! Many animals will react on coming into contact with a bloody corpse. Horses especially can be very sensitive and highly strung. The second was that the victim was not mutilated. No one can state with any degree of certainty that the killer ever intended to mutilate Stride. The killer may have planned well in advance that he was to kill two victims on 30 September 1888.

If Diemschutz had indeed found Stride at 1.00am then she had been dead for some minutes and the killer was long gone. It is not correct that Stride was attacked by her killer at 12.45am and that he was disturbed by Diemschutz at 1.00am before he had time to mutilate her, yet this is what we are asked to believe.

Let us assume for argument's sake that Diemschutz had found the body at about 12.53am and he poked about in the yard and calmed down his pony. He then went to check on his wife in the club. At this point someone went upstairs to alert the club members. Diemschutz then returned to the yard. A minute or so must have elapsed by this time making it 12.55am.

Common sense dictates that the killer's plan was compromised by Schwartz and the attacker. It certainly wasn't due to Diemschutz, who arrived later. This meant that the killer could not

THE FIFTH VICTIM OF THE WHITECHAPEL FIEND.

Mr Diemschutz discovering the body of Stride lying just inside the entrance to Dutfield's Yard. Note how the press has put Stride as victim No. 5 and not, correctly, as victim No. 3

stay on the scene knowing that Schwartz could be back at any moment with help. Therefore, the killer only had enough time to render Stride unconscious before he cut her throat. He would then have left the scene right away even if it were his original intention to mutilate Stride.

More factual reasons exist which can explain why Stride was not mutilated. Berner Street was the most dangerous site of all for the killer. People were coming and going to and from the club during the early hours. One only needs to view all the witness statements to realise the truly precarious nature of the murder site chosen. In fact, events proved this.

To spend time mutilating a victim at Dutfield's Yard would be to court trouble and risk detection. Jack may well have planned to kill another victim in Mitre Square within the hour. He knew that he could perform any mutilations on that victim if not on Stride. Occult ritual murder dictates that ritual mutilations of the dead can be performed on the next victim if they cannot be performed on the previous one.

Joseph Lave stated at the inquest that he was in the immediate area of Dutfield's Yard from 12.30am to 12.40am. Stride was not to be seen in the yard or at the entrance to it at 12.40am. Furthermore, Dr William Blackwell arrived on the scene at precisely 1.16am and he stated that the victim had been dead no longer than 20 minutes, at most 30 minutes. This would put the time of death at between 12.46am and 12.56am which is in keeping with the known facts and the realms of reality.

James Brown, of 35, Fairclough Street, stated that he saw Stride in Fairclough Street talking to a man at 12.45am. Lave, Brown, Blackwell and others enforce my belief that Israel Schwartz and Louis Diemschutz got their times wrong. Was the man in the long coat seen by Brown at 12.45am the same man that Schwartz saw wearing a long coat lurking in the pub doorway? There is far more evidence pointing towards Stride being dead by 12.55am than there is to suggest that the killer was disturbed on the job at 1.00am by Diemschutz.

Further evidence that Diemschutz was wrong in his time of 1.00am can be found in the statement made by Morris Eagle at the inquest on Stride. Morris gave evidence to the effect that he left the club to walk his girlfriend home. He returned to the club at 12.35am. At 12.55am members upstairs in the club were alerted to the fact that a dead woman was found in the yard.

The Times, 2 October 1888, reported that Eagle returned to the club at 12.35am and had passed along the alleyway, where Stride's body was found, and had seen no sign of a body at the time. He had been in the club for 20 minutes when a member reported a dead woman lying in the yard.

The Guardian, 1 October 1888, reported the same story and added that on his return to the club there were plenty of people about, both men and women. The front door of the club was closed when he returned so the only access to the club was through the alleyway where the body was found. He saw nothing amiss. He was in the club for 20 minutes when the steward named Gilleman raised the alarm. The steward of the club was in fact Diemschutz.

The *Weekly Herald*, 2 October 1888, carried the story that at 12.55am a passer-by named Joseph Koster was accosted by a little boy who came running up to him as he was passing on the opposite side of the road to the yard and told him that a woman was lying on her side in the gateway leading into Dutfield's Yard.

While certain newspaper stories differ on several points all appear to agree on the fact that Stride was found at around 12.55am. *The Times* of Tuesday, 2 October 1888 gave the inquest evidence of Diemschutz after finding the body. He went into the club and saw his wife in the front room on the ground floor. He told his wife, and several members who were in the room, that a woman was lying in the yard, but that he was unable to say whether she was drunk or dead.

He then got a candle and went into the yard. He saw blood but did not touch the body, and went at once to fetch the police. It makes no mention that Diemschutz went upstairs to alert club members.

Caution is required when dealing with Packer, the shopkeeper. Police made house-to-house enquiries on Sunday, 30 September, the day of the murder. Sergeant Stephen White of H Division was the first detective to interview Packer. White in company with another officer called at Packer's address at 44, Berner Street at 9.00am on 30 September.

Packer informed White that he had closed up his shop at half past twelve, due to the wet weather being bad for business. He informed the detectives that he saw no one standing about the street neither did he see anyone go up the yard. He saw nothing suspicious nor heard the slightest noise.

Two days later on Tuesday two private detectives, Grand and Batchelor, employed by the Whitechapel Vigilance Committee interviewed Packer. On 4 October Grand and Batchelor took Packer to identify Stride at the mortuary in St George's-in-the-East. They then took him to meet with Warren in person, whereupon Warren took a statement from Packer.

This involved Packer's story about selling grapes to a suspect who was in company with Stride. The statement he made to Sir Charles Warren differs by a time period of one hour when compared to events which took place in his other statements. He was inconsistent with the age of the suspect. Packer stated that the suspect was middle-aged, then between 30 and 35, changing it again to between 25 and 30.

More damning is the fact that Dr Phillips stated: 'Neither in the hands nor about the body of the deceased did I find any grapes, or connection with them. I am convinced that the deceased had not swallowed either the skin or seed of a grape within many hours of her death.'

Packer stated that the suspect with Stride bought black grapes. Yet no witness, including PC Smith, saw Stride, or the suspect, holding or eating grapes. More to the point, Packer made several conflicting reports to the police and the press after Stride was murdered.

One story involved a man who called at his premises to buy rabbits. Packer alleged that the customer told him he suspected the killer to be his cousin. The police concluded that the original statement made by Packer would be worthless in a court of law. Thus, he was never called to the inquest.

His reasons for injecting himself into the case may well have been to claim any reward placed on offer for information leading to the apprehension of the killer. The thought of being involved as the man who conversed with and sold grapes to the killer may well have boosted his ego.

It is interesting to note that the changes in Packer's statements appear to have been made in keeping with other witness statements as they were reported. When one views all the available evidence concerning Packer with the case, it appears that he was nothing more than a publicity seeker.

I remember the case of a police officer in recent years who was on patrol in Farnborough, Hampshire. He stated that an IRA gunman had shot at him from a car which police were looking for. One can imagine the set of events which then took place. It transpired that the car in question had never left Ireland. The policeman had been bored and he wanted some limelight. He invented the entire story to satisfy his own self-gratification.

Stride could have been soliciting in Berner Street (although she was heard to say 'No' to a man in Fairclough Street who may have

Press print showing armed Whitechapel prostitutes

The corner of Berner Street and Fairclough Street looking towards Commercial Road as it appears today. The man in the doorway (site marked 'D') was undercover from the rain. More to the point he stood at a perfect lookout position which gave him unobstructed views in all directions

been a potential client) or met the killer by arrangement on site. Stride was seen to be attacked only a yard or so from where her body was later found. Two men, apart from Schwartz, were on the scene. Only one of these men was the killer. Schwartz felt so threatened by events he fled the scene.

Was the man in the doorway Jack the Ripper? If not, then why didn't he come forward as a witness as Schwartz had done? Until this man is eliminated from the enquiries he must be considered as a suspect. Schwartz was scared and concerned for his well being, but in spite of this he came forward as a witness.

We are informed that the knife that killed Stride was not the same weapon that was used on the other victims. It was stated that the knife used by the Ripper was of the type used in post-mortem examinations (which was pointed at the end).

In the *Star* report it stated: 'A second man came out of the doorway of a public house a few doors off, and shouting out some sort of warning to the man who was with the woman, rushed forward as if to attack the intruder.' It does not specify who the intruder is.

Schwartz could be interpreted as intruding on the scene. Victim four, Eddowes, was found to be in possession of a domestic knife. Many people who lived in doss houses carried with them what little they owned, cutlery included. This was a safeguard against theft by others.

The Ripper scare was responsible for encouraging women to carry weapons for protection. So it is plausible that Stride carried her own protection in the form of a knife. Was she disarmed by guile, by the man in the doorway, who then used her own knife to cut her throat?

The attack on Stride witnessed by Schwartz was far from the realms of Jack's MO. The man who was seen to attack Stride did not kill her, neither was he the same man who killed Eddowes. Some writers have listed several details (some incorrect) differentiating Stride's murder from the other four Whitechapel victims:

1. A different type of knife was used to kill Stride.
2. The position of the body indicated that it fell on its left side, rather than on its back as in the other cases.

Incorrect: The evidence shows that it was placed on its side. Victims one, two, four and five did not fall on to their backs; they were placed in that position by the killer. They could hardly be mutilated if they were face down or on their sides. Victim three was not to be mutilated.

3. No extravasation of blood in the neck and head region, which would indicate asphyxiation before throat-cutting.

Incorrect: Medical evidence, clenched hands, a swollen, protruding tongue and a lack of blood on the scene did indicate asphyxiation.

4. No abdominal mutilations.

There is more than enough evidence to show why Stride can be termed a Ripper victim. The killer's MO shows up in many instances. Jack laid his victims down. Dr Phillips stated that Stride had been placed on the ground. PC Lamb who was the first police officer on the scene stated, 'She looked as if she had been laid quietly down.' The victim was murdered facing due west. We now have three victims killed at the three points of the compass.

Stride had been asphyxiated as in other Ripper cases. Her throat was cut from left to right after being laid down on her side. Like the other four victims she was a prostitute. She was murdered after 12.30am and before 6.00am. The body was placed close to a wall. The victim was found on her left side facing a wall, the position the killer placed the other victims in before cutting their throats and before laying them on to their backs prior to mutilating them.

Stride was not laid on her back because the killer had no intention of mutilating her. More to the point her murder scene had been located and pinpointed by her killer on a map in advance and was exactly the same distance from Victim five and Victim four, 950 yards! Nichols was found due east. Chapman was found due north. Stride was found due south. So our next victim should be found due west to complete the pattern.

There is a pressure point by the right shoulder near the collarbone, which can be manipulated to control violent individuals. If the killer had medical experience then he would have known about such pressure points, which can immobilise.

As an experiment I reconstructed the killer's MO with the help of a male prison nurse from HMP Wandsworth, who had previous experience in dealing with violent patients. He approached me from behind and placed his left hand over my nose and mouth. With his right hand he applied pressure to the point mentioned near the collarbone. I was completely and utterly immobilised. It had a paralysing and constricting effect on me and I could not move. This was probably the method used by the killer. This would explain why Stride still held cachous in her hand. Bruising was in evidence by Stride's right shoulder.

Dr Phillips attended Leman Street Police Station at 1.20am, on 30 September 1888. On arrival he was directed to attend the crime scene at Berner Street, arriving at approximately 2.00am. He attended Stride's inquest on 3 October, where he reported:

The body was lying on the near side, with the face turned toward the wall, the head up the yard and the feet toward the street. The left arm was extended and there was a packet of cachous in the left hand ... The right arm was over the belly. The back of the hand and wrist had on it clotted blood. The legs were drawn up with the feet close to the wall. The body and face were warm and the hand cold. The legs were quite warm. Deceased had a silk handkerchief round her neck, and it appeared to be slightly torn. I have since ascertained it was cut. This corresponded with the right angle of the jaw. The throat was deeply gashed, and there was an abrasion of the skin about $1\frac{1}{2}$ inches in diameter, apparently stained with blood, under her right brow. At 3pm on Monday at St George's Mortuary ... Dr Blackwell and I made a post-mortem examination ... Rigor mortis was still thoroughly marked. There was mud on the left side of the face and it was matted in the head ... The body was fairly nourished. Over both shoulders, *especially the right, and under the collarbone and in front of the chest there was a bluish discoloration, which I have watched and have seen on two occasions since.* There was a clean-cut incision on the neck. It was 6 inches in length and commenced $21\frac{1}{2}$ inches in a straight line below the angle of the jaw, $\frac{1}{2}$ inches over an undivided muscle, and then becoming deeper, dividing the sheath. The cut was very clean and deviated a little downwards. The artery and other vessels contained in the sheath were all cut through.

The cut through the tissues on the right side was more superficial, and tailed off to about 2 inches below the right angle of the jaw. The deep vessels on that side were uninjured.

From this it was evident that the haemorrhage was caused through the partial severance of the left carotid artery. Decomposition had commenced in the skin. Dark brown spots were on the anterior surface of the left chin. There was a deformity in the bones of the right leg, which was not straight, but bowed forwards. There was no recent external injury save to the neck. The body being washed more thoroughly I could see some healing sores. The lobe of the left ear was torn as if from the removal or wearing through of an earring, but it was thoroughly healed. On removing the scalp there was no sign of bruising or extravasation of blood ... The heart was small, the left ventricle firmly contracted, and the right slightly so. There was no clot in the pulmonary artery, but the right ventricle was full of dark clot. The left was firmly contracted so as to be absolutely empty. The stomach was large, and the mucous membrane only congested. It contained partly digested food, apparently consisting of cheese, potato and farinaceous powder. All the teeth on the left lower jaw were absent ... Examining her jacket, I found that while there was a small amount on the right side, the left was well plastered with mud ...

It was Dr Phillips's opinion that the cause of death was undoubtedly from the loss of blood from the left carotid artery and the division of the windpipe. The inquest was resumed on 5 October when Dr Phillips stated that Stride had not swallowed the skin or inside of a grape within many hours of her death. He had examined the handkerchiefs found with the body and had drawn the conclusion that the stains on the larger handkerchief were from fruit.

He was of the opinion that the deceased was seized by the shoulders, pressed to the ground and that the perpetrator of the deed was on her left side when he inflicted the wound. The fatal cut was made from left to right. He went on to add that the knife was not sharp pointed, but round, and an inch across. There was nothing in the cut to show an incision of the point of any weapon. The injury was accomplished possibly in two seconds.

He believed that Stride was lying on the ground when the wound was inflicted [on her left side]. Therefore, the killer would have been behind her in a kneeling or crouched position. This indicates that Jack was right handed when he made his cut left to right.

Elizabeth Stride was interred in a pauper's grave in East London Cemetery. From the medical evidence accumulated it can be said with certainty that the killer possessed medical knowledge. How much medical knowledge did he possess? He knew enough to win the day and confuse the experts in the bargain. Jack fell back on his past experiences to achieve his goal just as I fell back on my past experiences to achieve mine. He wasn't a medical orderly; he wasn't a slaughterman; he wasn't a butcher; he wasn't a barber; he was Jack of all trades, surgery being but one.

The Swanson Marginalia are pencil notes in Supt (deceased) Swanson's hand, written in his personal copy of Sir Robert Anderson's memoirs (*The Lighter Side of My Official Life*, 1910). Assistant Commissioner to the Metropolitan Police CID Anderson stated in writing that the identity of Jack the Ripper was known. He said it would serve no purpose if he made this knowledge public! Anderson stated: ' ... the only person who ever had a good view of the murderer unhesitatingly identified the suspect the instant he was confronted with him, but he refused to give evidence against him.'

Swanson then elaborated:

Because the suspect was <u>also a Jew</u> and also because his evidence would convict the suspect, and witness would be the means of murderer being hanged, which he did not wish to be left on his mind. And after this identification which suspect knew, no other murder of this kind took place in London.

(Which is hardly surprising – the murders stopped 18 months before this identification took place!)

Swanson also noted:

After the suspect had been identified at the Seaside Home where he had been sent by us with difficulty, in order to subject him to identification, and he knew he was identified. On suspect's return to his brother's house in Whitechapel he was watched by police by day and night. In a very short time the suspect with his hands tied behind his back he was sent to Stepney Workhouse and then to Colney Hatch and died shortly afterwards – Kosminski was the suspect.

Kosminski was in fact insane. In 1888 an insane person would not have been executed for murder, therefore the identification of the witness would not have meant Kosminski would hang, if indeed Kosminski was the suspect. The police would have gone to great lengths to tell the witness the suspect would not hang. This story has more holes in it than a Swiss cheese.

Other errors occur in this story. Kosminski lived until 1919 and was still alive when Swanson made these notes. There is no record of Kosminski being sent to Stepney Workhouse. The Kosminski story can only refer to Schwartz on Site 3 or Lawende on Site 4. Lawende doubted that he would know the man again. Taking all the evidence into account Site 3 is the most plausible site of the two.

Because of the conflict in the testimony of Schwartz to the police and the press, and taking into consideration the story mentioned in the Swanson Marginalia, I have sought to clarify the situation and propose the following scenario at Berner Street. Stride was standing at the entrance to Dutfield's Yard.

Kosminski was walking down the road towards Stride from Commercial Road. He may have known Stride and for some unknown reason he may well have held a grievance against her. He may simply have been ninety pence short of a pound and tipsy. For whatever reason, on drawing level with Stride he stated something to her and then physically assaulted her. He may not have been aware that Schwartz was walking behind him.

After Stride was thrown to the ground Schwartz passed across to the other side of the road, not wanting to get involved. However, the situation worsened and he turned to view the row. Kosminski then noticed that Schwartz was taking an interest in events.

The man in the doorway (waiting for the all clear to kill Stride) shouted a warning at the attacker. Schwartz then saw a man rushing towards him from the direction of the doorway of Nelson's Beer Shop on the corner and fled the scene.

This suspect then turned his attention on the attacker after scaring away the witness. Faced with the threat of a man with a knife rushing towards him, Kosminski decided it prudent to withdraw in a hurry.

Even a so-called lunatic can think logically when his own welfare is at stake. One must expect the unexpected when crime is involved. At this moment in time someone was attacking the victim that Jack intended to murder. After scaring off her attacker the killer may have consoled Stride and, thinking that this man had come to her rescue, she would quite naturally have dropped her defences and would have been more than grateful for his intervention.

Having no time left before Schwartz could return with help, Jack killed Stride. Maybe with her own knife, if she carried one, which he took from her by guile after scaring off her attacker. He then left the scene, knowing full well that the witness, Schwartz, would identify the attacker as the killer.

Diemschutz then arrived at Dutfield's Yard at about 12.53am and discovered the body. Club members upstairs were alerted at 12.55am. The man in the doorway was in a safe position; he was seen by Schwartz but was not seen as the attacker. If the man in the doorway was ever traced all he had to say was that he had left the scene as Schwartz had done.

All he had to do was to point the finger at poor backward Kosminski stating, 'There is the man who killed Stride.' Schwartz's story backed him up. Just as Reginald Christie pointed the finger at Timothy Evans when he stood in the dock. The man who was seen to attack Stride can't say, 'Yes, I did attack her but I didn't kill her. The man in the doorway did it.' No one would believe him and he would end up being found guilty.

It would be akin to the case of Timothy Evans (who was rather backward) stating in court that he didn't kill his wife or child. No one believed poor innocent Evans and he was hanged. Christie was to get his come-uppance later but that was no help to Evans. It is ironic that the witness at the Seaside Home (the Seaside Home was a police convalescent home in west Brighton the first of which was located at 51, Clarendon Villas in March 1890) who identified Kosminski as the attacker could well have saved an innocent man from prison by not identifying him.

Three men were at the murder scene; only one can be accounted for. Out of the two men left on the scene only one wore an overcoat, the man in the doorway. Dr Bond (police surgeon) stated that he believed the killer wore an overcoat to hide any bloodstains. Many poor Jews could not afford such a luxury as an overcoat. Reversible coats (waterproof or otherwise) were on the market in 1888. Such a coat could transform the appearance of any individual.

A change of headgear would also be advantageous to the killer, and would cause confusion in witness statements. It is possible that Schwartz was the man who identified the attacker at the Seaside Home, if in fact the Seaside Home saga is correct. It was dark and overcast when Stride was murdered, so how could the witness identify the suspect unhesitatingly under such conditions and after a period of 18 months? Try that one out on a Crown Court today – it would be laughed out of court.

Also, I find it difficult to believe that the police would let a witness go after he or she had potentially identified Yours Truly, Jack the Ripper, and then refused to state this in a court of law. The police would have asserted a great deal of pressure on the witness if only to save their own reputations.

THE FOURTH VICTIM

SUNDAY, 30 SEPTEMBER 1888, ALDGATE

Alias: Catherine Conway
Age: 46
Height: 5ft
Profession: Prostitute
Hair: Dark Auburn
Eyes: Hazel
Nose: –
Complexion: bronzed
Dress: Black cloth jacket, imitation fur edging. Black straw bonnet, brown linsey bodice dress. Pair of men's lace-up boots. Brown ribbed stockings. Very old ragged blue skirt and a white calico chemise

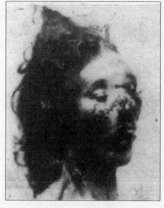

CATHERINE EDDOWES, ALIAS Mary Ann Kelly, was born in Wolverhampton in 1842. She moved to Flower and Dean Street in 1881 with John Kelly, who knew her as Catherine Conway. Her occupation was listed as a hawker who sold matchboxes and other small items.

In September 1888, she returned from a few weeks' hop-picking at Hunton, Nr. Coxheath, Kent. She walked back on foot with John Kelly.

They arrived back in London on 28 September. Catherine stayed at Shoe Lane Workhouse while John Kelly slept at 55, Flower and Dean Street. The newspaper story below, which relates to Eddowes knowing the identity of the killer, is not supported by any known police evidence.

Upon her arrival at the workhouse she told the superintendent she knew the identity of Jack the Ripper and that she was after the reward. The superintendent warned her to be careful that she was not murdered herself. Her reply was, 'Oh, no fear of that.'

On 29 September at 8.00am she arrived at 55, Flower and Dean Street after she was thrown out of Shoe Lane Workhouse. She spent her time with John Kelly until 2.00pm at which time they parted company. PC Robinson saw her at 8.30pm outside 29, Aldgate High Street causing a drunken disturbance.

Robinson, with assistance from PC Simmons, took her to Bishopsgate Police Station. She gave her name as 'Nothing' on admittance and Station Sergeant Byfield locked her in a cell. At 1.00am she was released, giving her name as Mary Ann Kelly residing at 6, Fashion Street, Spitalfields. When released by PC Hutt she asked the time and was told that it was too late for her to obtain drink.

She was seen to turn left on leaving the station and proceeded to walk in the direction of Aldgate, where she was supposedly picked up. To go in the direction of her home she should have turned right on leaving the station.

From Bishopsgate Police Station to Mitre Square it is a walk of about eight minutes. Harry Harris, Joseph Hyam Levy and Joseph Lawende had been drinking in the Imperial Club at 16–17, Dukes Place, Aldgate. Because of the foul wet weather they were late in leaving. Lawende checked the time by the club clock and his own watch and stated the time was exactly 1.30am when they got up to leave. Lawende said they finally left the club about five minutes later. Levy stated they got up to go at 1.30am but left the club three to four minutes after the half-hour.

Seconds after leaving the club at 1.33–35am they saw a man and a woman in Duke Street standing at the entrance to Church Passage; this was a covered passage which led into Mitre Square. According to

Lawende, the club was 15–16ft from the entrance to Church Passage. Lawende was the only witness to take in the suspect's appearance.

The woman was facing the man with her hand on his chest and was talking amicably to him. He was of medium build and was of a 'sailor's appearance', wearing a pepper-and-salt-coloured loose jacket, grey cloth cap with a peak of the same colour and he had a red neckerchief. He was 5ft 7-8in tall, aged about 30, with a fair complexion and he had a moustache.

The square was checked at 1.30am by PC Watkins walking in from the Mitre Street entrance, and all was clear. At 1.41–42am PC James Harvey walked up Church Passage from Duke Street and stood viewing the square from the end of the passage, but he did not enter the square.

Mitre Square showing the view from the entrance to Church Passage, the spot where Eddowes was seen with the suspect by Mr Lawende and company. The body was found at the spot marked 'X'. The original line of the old enclosed passage is still visible today. PC Harvey walked to the end of this passage at 1.41–42am. The end of the original passage can be seen 12 inches past the bollard on the far left. This gives a good indication of the distance involved. It took me 29.78 seconds to walk from the entrance to the passage in Duke Street to the spot where the victim was found. The killer may well have used one of the empty houses (located where the brick enclosure now stands, to the rear of the spot marked 'X') weeks in advance to check on the police beat times. The square still retains the old cobblestones which were in evidence in 1888. The line of the square is much as it was at the time of the murders. Nothing remains of the buildings which stood silent witness to such an infamous murder. The killer left this site to get straight back on to Aldgate High Street

He stated that all was clear. PC Harvey took his time from the post office clock in Aldgate at 1.28–29am.

At 1.44–45am, PC Watkins again entered the square from the Mitre Street entrance and found the body. He stated that the body was not there at 1.30am when he last checked the square on his beat. PC Watkins called George Morris, the watchman from Kearley & Tonge's, to assist him. Morris ran into Aldgate finding Constables Harvey and Holland. Harvey brought Dr Sequeira from Jewry Street on to the scene.

News of the murder reached Inspector Edward Collard at Bishopsgate Police Station about 10 minutes after the body was

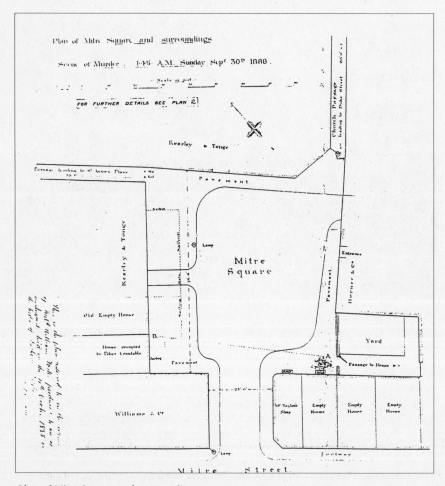

Plan of Mitre Square and surroundings

Drawing of Mitre Square and the body of Eddowes

Police Constable Edward Watkins of the City Police discovering the mutilated remains of Catherine Eddowes in the corner of Mitre Square

discovered. Police surgeon Dr Gordon Brown was then summoned to attend the crime scene. He arrived at Mitre Square just after 2.00am. Sergeant Foster, Superintendent McWilliam and Commissioner Warren, among others, would be attending the scene before daybreak; this was the only murder site Warren attended.

A brief summary of the sight which confronted Watkins can be found in the following extracts taken from Dr Brown's medical report:

The body was found on its back, the head turned to the left shoulder. The right leg drawn up, the other leg in line with the body. The arms were by the side of the body as if they had fallen there. Her throat was cut across twice to the extent of about six to seven and a half inches. Her face had been badly mutilated. Mutilations were carried out to the body and the intestines were found placed over her right shoulder – they were smeared over with some feculent matter. A piece of about two feet was quite detached from the body and placed between the body and left arm, apparently by design. The lobe and auricle of the right ear was cut obliquely through. No sign of superficial bruises. No secretion of any kind on the thighs. No spurting of blood on the bricks or pavement around the victim. No blood on the front of the clothes. No traces of recent connection. Body parts, including the left kidney and the womb, were taken. A portion of the victim's apron had been cut away and was missing. There was no sign of a struggle.

Dr Brown concluded that there would not be much blood on the murderer.

The body was taken to Golden Lane Mortuary for a full examination by Dr Gordon Brown. The full post-mortem report by Dr Brown can be seen in the Corporation of London records. This victim was asphyxiated standing up and then placed on her left side. The left side of her face had mud on it, which supports this. Her throat was then cut twice, left to right. The killer was placed behind her at this stage. She was mutilated after being placed on her back.

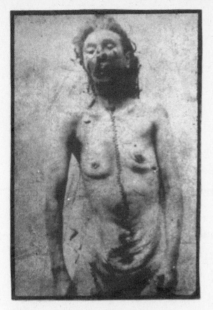

Mortuary photograph of Eddowes

It has been suggested that the killer cut a piece from the victim's apron at Mitre Square and then walked to Goulston Street where he cleaned his knife and left the apron piece in the doorway. This assumption is incorrect. The killer is not going to use his knife, conceal it before cleaning it, then take a walk to Goulston Street to clean it. He would have cleaned his knife (and hands) in Mitre Square. He did not take the apron piece for the purpose of cleaning his knife

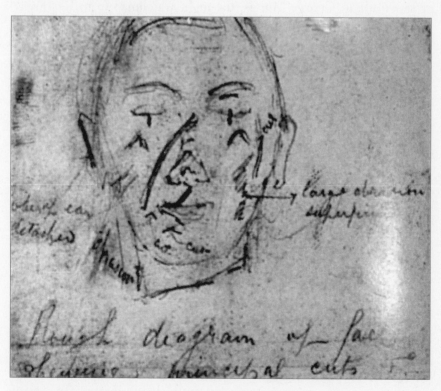

Diagram drawn at the time of the murder showing the cuts to the face and symbols cut into the eyelids and cheeks

73

elsewhere. Neither did he do as one would expect and wipe his hands and knife on the apron and leave it intact.

He needed the apron piece for three reasons, one of which is dealt with here; the other two reasons are included later. According to Dr Brown the victim's apron which had originally been white was, at the time of her demise, black with dirt and grime. A very large piece of the victim's apron had been taken with a clean cut of the killer's knife. Certain items taken by Jack were fouled with faecal matter.

To overcome the problem of contaminating his person Jack wrapped the stolen body parts in the large piece of apron cut from the victim to carry them off in. When found at Goulston Street the apron piece did contain traces of blood and faecal matter.

I do not believe that Jack killed Eddowes without prior knowledge of police activity in Mitre Square. A City of London policeman, PC Pearse, actually lived at No. 3 Mitre Square with his wife and they heard or saw nothing. George Morris, the night watchman from Kearley & Tonge's in Mitre Square, was an ex-policeman!

In spite of the presence in the square of one serving policeman, one ex-policeman and police activity to and from the square, Jack still achieved his objective. This was not achieved by sheer speculation or luck on the part of the killer. A cautious planner would have undoubtedly checked out the beat times on this site.

Only a fool would kill on speculation without finding out that the site was checked by police at 1.30am, 1.41–42am and 1.44–45am. To even contemplate such a move would

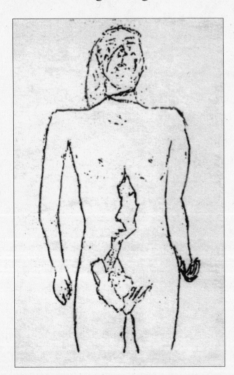

Sketch taken at the mortuary showing cuts to the body

The corner of Wentworth Street looking down Goulston Street. The doorway is marked 'X'. It is sometimes incorrectly assumed that the door to the left of the 'X', with the awning, is the correct doorway

be akin to suicide. Failure would have meant death by hanging (if the killer was proven sane) if caught. We are not dealing with the village idiot here.

At exactly 2.55am, one hour and 19 minutes after the body was found, PC Long found the missing apron piece at Goulston Street. Placed above it on the wall was a message from the killer. It was misinterpreted as 'The Juwes are the men that will not be blamed for nothing.' This will be discussed in depth later.

The killer on leaving Mitre Square would have wanted to go to ground as soon as possible with the incriminating stolen body parts covered in the apron piece. He would have known that it would only be a matter of minutes before the victim was found by the beat constable. He could not afford to be on the streets heading towards Goulston Street when the hue and cry went up. He did the sensible thing by going straight to a bolthole near the centre of the main junction which he reached about seven minutes after leaving Mitre Square.

He did what he had to do at his bolthole, possibly changing clothes. He then waited until he thought it safe before venturing forth to leave

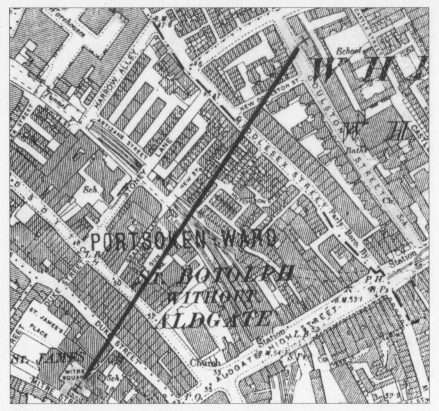

Map showing Mitre Square in relation to Goulston Street. At the ends of the black line marked with '+' appear the locations of the victim at Mitre Square and the doorway in Goulston Street where the writing and apron piece were found

the apron piece and message at Goulston Street. On leaving his bolthole he would be free of any blood on his person so would be safe in that respect. The police were looking for a killer with blood on him.

We also know that some suspects stopped after the murder of Eddowes were not searched. One misconception relating to the killer is that he was left-handed. Such a conclusion has been drawn by those who misinterpret the known facts. Due to the killer's MO and the medical evidence I believe Jack was right-handed.

Professor James Cameron, a specialist in forensic medicine who has investigated this aspect of the case, agreed with my conclusion recently by stating that the killer was right-handed.

Eddowes was buried in an unmarked grave in Ilford on 8 October 1888. Ripper expert Philip Sugden, author of *The Complete History of*

Jack the Ripper, believes that in the case of Chapman and Eddowes there does seem to have been some eerie ritualistic element in evidence.

Rewards were offered by the City police and a Vigilance Committee presided over by Mr Lusk of Alderney Road, Mile End. Mr Lusk received a three-inch-square box wrapped in brown paper on 15 October 1888. The postmarks on the parcel were indistinct so that it was impossible to state whether the package was posted in the E or EC districts. The parcel contained half of a human kidney.

The kidney was submitted to Dr Openshaw, curator of the London Hospital Anatomical Museum who pronounced it to be a human kidney preserved in spirits of wine. The kidney was then handed over to the City police. The kidney was then examined by Dr Gordon Brown of the City police.

He stated that he could not tell if it was a left kidney. He went on to add that it must have been cut previously to its being immersed in the spirit for more than a week. Brown added that there was no portion of the renal artery adhering to it, it having been trimmed up, so consequently there could be no correspondence established between the portion of the body from which it was cut. No proof was ever shown that the kidney came from Eddowes.

The box contained a letter, which read:

From hell
Mr Lusk
Sor
I send you half the
Kidne I took from one women
prasarved it for you. tother piece I
fried and ate it was vey nise. I
may send you the bloody knif that
took it out if you only wate a whil
longer
signed Catch me when
you can
Mishter Lusk

The *Daily Telegraph* of Saturday, 20 October 1888, reported:

A statement which apparently gives a clue to the sender of the strange package by Mr Lusk was made last night by Miss Emily Marsh, whose father carries on business in the leather trade at 218, Jubilee Street, Mile-end-road. In Mr Marsh's absence Miss Marsh was in the front shop, shortly after one o'clock on Monday last when a stranger dressed in clerical costume entered, and, referring to the reward bill in the window, asked for the address of Mr Lusk, described therein as the president of the Vigilance Committee. Miss Marsh at once referred the man to Mr J. Aarons, the treasurer of the committee, who resides at the corner of Jubilee Street and Mile-end-Road, a distance of about thirty yards.

The man, however, said he did not wish to go there, and Miss Marsh thereupon produced a newspaper in which Mr Lusk's address was given as Alderney Road, Globe Road, no number being mentioned. She requested the stranger to read the address, but he declined, saying, 'Read it out', and proceeded to write something in his pocket book, keeping his head down meanwhile. He subsequently left the shop, after thanking the young lady for the information, but not before Miss Marsh, alarmed by the man's appearance, had sent the shop-boy, John Cormack, to see that all was right. This lad, as well as Miss Marsh, gave a full description of the man, while Mr Marsh, who happened to come along at the time, also encountered him on the pavement outside. The stranger is described as a man of some forty-five years of age, fully six feet in height, and slimly built. He wore a soft felt hat, drawn down over his forehead, a stand up collar, and a very long black single-breasted overcoat, with a Prussian or clerical collar partly turned up. His face was of a sallow type, and he had a dark beard and moustache. The man spoke with what was taken to be an Irish accent. No importance was attached to the incident until Miss Marsh read of the receipt by Mr Lusk of a strange parcel, and then it occurred to her that the stranger might be the person who had despatched it. His

	Man seen in pub doorway	Man who spoke to Miss Marsh	My suspect
Age	about 35	about 45	47
Hair	light brown	dark	light brown
Height	5ft 11in	6ft	5ft 11in
Hat	black felt, wide-brimmed	black felt, wide-brimmed	black felt, wide-brimmed
Coat	long black overcoat	long black overcoat	long black overcoat
Complexion	fresh	sallow	sallow
Build	not known	slim	lean & slim
Smoker	seen lighting a pipe	not known	known pipe smoker
Moustache	light brown	dark	light brown

inquiry was made at one o'clock on Monday afternoon, and Mr Lusk received the package at 8pm the next day. The address on the package curiously enough gives no number in Alderney Road, a piece of information which Miss Marsh could not supply. It appears that on leaving the shop the man went right by Mr Aaron's house, but did not call. Mr Lusk has been informed of the circumstances, and states that no person answering the description has called on him, nor does he know any one at all like the man in question. The letter sent with the kidney show the word's 'mishter', 'prasarved', 'Sor' and 'tother' which is how some Irish people would pronounce such words. The Lusk letter was possibly written to give the false impression that it was written by an Irish person. Miss Marsh stated the stranger spoke with what was taken to be an Irish accent and she was very suspicious of him. It is possible that he intended to give the false impression that he was an Irishman.

Combined police and medical opinions thought it possible that the 'Lusk kidney' could be a hoax. The kidney could have been taken from any person upon whom a post-mortem had been made for any cause by students or a dissecting room porter. In fact it could have been taken by anyone in a hospital with access to organs. Such body parts could also be bought for cash.

If the man seen by Miss Marsh were the killer, or someone who sent the kidney as a hoax, then it would stand to reason that they would wish to alter their true appearance before putting themselves 'on offer' in person, by asking questions. After all, the stranger did bring suspicion upon himself by doing so. Did he disguise himself, hence the dark beard?

The *Standard*, dated 13 November 1888, quoted the Home Secretary Henry Matthews as stating:

> The failure of the police, so far, to detect the person guilty of the Whitechapel murders is due, not to any new reorganisation in the department, but to the extraordinary cunning and secrecy which characterise the commission of the crimes.

Surely such a cunning murderer would disguise himself if only for the following reasons: several murders were to be committed in a public place so there was a high risk of being seen. He would not wish to be recognised if disturbed on the job or if seen in the company of a victim minutes prior to her murder. He would wish to dress in an attire to throw people off his true occupation or class (i.e. dress to give the appearance of a sailor or clerk so that the police would look for a different person), to blend in with his surroundings more easily. If caught later no witness could identify him. He could clean up more easily, go to ground minutes after each murder and change from the disguise into his own clothes thus no blood on his person.

If we work on the supposition that Jack killed Eddowes between the police beat times of 1.30am and 1.41–42am then ideally she should have been murdered by 1.35–36am. Thus evidence must be shown that the killer was in the company of Eddowes just prior to 1.35–36am. We do have such evidence. I believe it possible that she was dead and being mutilated by 1.36am.

We are very fortunate that we can place Eddowes on the scene some minutes previously, because she was last seen between 1.33am and 1.35am with a suspect (a 29-second walk from where the body was found) at the entrance to Mitre Square. If seen at 1.33am the victim could have been dead by 1.34am. Two minutes for the mutilations and the killer could have left at 1.36am. This would have left him five to six minutes to spare.

If seen at 1.35am Eddowes could have been dead by 1.36am and Jack could have fled the scene by 1.38am. This would give him three to four minutes before the scene was checked again at 1.41–1.42am. I have used the basis of my times on the written evidence of both Levy and Lawende.

Clocks and watches in 1888 were mechanical and, if not properly maintained, they had a tendency to run either fast or slow. So, if Lawende's watch and the clock in the club were running a minute or two slower they could have seen Eddowes a minute or so sooner than 1.33am.

Dr Brown believed the mutilations took at least five minutes to perform. However, because the killer was working at great speed, the mutilations could have been achieved in less time. Dr Sequeira thought it would only have taken three minutes. From my own experiences of gutting thousands of livestock on piece work, before the industry was mechanised as it is today by ECU standards, and of observing others, the killer could well have achieved his task in two minutes. Dr Iain West, forensic pathologist at Guys Hospital, London, recently stated that in his opinion the mutilations took about two minutes.

Question. What type of surgeon could work in poor light at speed in such conditions?
Answer. One with experience in adverse or battlefield conditions.

Although it was dark, Jack could see well enough to cut very fine symbols into the victim's eyelids and face. Dr Brown believed that the killer had sufficient time or he would not have nicked the lower eyelids. The speed at which the killer worked could be attributed to the fact that he knew he had to leave before the crime scene was checked at 1.41–42am. Precise timing and speed on this site were of the essence.

When we turn to the motive for the crimes, again misconceptions seem to be the order of the day. It is interesting to note that Dr Brown stated that there was definitely no sign (as in the other cases) of any sexual connection. In other words there was no conclusive medical evidence to support the theory that the motive for murder was of a sexual nature.

Professor Jeremy Coid, forensic psychiatrist, recently stated of the murders, 'there's nothing in terms of the evidence available at that time which shows without a doubt that these crimes were committed by somebody in a state of sexual arousal. There weren't actually objects inserted into the body; there was no evidence of semen at the scene of the crime.'

Coroner Wynne Baxter, presiding over the inquest on Chapman, stated that the desire to possess the missing organ had been the object of the attack and the theft of the two rings was an attempt to disguise the true motive which was simply to obtain her womb. So what use could be made from the missing organs?

At the time of the murders, an unknown American doctor was doing the rounds of certain hospitals with the intention of obtaining wombs to illustrate his lectures. Dr Brown wrote, 'the parts removed would have no use for any professional purpose'. No one would deliberately achieve infamy while searching for specimens, and then kill five prostitutes to obtain two wombs when they could have purchased them legally.

Dr Brown was of the opinion that the killer had a great deal of medical knowledge to have removed the kidney and considerable knowledge of the positions of organs in the abdominal cavity and how to remove them.

Let us take into account the beat times at Mitre Square, the precise timing which had to be involved on the part of the killer, the boldness by which it was all achieved and the elaborate surgery performed at speed in such conditions. Added up, these indicate that the killer must have planned in advance, was cool, calculating, bold, was not perturbed by danger and had a great deal of experience in surgery. It is obvious that he needed the body parts or he would not have taken them. They were more than just trophies. Not enough thought has gone into why he took them.

One avenue which was never explored by the police of the day, mainly due to their ignorance of it, was occult ritual murder, including the doctrine that certain organs should be removed from murdered harlots, killed at pre-arranged sites, which were to be located at the four points of the compass. Certain organs could be made into holy candles for use in an occult ritual, while other organs could be made into potions for use in the occult.

Sergeant Jones found three boot buttons, a thimble and a mustard tin containing pawn tickets for a man's shirt and John Kelly's boots lying beside the body. It would help to know whether or not the items were placed in a neat and deliberate fashion.

The killer cut a line into each of Eddowes's eyelids. He also cut two symbols into her cheeks (^ ^). I was told by an investigator with 30 years' experience (who should have known better) that the marks on the face of this victim could have been caused by her falling over! (She was laid down by the killer.) My answer to such a remark is that the victim may also have stabbed herself twice in the face with a potato peeler moments before her murder!

The two marks in question are occult symbols, which were placed by the killer for a purpose. The two brass rings taken from Chapman's fingers also have significance in the occult. Metal is removed from contact with the skin so that certain forces or energies called upon to aid the killer will not be interfered with by their conductive properties.

When a Mason takes his oath he is symbolically stripped of such metal objects as rings and watches. It is believed that a similar ritual went back to the initiation into the temple in Egypt. Once stripped of all metal, a rod was placed on a particular spot on the body and a small charge of energy was passed through the rod. A Mason's oath is simply mentioned here as an example.

Many secret societies, including occult groups, believe in unseen forces or energies. My suspect belonged to one such group if not more.

I simply wish to point out that certain societies share certain beliefs in relation to certain doctrines. In fact, I can see why Masons are concerned that certain knowledge should not get into the wrong hands for it can be abused by unscrupulous people.

My beliefs, and those of the general reader, on the subject of black magic or the occult are neither here nor there. What matters is the fact that many individuals involved in voodoo, the occult or black magic do believe in such mumbo jumbo, for many it is a form of religion and some commit murder because of such beliefs. Such murders continue to happen up to the present day as will be shown later.

The man that Schwartz saw attacking Stride was not her murderer. Neither was he the same man that killed Eddowes. Not unless he went home, sobered himself up and took a 10-minute crash course on how to approach a woman without attacking her first.

Dr William S. Saunders was a doctor of medicine, Fellow of the Chemical Society, Fellow of the Institute of Chemistry and public analyst of the City of London. He received the stomach of Eddowes from Dr G. Brown. It had been sealed and had not been interfered with. The stomach and the contents had been examined for poisons of a narcotic nature. There was not the slightest trace of any poison or narcotic. In fact none of the victims was either poisoned or drugged. No evidence however slight has ever been produced to show otherwise. Despite this fact and taking into account the police and medical evidence available, some individuals still persist in believing otherwise.

Others erroneously assume that the killer would have been covered in blood after performing his operations on any of his first four victims. It would also be incorrect to deduce that blood would have soiled his clothing to a high degree when he hid the body parts on his person. Jack the Ripper was no novice when it came to operating and he knew how to avoid being soiled with blood under such circumstances.

He knew that, if he asphyxiated his victims prior to cutting their throats and before mutilating the corpse, such action would eliminate the problem of blood. He dealt with his first four victims as a slaughterman would deal with cattle. The principle is the same and so are the end results.

I have gutted hundreds of animals in a single shift and at the end of the day I may have had a few smears of blood on my whites. When working with livestock, after the correct procedures have been observed, it is far from a bloody job. In fact, it is surprisingly blood-free after the initial blood-letting stage.

Vital organs such as the heart, lungs, liver and pancreas are not bloody to handle. A small film of fluid and a smear of blood would be the limit. The vital organs removed from the victims would be no bloodier than what you would buy from a butcher. However, any appendages also taken could be soiled with other matter. Such items would need to be handled more carefully.

A kidney taken from a person or animal could be placed straight into a pocket without blood visibly soaking through the pocket and appearing on clothing. All Jack the Ripper had to do was to wipe his hands after working and, if he were wearing dark clothing, any spots of blood would be difficult to see. It would just be a matter of wiping any spots away. In fact, my suspect stated this to be the case.

He also smoked a pipe so could quite easily have placed any body parts he took in a waterproof tobacco pouch before concealing them

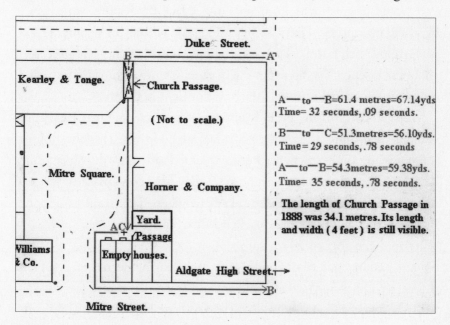

Distances in relation to Mitre Square, Aldgate. Victim denoted by '+'

Photograph showing access and distance from Mitre Square to Aldgate High Street, looking down Mitre Street

about his person. In fact, he need not have wrapped them in anything. If the latter had been the case then a possible slight smear of matter could have appeared inside a pocket or wherever the item was hidden.

It would be misleading to maintain that Jack the Ripper worked in a blind and uncontrolled frenzy while killing and gutting his victims. When performing such fast work, concentration, control, ability and precision are of the essence. The operations performed on the victims were carried out in a professional manner, which was evident in the work.

We have two missing periods of time, which indicate that Jack went straight to ground after killing Stride and Eddowes. The question of these missing times has never been explained satisfactorily. More often than not, like other aspects of the case, they have been passed over as a mystery. The first missing time relates to where Jack went on leaving Berner Street and before he reached Mitre Square.

It has been incorrectly assumed that Jack went straight to Mitre Square, picking up a victim on the way, after leaving Berner Street. I left the site of Dutfield's Yard at 12.55am and walked at a very fast pace to Mitre Square via Commercial Road and Aldgate High Street. This is one of two possible routes Jack took. The other route is no longer possible to travel due to redevelopment. I stopped at the old prostitute's church, St Botolphs, Aldgate, for two minutes to reconstruct Jack's timing.

In 1888 prostitutes congregated outside the church, which was a well-known area for soliciting prostitutes. While prostitution was not illegal, loitering for that purpose was. To overcome this problem the prostitutes would keep on the move by walking around the church.

It would make sense for Jack to pick up Eddowes in the vicinity of the church in Aldgate High Street which was only 46 yards from Duke Street which led into Mitre Square. He is only in the company of this victim for several minutes. It would also make sense for Jack to arrange to meet both Stride and Eddowes on site due to the measures taken to catch him. Stride was seen waiting around for some reason and in the process she was heard to turn down a potential client.

It should have taken Jack no longer than two minutes to pick up a prostitute in Aldgate if he did not agree to meet with Eddowes on site. On leaving the church Jack should have been at the entrance to Church Passage (now St James Passage) with Eddowes between one and two minutes later. Thus, he would be in her company for only a minimum amount of time.

I reached the entrance to Church Passage from Berner Street in just under 12 minutes. The time was nearly 1.07am. But Jack was not seen at the same place until about 1.33–35am. He certainly was not talking to Eddowes at the entrance to the passage for nearly 26–28 minutes, neither did he spend the missing time looking for a prostitute. Nor would he have gone into a pub to pick up a victim. So where did he go on leaving Berner Street and before reaching Mitre Square? I believe that he went to ground at a bolthole halfway between Berner Street and Mitre Square to alter his appearance, owing to the fact that he was seen at Berner Street.

The second missing time relates to where Jack went on leaving Mitre Square and before he went to Goulston Street. When Eddowes was murdered it was incorrectly assumed that the killer proceeded to Goulston Street where he wrote the message on the wall and left the piece of the victim's apron to show evidence that the writer was the killer.

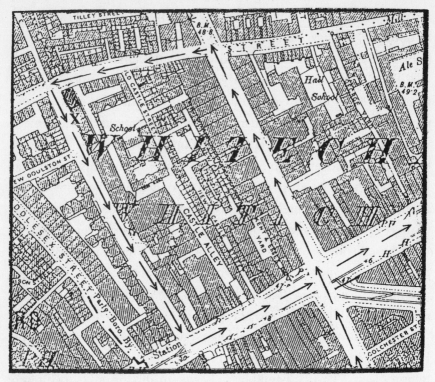

Map showing the route which I believe the killer took from his second bolthole in Leman Street to write the chalked message and to drop off the piece of the victim's apron in the doorway at Goulston Street, which is marked 'X' on the map

Mitre Square to Goulston Street is a walk of less than ten minutes, so the writing on the wall and the apron piece should have been on site no later than 1.55am if the murderer had gone directly to Goulston Street from Mitre Square. According to the police, the writing was not on the scene at 2.00am, nor was it on site at 2.20am, when the beat constable passed the spot. PC Alfred Long found it at 2.55am. PC Long was most adamant that the writing and the apron piece were not on site prior to 2.20am.

Some time between 2.20am and 2.55am Jack the Ripper wrote the message in Goulston Street. So it stands to reason that the killer went elsewhere on leaving Mitre Square. I believe that he went to his bolthole near the centre, which he could reach quite quickly after murders two, three, four and five.

The doorway at Goulston Street. Entrance to numbers 108–119, Wentworth Model Dwellings, Goulston Street. The lack of certain detail in relation to the crimes leaves a lot to be desired. For example no record exists of which doorjamb the killer left his message on, or where precisely on the doorjamb the writing was located. In his letter to the Home Office, Warren never mentioned these facts. Neither did Detective Halse. However, I believe the message was written on the right doorjamb, as one would face it from the street. The killer being right-handed would, I presume, stand in the cover of the entrance when writing the message on the doorjamb
Photo courtesy of Richard Whittington-Egan

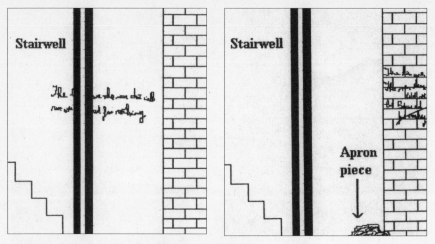

Two alternative drawings of wall, stairs and writing

The Goulston Street Graffito

I believe that the chalked message was written on the black brickwork of the doorjamb at the entrance to Wentworth Model Dwellings. It was not written in the inside of the stairwell as stated by some writers on the subject.

Detective Officer Daniel Halse stated: 'I and Detective Hunt went on to Goulston Street and the spot was pointed out to me where the apron was found. I saw some chalked writing on the black facing of the wall.'

I believe it is possible to deduce the following from the given facts:

1. One uses a black background if possible when writing with chalk, and the only black background available to the killer was on the doorjamb.

2. It is usual practice to place a message in a position where it can be viewed by the maximum number of people. If written on the doorjamb then the message would have been viewed by people in the street or by those leaving and entering the building. If the message were in the stairwell then fewer people would have seen it.

3. The manner in which the message was laid out suggests that the killer had limited space on which to write his message. The only

limited space available was on the black brickwork of the doorjamb at the entrance to the building. I do not believe that the killer carried chalk on his person at all times. Therefore I view the message as not being written on the spur of the moment but rather planned well in advance of the murder.

4. If the message was written on the wall inside the stairwell then it is most probable that it would have appeared on the wall in a similar fashion as shown (previous page left). If written on the black brick doorjamb then it would have appeared as copied by the police (previous page right).

In his article titled 'On the Danger of Writing Graffiti Too Cleverly', Jeffrey Bloomfield wrote:

Ever hear of Arthur Lambton? He was a leader in liberalising British divorce laws, and a founder of Our Society. In 1931, he wrote *Echoes of Cause Célèbres*. In it he relates the story of the Dalton Murder of 1882. PC George Cole was mortally wounded by a burglar he caught. The burglar's chisel was found with the word 'rock' on it. Two years later closer examination showed the letters 'O' and 'R' preceded the word. This helped identify one Thomas Henry Orrock as the murderer. Lambton's friend, Sir Arthur Conan Doyle, admitted to him that this clue was used in the first Sherlock Holmes novel, *A Study in Scarlet*. Holmes and Watson are examining the body of Enoch J. Drebber. Inspector Lestrade shows a clue. The letters 'R', 'A', 'C', 'H', and 'E' have been written in blood on a nearby wall. Lestrade believes the killer was writing the name 'Rachel'. Holmes points out that 'rache' is German for 'revenge'. Later Holmes is proved right.

Researches by various Sherlockians tend to support Lambton's claim. The novel, set in 1881, has many references and inferences to that period. Thomas Carlyle, who died in 1881, is mentioned. Watson, referring to Holmes's violin playing, uses the phrase 'trials upon my patience'. This may refer to the early Gilbert and Sullivan operettas, culminating in *Patience* (1881). A second murder victim, Joseph Stangerson, may owe his name to one Urban Napoleon Stanger, who disappeared in 1881. Even Lestrade's reference to a 'Miss Rachel' may be based on a notorious swindler, 'Madame' Rachel Leverson, who died in prison in 1880.

Doyle must have been proud of this clue with a hidden meaning. It seems likely that he was consulted regarding illustrations. When the novel (sic) appeared in *Beeton's Christmas Annual* of 1887, it was illustrated by one D.H. Friston. The writing on the wall was chosen as the frontispiece facing the opening page. It shows Holmes and the others studying the clue.

On 30 September 1888, a prostitute named Catherine Eddowes was murdered. It was the second vicious killing of that night. Near the site of the killing, on a wall on Goulston Street, was written, 'The Juwes are the men what [sic] will not be blamed for nothing.' The killer (we presume) must have thought the public would think the murders were done by a Jew.

Prior to 1888, I have found only one notorious crime where writing was near the victim's body: In the De La Rue Murder of 1845, Thomas Hocker left a *letter* near the victim to mislead the police. Among factual cases none seem to have killers' writing on walls. But not in fictional cases. I do not think it is a coincidence that nine months after Holmes examined 'Rache' (and was glaringly shown doing it by his illustrator) the Metropolitan Police were examining 'Juwes'. Both times the writing is on a wall near a murder scene, and the key word has a cryptic meaning. I feel Jack read *A Study in Scarlet*, and filed away a trick for future use. Far-fetched? Then please tell me of any other actual pre-1888 murder with a similar cryptic clue written on a wall.

Now let us look deeper into the matter. Part 1, Chapter 6, paragraph 2 of *A Study in Scarlet* reads:

The *Daily Telegraph* remarked that in the history of crime there had seldom been a tragedy which presented stranger features. The

German name of the victim, the absence of all other motive and the sinister inscription on the wall all pointed to its perpetration by political refugees and revolutionists. The socialists had many branches.

This, of course, is fiction. It resurfaced in 1888 when the tabloids were covering the real-life crimes of Jack the Ripper. Jack replaced the German word 'Rache' with the French word 'Juives', which means Jews. Police Commissioner Warren made a statement on 12 October 1888, while he was reflecting on the writing on the wall.

As Mr Matthews is aware, I have for some time past been inclined to the idea that the murders having been done by a secret society is the only logical solution to the question. But I could not imagine them being done by someone desiring to bring discredit to the Jews and socialists or the Jewish Socialists.

This statement could have come directly from *A Study in Scarlet*. In Part 1, Chapter 7, Holmes states, 'This murder would have been infinitely more difficult to unravel had the body of the victim been simply found lying in the roadway.' Three Ripper victims were found in just those circumstances.

In the murder investigated by Holmes we have blood left in a sink, after the killer has washed his hands, and marks on a sheet where the killer cleaned his knife before writing on the wall. In the murder of Eddowes, mentioned by Mr Bloomfield, we also have blood allegedly left in a sink.

Chief Superintendent Major Henry Smith, City of London police, stated he found blood in a sink shortly after the killer had wiped his knife on a piece of the victim's apron and left his message on the wall. Apparently Major Smith got confused and also placed the 'sink' incident as occurring after the Kelly murder (see *From Constable to Commissioner*, published 1910).

Police top brass of the period, and many Ripperologists since, are also guilty of placing certain incidents which occurred on one site at

Fiction: the frontispiece from A Study in Scarlet *(1887), by D. H. Friston*

Fact: an illustration taken from the Illustrated Police News, *Saturday, 20 October 1888. It shows Sir Charles Warren viewing the writing on the wall at Goulston Street*

another. My suspect did the same but his motives for doing so were far more devious as will be shown.

The Sir Arthur Conan Doyle stories are the fictitious reminiscences of John H. Watson MD, late of the Army Medical Department. The suspect named in my research held the post of surgeon major, with the rank of lieutenant in the Army of Garibaldi. He moved in the same circles as Doyle and they shared common interests, Madame Blavatsky being but one. She had also fought in Italy with Garibaldi, as did my suspect, but she fought in a later campaign.

Why shouldn't my suspect read the works of Conan Doyle? The quote I used at the beginning of this work, which I attribute to Jack the Ripper, was taken from a letter sent by my suspect to the *Pall Mall Gazette* in November 1888, which appeared in the same issue as a letter written by Conan Doyle. The quote given by the suspect is very Holmesian. I would have to agree with Jeff Bloomfield that the Ripper got the idea to write the message on the wall at Goulston Street from *A Study in Scarlet*, published in 1887.

Instead of using a German as Doyle did, the suspect plumped for a Frenchman. He had many French connections, including the use of the name Roslyn. He stated that the purpose of the missing womb in relation to the occult could be found in a French book. It is interesting to note that the offices used by my suspect were to be found in Baker Street opposite the fictional address used by Sherlock Holmes.

It is necessary at this point to give credit where credit is due. Jeffrey Bloomfield is the only person in over 100 years who has given us the answer to the question, 'Where did the killer get the idea for the Goulston Street Graffito?' I have yet to read any comment from any quarter recognising Jeffrey Bloomfield's achievement, which has been ignored. This a very unsatisfactory state of affairs but one which I do not altogether find surprising taking into consideration the prevailing attitude among many involved in Ripper research.

The stolen apron piece was used to wrap the faecal-soiled body parts in. The killer had two other reasons for taking it. His plan had two basic components.

1. Leave a message blaming the Jews.
2. Leave a trail to Dorset Street

The only way to prove that the killer left the message would be to leave evidence with the message that could be associated with the killer, and a piece of the victim's apron covered in gore would do the trick. The killer did not expect that the message would be misunderstood simply because it was not copied in its full context. When this man left a clue, it was left with the intention of leading police away from him and not to him.

Because of the confusion created over the word 'Juwes', the killer decided to write to the City of London police to clarify the true meaning of the message! The only person who knew the true meaning and spelling of the message was the killer himself. He even went so far as to explain to the police how they managed to get it wrong. This man has been the only person since 1888 to explain the true situation about the writing. We have a piece of damning evidence which has been either ignored or overlooked by Ripperologists for various reasons. The letter sent by the killer to the police on 16 October 1888 is shown below.

The London Hospital
Sir,
Having read Sir Charles Warren's Circular in yesterdays papers that 'It is not known that there is any dialect or language in which the word Jews is spelt Juwes', I beg to inform you that the word written by the murderer does exist in a European language, though it was not JUWES.

Try it in script———Thus,

The Juwes, &c

Now place a dot over the third upstroke (which dot was naturally overlooked by lantern light) and we get, plainly, The Juives which, I need not tell you, is the French word for Jews.

The murderer unconsciously reverted, for a moment, to his native language.

Pardon my presuming to suggest that there are three parts indubitably shown (2 another, probably) by the inscription.

1. The man was a Frenchman.

2. He had resided a long time in England to write so correctly; Frenchmen being, notoriously, the worst linguists in the world.

3. He had frequented the East End for years, to have acquired, as in the sentences written, a purely East End idiom.

4. It is probable (not certain) that he is a notorious Jew-hater, though he may only have written it to throw a false scent.

May I request an acknowledgement that this letter has safely reached you, & that it be preserved until I am well enough to do myself the honour to call upon you personally.

I am sir,

Yr. Obedt. Servant

(Killer's signature)

PS. I can tell you, from a French book, a use made of the organ in question d'une femme prostituee, which has not been suggested, if you think it is worth while.

Left: The message as copied by the police

Right: The message as it was written by the killer and as described by him. We can clearly see Juwes in the first example change to Juives simply by adding the missing dot above the letter i

The suspect let the police know that he was a patient in a hospital and was not well enough to call upon them, let alone commit five murders. One opinion, that the killer is a Frenchman, is a red herring while the other is true about a false scent, i.e. 'that it is possible but not certain that the killer was a Jew hater, although he may have only written the message to throw a false scent'.

In writing this letter to the police, he was playing a game and showing an egotistic tendency. A weakness is showing in his makeup because he is feeling the need of communicating his methods to the police. He is basically saying to the police 'See how clever I am?', but without telling them that he is the killer. He believed in his own superiority while believing others to be stupid. To a certain extent the situation proved such an assumption correct.

Jeffrey Bloomfield, an American Investigator-Specialist, wrote:

The problem with being in the position of Jack the Ripper, if you were an egomaniac, was that you had one of the greatest secrets of the world in your pocket, but could not reveal it to anyone. The murderer's position would have been impossible, unless he discovered that he would die shortly, and it did not matter if the world knew. As he lived past the year 1893 (when he repented) he would have had a perfect chance to see first hand what happens when you open your mouth too much. In 1891–92 a series of poisonings hit the area of Lambeth and Stepney and they were of prostitutes. The killings were at such a random pacing that little notice was made of them, until the killer, Dr Thomas Neil Cream, kept writing to various people (members of Parliament, doctors treating the Royal Family, divorced peeresses) revealing that he knew too much about the crimes. Though he used pseudonyms, his big mouth led the police to him and him to the scaffold. It would be curious to know what Jack the Ripper thought of Cream.

The intentions which lay behind the writing on the wall have been explained by the suspect. The message succeeded in confusing the police further than intended because it was copied down incorrectly. The suspect knew full well he had perpetrated the crimes and that he left the message at Goulston Street.

I view the message for what it was, a red herring. It is incorrect to believe that the writer was a Jew who wished to lead police to him. If Warren had taken a photograph of the writing, years of debate may have been avoided. It was believed by the police at the time that the writing was definitely the work of the killer and it has been generally accepted as so.

The writing on the wall is another classic example of the misinterpretation of the facts. The true situation at Berner Street was misinterpreted into two different stories. Fact has been substituted for fiction in many aspects of the case. A report written on 6

November 1888 by Chief Inspector Donald Swanson, in charge of the murder investigation from 1 September to 6 October 1888, stated that the medical evidence showed that the murder of Eddowes could have been committed by a properly trained surgeon or a student in surgery.

Acting Commissioner, City of London police, Sir Henry Smith was quoted in *The People of Sunday*, 9 June 1912, as saying that the killer was a gentile and possessed anatomical knowledge leading one to the conclusion that he was a medical man. From my own interpretation of the known facts and from my own past experiences I concur with such opinions.

Unfortunately, since 1888 many untrue stories have accumulated and have emerged in relation to the murders. Misinformation and misinterpretation of the truth have all played their part in obliterating the realms of reality and have substituted the truth of the matter with myth and misconceptions.

The medical profession gave varying opinions as to Jack's surgical ability. But the medical profession has always had a reputation for closing ranks. It is no different from the reaction from certain Masons when any mention is made of a Masonic connection to the murders. I have known blatant untruths to be told in defence of such ill-founded stories. From those, I might add, that should know better and who are a disgrace to their craft.

When Warren decided to erase the chalked writing at Goulston Street he came under a lot of criticism from all sides. Below is a copy of the letter sent by Warren to his superiors to justify his actions.

4 Whitehall Place,
S.W.
6 November 1888

Confidential
The Under Secretary of State
The Home Office

Sir,

In reply to your letter of the 5th instant, I enclose a report of the circumstances of the Mitre Square Murder so far as they have come under the notice of the Metropolitan Police, and I now give an account regarding the erasing the writing on the wall in Goulston Street which I have already partially explained to Mr Matthews verbally.

On the 30th September on hearing of the Berner Street murder, after visiting Commercial Street Station I arrived at Leman Street Station shortly before 5am and ascertained from the Superintendent Arnold all that was known there relative to the two murders.

The most pressing question at that moment was some writing on the wall in Goulston Street evidently written with the intention of inflaming the public mind against the Jews, and which Mr Arnold with a view to prevent serious disorder proposed to obliterate, and had sent down an inspector with a sponge for that purpose, telling him to await his arrival.

I considered it desirable that I should decide the matter myself, as it was one involving so great a responsibility whether any action was taken or not.

I accordingly went down to Goulston Street at once before going to the scene of the murder; it was just getting light, the public would be in the streets in a few minutes, in a neighbourhood very much crowded on Sunday morning by Jewish vendors and Christian purchasers from all parts of London.

There were several Police around the spot when I arrived, both Metropolitan and City.

The writing was on the jamb of the open archway or doorway

visible in the street and could not be covered up without danger of the covering being torn off at once.

A discussion took place whether the writing could be left covered up or otherwise or whether any portion of it could be left for an hour until it could be photographed; but after taking into consideration the excited state of the population in London generally at the time, the strong feeling which had been excited against the Jews, and the fact that in a short time there would be a large concourse of the people in the streets, and having before me the Report that if it was left there the house was likely to be wrecked (in which form my own observation I entirely concurred). I considered it desirable to obliterate the writing at once, having taken a copy of which I enclose a duplicate.

After having been to the scene of the murder, I went on to the City Police Office and informed Chief Superintendent of the reason why the writing had been obliterated.

I may mention that so great was the feeling with regard to the Jews that on the 13th ulto. the Acting Chief Rabbi wrote to me on the subject of the spelling of the word 'Jewes' on account of a newspaper asserting that this was Jewish spelling in the Yiddish dialect. He added 'in the present state of excitement it is dangerous to the safety of the poor Jews in the East [End] to allow such an assertion to remain uncontradicted. My community keenly appreciates your humane and vigilant action during this critical time.'

It may be realised therefore if the safety of the Jews in Whitechapel could be considered to be jeopardised 13 days after the murder by the question of the spelling of the word Jews, what might have happened to the Jews in that quarter had that writing been left intact.

I do not hesitate myself to say that if that writing had been left there would have been an onslaught upon the Jews, property would have been wrecked and lives would probably have been lost; and I was much gratified with the promptitude with which Superintendent Arnold was prepared to act in the matter if I had not been there.

I have no doubt myself whatever that one of the principal objects of the Reward offered by Mr Montagu was to show to the world that the Jews were desirous of having the Hanbury Street Murder cleared up, and thus to divert from them the very strong feeling which was then growing up.

I am, Sir,

Your most obedient Servant,
(signed) C. Warren

If Warren had obliterated the word 'Jewes' then I cannot see any logical reason why a riot should have taken place. Such a decision undoubtedly brings his judgement into question. Sir Charles Warren was to resign his post on 8 November 1888. This was the day before Mary Kelly was found murdered.

The Times of Tuesday, 13 November 1888 wrote that 'relations between Warren and the Home Office have for some time been strained'. The report added 'that the resignation of Sir Charles Warren practically arose out of a difference of opinion with Mr Monro'. The latter was assistant commissioner and was head of the CID. He resigned in August 1888, and became 'Head of Detective Service'. He was replaced by Anderson. Monro replaced Sir Charles Warren.

THE FIFTH VICTIM

FRIDAY, 9 NOVEMBER 1888, SPITALFIELDS

Alias: Marie Jeanette Kelly
Age: 25
Height: 5ft 7in
Profession: Prostitute
Eyes: Blue
Build: Stout
Complexion: Fair
Hair: Fair
Dress: Usually wore a black silk dress and often a black jacket, and red crossover shawl

A LOST WOMAN
MARY KELLY
IN MILLER'S COURT

MARY JANE KELLY, also known as Marie Jeanette or Black Mary, was alleged to be 25 years of age, stout and very attractive. Eddowes had a mustard tin with a pawn ticket inside which had been found near her body. The ticket was in the name of Mary Ann Kelly. Victim five is an enigma, for little is known of her early days. No records in births or marriages are known to exist.

Joseph Barnett, her boyfriend, made a statement to police on 9 November 1888, stating: 'She left her home about 4 years ago, and she was married to a collier, who was killed through some explosion. I think she said her husband's name was Davis or Davies.'

Moving to London in 1884 it was alleged that she had worked in a high-class French brothel in Knightsbridge. She stated to Barnett that a gentleman had taken her to France. She did not like it there and had returned to London after a fortnight. The suspect named in this book spent time in France and had French connections. The Goulston Street graffito indicates his knowledge of French.

Barnett stated that on her return from France she moved to Ratcliffe Highway for some time. Then she was living near Stepney Gas Works with a man named Morganstone. She then moved to Spitalfields, where she was picked up in Commercial Street by Barnett. He then took lodgings in George Street, Spitalfields.

Barnett said that Kelly was frightened of a man or men and often had him read accounts of the murders to her. This could indicate that Kelly could not read. However, a witness named Harvey of New-Court, off Dorset Street, said she had been on good terms with the deceased, whose education was much superior to that of most people of her position in life!

Kelly visited Harvey in New-Court on Thursday night. After drinking together they parted company at 7.30pm. Kelly went off in the direction of Leman Street, which she was in the habit of frequenting. Kelly had been living with Joe Barnett for 18 months until 30 October 1888. Eight months of these were spent at 13, Millers Court, 26, Dorset Street. Barnett and Kelly had a row over Kelly resuming prostitution and letting other prostitutes stay overnight.

A widow and resident of 1, Millers Court, and a close friend of Kelly's, Julia Venturney, mentioned in her statement dated 9 November 1888 that a few weeks previously Kelly was drunk and had broken the windows in room 13. The key to 13, Millers Court also disappeared (lost or stolen?) prior to the murder.

After Barnett moved out of 13, Millers Court, No. 26, Dorset Street, a German girl named Julia stayed. After a few days Julia left, her place being taken by Mrs Harvey. She stated that she had stayed over with Kelly on the Monday and Tuesday prior to the murders (5 and 6 November). She also stated that she had left a man's overcoat, two shirts, a boy's shirt, a black crepe bonnet, a child's petticoat and a pawn ticket in Kelly's room.

So Kelly, who for the last eight months had been living with Barnett in Dorset Street, now found herself living alone in a room only three days before her murder. This is very convenient for her killer. Many assumptions have been made in relation to the time lapse (nearly six weeks) between murders four and five. The killer had to wait for the right moment to kill Kelly after killing Eddowes.

Kelly had to be killed in her room and the killer could not proceed with his plans while Kelly was sharing her room with Barnett, Julia or Mrs Harvey. This simple fact explains the long period of time between the double event of 30 September and the Kelly murder. The killer had his eye on this victim and planned her murder well in advance. However, he had to wait for the opportunity before he could proceed to murder her in her room.

Several minutes prior to 2.00am on 9 November 1888, George Hutchinson was walking north along Commercial Street. After

Dorset Street circa 1890, looking east towards Commercial Street

Commercial Street, circa 1898. The entrance to Dorset Street is to be found bottom left by the Britannia public house. The Ten Bells public house can be seen on the corner, middle right. Spitalfields market is the building with the gables

passing the corner of Thrawl Street, and on approaching Flower and Dean Street, he met Kelly walking towards him. Hutchinson had known Kelly for about three years. She said to Hutchinson, 'Mr Hutchinson, can you lend me sixpence?' Hutchinson replied, 'I spent all my money going to Romford.' They then parted company, Kelly walking in the direction of Thrawl Street.

After parting company with Kelly, Hutchinson then turned round
and looked in the direction that Kelly had taken. Hutchinson said he
saw a man reach out and tap her on the shoulder, he then said
something to her, and they both burst out laughing. Kelly said, 'All
right,' to which the man replied, 'You will be all right for what I have

The same scene as it appears today

told you.' (Was he referring to a promise made previously?) He then placed his arm around her shoulders. He was carrying a kind of small parcel of American oilcloth in his left hand, tied with a strap. (Change of clothes or an oilcloth apron?) This night was cold and very wet, and oilcloth would keep a change of clothes dry.

Hutchinson was so surprised at the dress of this man that he decided to follow him. Kelly and the man walked towards Dorset Street. Hutchinson stopped under the lamp on the corner of Fashion Street and eyeballed the man as he walked by. Hutchinson stated that the man gave him a stern look on passing. The couple stood at the entrance to Millers Court. The man spoke to her and Kelly was heard to say, 'All right, my dear, come along, you will be comfortable.' Kelly then kissed him saying, 'I have lost my handkerchief.' The man then gave her a red one.

Hutchinson had alleged that he not only saw the colour of the handkerchief but had also heard what the couple had said. Under such dark and overcast conditions he must have been only a few yards away from them to notice the colour of the handkerchief. Therefore they must have noticed that Hutchinson was on their case.

The couple then went into Millers Court at about 2.05am. Hutchinson was so interested in the man that he stood opposite the court waiting for the suspect to appear. When this did not transpire, Hutchinson left the scene at 2.45am. The suspect was about 35, had a dark complexion, heavy moustache turned up at the ends, bushy eyebrows, dark eyes, long dark coat trimmed with astrakhan, soft felt wide-brimmed hat, white collar, black tie fixed with a horseshoe pin, dark spats, light button overboots and a massive gold chain was showing in his waistcoat.

Mary Anne Cox, No. 5, Millers Court, made a statement to police on 9 November 1888. She stated that she had last seen Kelly at about 11.45am when she came into Dorset Street from Commercial Street, and saw walking in front of her Mary Jane with a man. They turned into the court and as Cox entered the court they went indoors, as if they were going into Kelly's room. Cox stated that she said goodnight to Mary Jane, and that she was very drunk and could scarcely answer

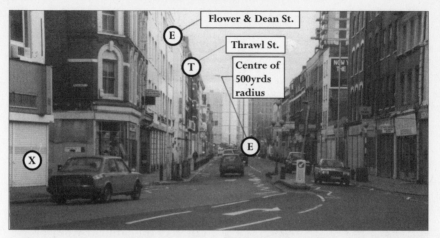

Flower & Dean St.

Thrawl St.

Centre of
500yrds
radius

E

T

E

X

Looking down Commercial Street from the North corner of Dorset Street towards the main cross-roads and the centre of the 500-yard radius. Fashion Street is to the far left of the picture. The shuttered shop (marked with an 'X') on the corner was once the Queen's Head Public House. It was on this corner that Hutchinson stopped under the lamp to get a good look at the suspect as he walked past with Kelly and crossed the street to Dorset Street. It was between Flower and Dean Street and Thrawl Street that Kelly was picked up by the suspect

her, but said goodnight. Cox heard Kelly singing shortly afterwards.

The man seen by Cox was about 36 years old and about 5ft 5in tall. His complexion was fresh, although he had blotches on his face, and he had small side whiskers and a thick carrotty moustache. He was dressed in shabby, dark clothes, a dark overcoat and a black felt hat. Kelly was wearing a linsey frock, a red knitted crossover around her shoulders and no hat or bonnet. Cox left the court shortly after midnight and returned at about 1.00am and Kelly was still singing in her room.

Catherine Pickett, a friend and neighbour of Kelly's, was annoyed by her singing and intended to complain about it at the time. David Pickett, her husband, persuaded her from doing so. Cox left the court again shortly after 1.00am returning at 3.00am (15 minutes after Hutchinson had left the scene) all was quiet and no sign of a light or fire was seen to come from room 13. Sarah Lewis, of 34, Great Pearl Street, Spitalfields (who was staying the night at No. 2, Millers Court), and Elizabeth Prater, of No. 20, room 27, Dorset Street, both stated that they heard a cry of 'Murder' come from the direction of Kelly's room between 3.30am and 4.00am.

Room 13, Millers Court, 26, Dorset Street, Spitalfields, taken on 9 November 1888. Elizabeth Prater, one of the women who heard a cry of 'Murder', lived above Kelly's room. The two broken windows are those nearest to the drainpipe. It was from this window that Mr Bowyer discovered the body

At 7.30am Catherine Pickett knocked on Kelly's door with the intention of borrowing her shawl. She received no answer and left.

The body was found, by Thomas Bowyer, just after 10.45am on Friday, 9 November, the day of the Lord Mayor's Show. (Bowyer had been sent to collect the rent owed of 35 shillings, which was a lot of money. Why had she not been evicted? We have two victims that were turned out for not having 4d for the price of a bed.) After knocking on the door and receiving no reply he tried the door, but it would not open. He then went to the back window of the room and pulled aside a muslin curtain by placing his hand through the lower of the two broken panes of glass.

The first thing he saw was a pile of flesh on a bedside table. The victim, in a chemise lying on the bed, was barely recognisable as a human being. She had been gutted, dissected and partly skinned. This victim had had her heart removed and stolen. Was it taken for a personal reason? Did the killer intend to use it in a ritual?

Bowyer rushed to get his boss, John McCarthy, who stated, 'The sight we saw I cannot drive away from my mind. It looked more like the work of a <u>devil</u> than of a man. I had heard a great deal about the Whitechapel murders, but I declare to God I had never expected to see such a sight as this. The whole scene is more than I can describe. I hope I may never see such a sight as this again.'

The police did not enter the room until 1.30pm, at which time

The remains of Mary Kelly lying on the bed in room 13, Millers Court

access to the room was forced by breaking open the door. Signs of a roaring fire were in the grate, the ashes still warm. It was concluded that several items left by Mrs Harvey in the room were burned on the fire. The solder on the spout and handle of a kettle found in the grate had melted. It is not known whether or not this damage may have occurred prior to the murder.

The following post-mortem report was written by Dr Thomas Bond after his examination of Mary Kelly's body. The report was missing for many years until it was returned to Scotland Yard,

The table with the pile of flesh taken from the victim. Note the leg bone in the foreground stripped of all flesh. The victim was dissected

anonymously in 1987. A large proportion of Ripper-related paperwork in official files went missing for various reasons.

Position of body

The body was lying naked in the middle of the bed, the shoulders flat, but the axis of the body inclined to the left side of the bed. The head was turned on the left cheek. The left arm was close to

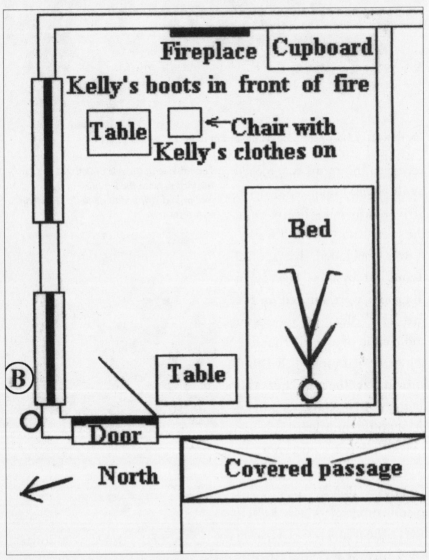

Plan of room 13, Millers Court. The broken windows from where Mr Bowyer saw the body is marked 'B'

the body with the forearm flexed at a right angle and lying across the abdomen. The right arm was slightly abducted from the body and rested on the mattress, the elbow bent and the forearm supine with the fingers clenched. The legs were wide apart, the left thigh at right angles to the trunk and the right forming an obtuse angle with the pubes.

The whole of the surface of the abdomen and thighs was removed and the abdominal cavity emptied of its viscera. The breasts were cut off, the arms mutilated by several jagged wounds and the face hacked beyond recognition of the features. The tissues of the neck were severed all round down to the bone.

The viscera were found in various parts viz.: The uterus and kidneys with one breast under the head, the other breast by the right foot, the Liver between the feet, the intestines by the right side and the spleen by the left side of the body. The flaps removed from the abdomen and thighs were on a table.

The bed clothing at the right corner was saturated with blood and on the floor beneath was a pool of blood covering about 2 feet square. The wall by the right side of the bed and in a line with the neck was marked by blood, which had struck it in a number of separate splashes.

Post-mortem examination

The face was gashed in all directions the nose, cheeks, eyebrows and ears being partly removed. The lips were blanched and cut by several incisions running obliquely down to the chin. There were also numerous cuts extending irregularly across all the features.

The neck was cut through the skin and other tissues right down to the vertebrae the 5th and 6th being deeply notched. The skin cuts in the front of the neck showed distinct ecchymosis.

The air passage was cut at the lower part of the larynx through the cricoid cartilage.

Both breasts were removed by more or less circular incisions, the muscles down to the ribs being attached to both breasts. The intercostals between the 4th, 5th, and 6th ribs were cut through and the contents of the thorax visible through the openings.

The skin and tissues of the abdomen from the costal arch to the pubes were removed in three large flaps. The right thigh was denuded in front to the bone, the flap of skin, including the external organs of generation and part of the right buttock. The left thigh was stripped of skin, fascia and muscles as far as the knee.

The left calf showed a long gash through skin and tissues to the deep muscles and reaching from the knee to 5 inches above the ankle.

Both arms and forearms had extensive and jagged wounds.

The right thumb showed a small superficial incision about 1 inch long, with extravasation of blood in the skin and there were several abrasions on the back of the hand moreover showing the same condition.

On opening the thorax it was found that the right lung was minimally adherent by firm old adhesions. The lower part of the lung was broken and torn away.

The left lung was intact: it was adherent at the apex and there were a few adhesions over the side. In the substances of the lung were several nodules of consolidation.

The Pericardium was open below and the heart absent.

In the abdominal cavity was some partially digested food of fish and potatoes and similar food was found in the remains of the stomach attached to the intestines.

According to Dr Bond the body was naked when, in fact, a chemise was in evidence. However, the chemise had been cut from the torso. Under such circumstances it is understandable why Dr Bond referred to the body as naked.

Ritual mutilation of the dead such as we find in this series of murders has a great deal of significance in occult murder. Such practices are still in evidence today on the west coast of Africa. In fact my suspect was known to have travelled to the West Coast of Africa in search of such occult knowledge. He even went so far as to write on the subject.

Certain superstitious religious beliefs world-wide also have a bearing on ritual mutilation of the dead. Several tribes world-wide held the belief that disembowellment of an adult enemy signified that the spirit of the deceased would go straight to the afterlife, thus ensuring that the spirit does not wreak revenge while remaining on the earthly plain.

In January 1879, at the Battle of Isandhlwana, over 800 Europeans were disembowelled and mutilated by Zulu warriors who held such religious beliefs. The Drummer boys at Isandhlwana, not considered as men by the Zulu, were not disembowelled. Instead they were hung on meat hooks. North American Indian tribes such as the Sioux and Cheyenne mutilated their dead enemies because of certain religious beliefs they held.

Mary Kelly could not be recognised by her facial features. It was stated that Joseph Barnett only recognised her by the colour of her eyes and her unusual ears. Yet Dr Bond stated that her ears had been partly removed. It was assumed that the body on the bed was Kelly because her clothing was found in a neat and deliberate pile on a chair, the body was found in Kelly's room, and nothing more was ever heard of Kelly after the murder.

Several people, including Mrs Maxwell and Maurice Lewis, stated that they either saw Kelly or spoke to her between 8.00am and 10.00am on 9 November 1888. This was six or eight hours after medical and other evidence suggested that she was murdered. Mrs Maxwell stated that she had known Kelly for some months and that she had seen her between 8.00am and 8.30am standing at the corner of Millers Court.

She said Kelly was dressed in a green bodice, dark skirt and a maroon crossover shawl (Kelly was seen wearing a shawl the previous day). Mrs Maxwell went on to say that she had a conversation with Kelly in which Kelly said she had been for a drink but had vomited it up. Maxwell went on to add that about one hour later she saw Kelly talking to a man outside the Britannia public house. I would like to know if the crossover shawl was ever found in Kelly's room. What happened to that shawl?

It is a matter of conjecture whether the killer went to Millers Court to meet Kelly or whether he met her in Commercial Street. We do know she was in bed when attacked and was awake at the time. The cry of 'Murder' heard by independent witnesses enforces this fact. A sheet had covered the region of her neck. The top part of the sheet was found to have knife cuts in it.

If she was in bed and awake when attacked she may have pulled the sheet up with her hands out of fright and in an attempt to protect herself. The victim's hands had defensive knife wounds on them. A great amount of blood was found at the head of the bed in the corner on the sheet and mattress and on the floor in the corner. The killer possibly cut her throat instead of rendering her unconscious like the other victims.

When her throat was cut she was lying on her right side facing the wall and in the process the blood went all over the area at the corner of the bed. Medical evidence showed that she had been placed on to her back, as were victims one, two and four, after death. I cannot see this killer creeping into her room on speculation. Thus I believe Kelly took the killer to her room after they had possibly met in Commercial Street. It is very feasible that she either knew her killer, or that the killer knew of her.

Kelly, like other Ripper victims, was killed in a corner, leaving her with no escape. Kelly was heard to say to her last customer, 'All right my dear, come along, you will be comfortable.' Did she mean by this remark that she would light a fire to dry their clothes and to keep them warm?

After spending time on the mutilations, the killer possibly placed any soiled items which had belonged to him on the fire. My suspect was known to carry alcohol in a flask so he may well have used this substance to soak items (evidence) he wished to burn. He may have worn one set of clothing to the scene (while carrying another set) then possibly burned the clothes he wore to the scene in Kelly's room, thus changing into a different attire on leaving.

This would have several advantages. Firstly, if someone had seen Jack enter Millers Court with Kelly and they (or someone else) had seen him leave it would be concluded that two different men were seen because two different descriptions would have been given. Secondly, once the killer left the scene he was safe; he would not be covered in blood after this slaughter and attract attention to himself.

Common sense dictates that he is not going to leave the scene covered in blood. I believe that he burned his own items on the fire and then placed other items he found in the room on the fire (items owned by Mrs Harvey). This was done to cover the fact that it was his own items that were burned.

Inspector Abberline, the Metropolitan Police Inspector in charge of detectives in the field investigating the Whitechapel Murders, stated that the items belonging to Mrs Harvey were in his opinion burned to give the killer light to work by! He did not take into consideration that the killer possibly burned his own items adding items of Harvey's to conceal the fact.

The key to Kelly's door had been missing for some time prior to the murder. The lock on Kelly's door was of the spring bolt type, which could lock automatically when the door was closed. Barnett stated access to the room was gained by placing a hand through the broken pane of glass in the window, and opening the door from the inside. It is more than likely that Kelly and her 'room mates' kept the lock on the latch when leaving the room so entry could be gained without the need of placing an arm through the broken window.

Needless to say this method would have been rather a hassle and dangerous if one was the worse off for drink at the time. If the lock had not been placed on the latch and the door was locked inadvertently by Kelly as she left the room then one would suppose that the window method was used to gain entry again.

When the killer left the room, he no doubt took the latch off the lock so that when he closed the door behind him the door locked automatically. This explains why the door was broken open. McCarthy either did not know that the door could be opened from the window or if he did then being in a state of shock at the time he did not think of it.

Although the killer was in the confines of a room while operating on Kelly he was still at risk. Although the door was locked there was nothing stopping a late caller doing as Mr Bowyer had done when he had discovered the body. Any such caller on receiving no answer on knocking the door could have gone to the broken windows and moved back the curtain. The killer would have been caught in the act with only one escape route possible.

It is my contention that the killer would have intended to spend a minimum amount of time in that room and would therefore have intended to leave at the earliest opportunity. I do not believe that he was working at a leisurely pace. He must have been aware of the precarious nature of his surroundings. As with the other mutilated victims he would have been working at speed to get the job done as soon as possible.

The police at the time believed that if they were to catch the killer in the act he would try to dispatch them while attempting to make good his escape. They were under no illusions on this matter. Kelly was to be the last victim in the series. Ripper author Martin Fido wrote: 'I've never heard of a sexual serial killer whose last victim was his last by his own choice.' This statement only adds to the evidence that Jack was not a sexual serial killer.

View from Commercial Streeet towards Dorset Street today. Kelly allegedly lived at the Providence Row Night Women's Refuge and Convent (marked 'P') in Crispin Street, directly at the end of Dorset Street, when she first came to Spitalfields. The street line shown on the right (north) is located further back than the original old street line of 1888. The original street line was located approximately at the point marked with an 'N' shown on the photograph. The original street line on the left (south) would have been located several metres further back from the street line marked with an 'S'. Crossinghams lodging house was located approximately opposite the arch on the right. Hutchinson stood at the entrance to this lodging house waiting for the suspect to leave Millers Court

Hutchinson went to the inquest two days after the murder and heard Sarah Lewis give evidence indicating that she had seen a stout man wearing a wide-awake hat, standing against Crossinghams lodging house opposite Millers Court at exactly 2.30am on the morning of the murder.

Hutchinson knew that he was on the same spot on the same morning. On realising that he had been seen by Sarah Lewis he went straight to the police after the inquest, and informed them that he was the man seen by Lewis. He also gave the reason why he was standing there at that time of the morning.

Hutchinson's behaviour in following Kelly and the suspect is explained in the words of Inspector Abberline.

Dated 12th November 1888.

Metropolitan Police.

CID Scotland Yard.

I beg to report that an inquest was held this day at the Shoreditch Town Hall before W. MacDonald (Coroner) on the body of Marie Jeanette Kelly found murdered at No.13, Millers Court, Dorset Street, Spitalfields. A number of people were called who clearly established the identity of the deceased, the Coroner remarked that in his opinion it was unnecessary to adjourn the inquiry and the jury returned a verdict of Wilful murder against some person or persons unknown.

An important statement has been made by a man named George Hutchinson, which I forward herewith. I have interrogated him this evening and I am of the opinion that his statement is true. He informed me that he occasionally gave the deceased a shilling, and that he had known her for about three years, also that he was surprised to see a man so well dressed in her company which caused him to watch them. He can identify the man, and arrangements have been made for two officers to accompany him round the district for a few hours tonight with a view of finding the man if possible.

Hutchinson is at present in no regular employment and he has promised to go with an officer tomorrow morning at 11.30am to the Shoreditch Mortuary to identify the deceased. Several arrests have been made on suspects of being connected with the recent murders. But the various persons detained have been able to satisfactorily account for their movements and were released.

signed. F.G. Abberline.

Insp.

Supt. T. Arnold.

Several reasons exist why the mutilations carried out on Kelly were more severe than those of the other four victims. I do not believe for a moment that the killer was getting psychologically bolder and

experimenting with his mutilations as time progressed. Neither do I believe that the progressive mutilations implied that a complicated sexual condition was worsening with each murder and which ultimately culminated in Jack's suicide.

Kelly's murder was to be the last in the series. Therefore it is possible that as the grand finale Jack wished to leave an everlasting impression, hence a far greater shock impact was required. Kelly may have been more of a personal matter to Jack for she is the odd one out in many respects.

Another reason for the nature of Kelly's murder may well have been certain occult beliefs held by the murderer. It may have been an accumulation of these reasons, which could explain the severity of Kelly's mutilations. It is simply not true that he never had enough time with any of the other victims. In Mitre Square he could have worked all night long in one of the empty houses, or in the unused yard, or the passage that led into it. All were only a metre or so from where Eddowes was found.

Kelly's territory was outside of the Ten Bells public house. She was also known to frequent Leman Street a lot. The competition in such a small area would have known each other. A witness, talking of Kelly, stated, 'If another woman encroached on Kelly's territory outside of the Ten Bells, then handfuls of hair would fly.' All five victims lived so close together in such a small area that they must have been rubbing shoulders daily. Photographs of the time show the community in the East End in 1888 was very close knit. Everyone knew each other.

Assistant Commissioner Anderson stated, 'The wretched victims belonged to a very small class of degraded women who frequent the East End after midnight.' So the killer did not take his pick from 1,200 prostitutes but from a very small number who worked the early morning hours. Thus making the chances that they knew each other even greater. All professional people in such a small area know each other and prostitution is the oldest profession of all.

ANALYSIS OF THE DEATH SITES

TO RECAP, THE murder scenes were as follows:

Victim No. 1

The alcove in Bucks Row afforded good cover. In 1888 the entrance to the stable was narrower and deeper than in later years. The two original houses next to the old stables were demolished. The entrance to the stable was then widened to take in this lost space. The killer was in a position to spot anyone walking up from the Brady Street end. The same can be said of anyone walking from the direction of the board school. Because this murder took place in a public road, the killer knew he was at risk of being disturbed at work.

Victim No. 2

This victim was taken into the back yard of 29, Hanbury Street which afforded better cover than Bucks Row. Although it was a private yard and not patrolled by the police it was still a high-risk site. There were 17 people living at this address, any one of which could be getting up at the time of the murder (5.30am) to go to work. The yard was used by prostitutes and clients, another reason that the killer could have been disturbed.

John Richardson also checked the property for security 45 minutes prior to the murder. Also, there was only one way (not including jumping over garden fences) in and out of the building, and that was through the front door. This was still a risky site, although the killer had privacy to perform elaborate mutilations. Cadosch was only a few yards away when he heard the attack take place but he never bothered to put his head over the fence. Jack certainly was at risk of being disturbed on this site.

Victim No. 3

When compared to the other four sites, this site was the most dangerous for the killer in terms of activity. The many witness statements prove this point. People were coming and going to the Working Men's Club, passing by in the street or just standing around. I believe that the precarious nature of this site was one reason for Jack only spending the minimum amount of time on this victim. This may explain why this victim was the least mutilated of the five. Of course he may have had no intention of mutilating Stride to begin with. It has been taken for granted that he intended to mutilate her. He was at great risk of being disturbed on this site.

Victim No. 4

This victim was found on the pavement in Mitre Square. Access into the square could be obtained from three different directions. She was found by a policeman who would have fallen over the killer if he had been at work. Yet this victim had mutilations which took several minutes to perform. He wanted the body to be found as soon as possible. If this had not been the case, the victim would have been left in the unused passage or in one of the empty houses, and may not have been found for a day or two. He was at risk on this site, which was a public square.

Victim No. 5

This victim was the only one to be killed under full cover, in the privacy of a room and had the largest number of post-mortem mutilations performed on her. This simply supports my belief that the time and cover factor on this murder was much greater than the others, hence the greater severity of the injuries. The killer also knew that Kelly was to be his final victim so he may have decided to create a lasting impression with this murder.

Each of these locations clearly came with risks attached, then. This suggests other motives other than simple convenience may have been in play here. On what other bases might the Ripper have chosen to carry out his work in these places? Why did the killer place himself at greater risk than necessary by committing murders in very precarious public places where the victims would be discovered within minutes? Why didn't he commit the murders in places where the victims would not be found for days or possibly years or never?

The killer had no alternative but to kill the victims where they were found. He had an occult plan from which to work and to this end he had various factors to take into account. One was that the first four victims killed had to be placed east, north, south and west (in that order). He would pick up his victim on a main road and take her down a side road. Then he would kill her at a chosen spot off the side road. He could get back on to the main road near the site so he could mix in with other people.

This is one reason why all the murder sites are laid out in the same manner from the centre of Whitechapel Junction (see killer's routes). In fact, the killer had to move two of the victims from their original planned sites because they were far too open and risky. However, these two victims were only moved a short distance to locations which afforded better cover.

The Victims' Addresses

Mary Anne Nichols (1845–88)
2–24 August 1888: 18, Thrawl Street.
24–30 August 1888: 56, Flower and Dean Street.

Annie Chapman (1841–88)
1886: 30, Dorset Street.
From May 1888: Mainly at Crossinghams, 35, Dorset Street.

Elizabeth Stride (1843–88)

1882: 32, Flower and Dean Street.

1886: Devonshire Street.

1885–88: 33, Dorset Street.

September 1888: 32, Flower and Dean Street.

The Times, Thursday, 4 October 1888, reported on the resumed inquest on Stride. It wrote that Elizabeth Tanner, 32, Flower and Dean Street, stated that Stride had lived in Fashion Street at one time. The report added that Catherine Lane, 32, Flower and Dean Street, stated that at one time Stride had lived in Devonshire Street, Commercial Road. Lane stated that Stride had also lived in Fashion Street where she frequently went to visit her. *The Times* quoted Kidney as saying, 'I live at 38, Dorset Street, Spitalfields, and am a waterside labourer. I have seen the body in the mortuary and it is that of a woman whom I lived with. I have no doubt whatever about it.'

For the last three years of her life, Stride had lived on and off with Michael Kidney. When away from Kidney she resided at 32, Flower and Dean Street. Kidney's address has been generally accepted as 33, Dorset Street, Spitalfields. Author Donald Rumbelow wrote that Stride had been living in Fashion Street with Michael Kidney. Author Philip Sugden gave Kidney's address as 35, Devonshire Street as reported in the Central News.

Lloyd's Weekly London Newspaper, 7 October, 1888, printed Kidney's inquest testimony giving 33, Dorset Street as his address. At the inquest he stated that on the day of the murder he expected Stride to return to his address. Various tabloids of the period including *The Daily News,* 6 October, 1888, also placed Kidney as living in Dorset Street. *The Times*, Saturday, 6 October 1888, quoted Sven Olsson, Clerk to the Swedish Church in Princes Square, as stating that Stride had lived in Devonshire Street in 1886.

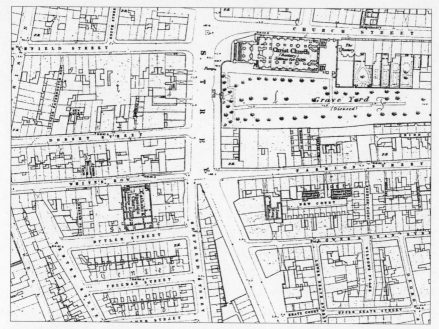

Map showing the small area in Spitalfields in which the five victims lived. The Ten Bells public house (Kelly's patch) can be seen middle top of the map on the corner of Church Street. Map O/S Scale 1in/88ft

Catherine Eddowes alias Mary Ann Kelly (1842–88)

1881: 55, Flower and Dean Street (next to Nichols) with John Kelly.
Also at one time lived in Dorset Street (*Daily Telegraph,*
10 November 1888).

Mary Jane Kelly alias Marie Jeanette (1863–88)

April 1887: Thrawl Street.
Paternoster Row, Dorset Street.
1888: Millers Court, Dorset Street (opposite Chapman).

All the above addresses (apart from Devonshire Street) are located within a very small area of Spitalfields.

After having located the exact spots on which the five victims were found, I transferred the locations on to several period Ordnance Survey Maps, scale 1/2500 and measured the distances from victim to victim. Victims three, four and five were all killed on the line of a 500-yard radius.

The scene of crime in the rear yard of 29, Hanbury Street

This is the first time since 1888 that anyone has measured the distances from victim to victim. The distances are accurate to within two metres and show that the murders were planned on a map. Kelly was the only victim who was killed indoors in her own room. So, if the murder sites were planned in advance on a map, then the killer knew in advance that a victim was to die in room 13, Millers Court. This can only mean that the killer either knew Kelly personally or knew of her. He knew enough to pinpoint her room on a map.

The killings were carried out on foot and the killer knew the area well. He resided in the area during the murders but he was not a native of the area. I know the area as well as the killer knew it and I do not reside there. The killer did his homework as I did mine. He used the four busy main roads in the area to move about on. Using these routes gave him the advantage of moving in the most efficient manner, in a straight line.

The main roads on which he moved were some of the busiest streets in London. Do not forget that on the Whitechapel Road in 1888 a market lined the pavement. When I went to the area in the small hours I was surprised to find it busy. In 1888 it was far busier than it is today. One only has to view the street traffic in old period photographs to realise how busy the main roads were.

We know that the killer moved about on weekends when the markets and main roads in the area (even early mornings) were very busy with people and traffic. The area was buzzing on weekends and it was a busy time for the prostitutes.

If the necessity of moving sites 1 and 2 a very short distance to achieve the required cover had not arisen then all distances from victim to victim (excluding site 5) when measured on an O/S map of the period, scale 1/2500, would be 950 yards forming a parallelogram.

There has never been any evidence to suggest that the killer used back alleys, it has only been assumed that he did. Hundreds of local people including undercover plainclothes detectives dressed in many diverse and various disguises, private detectives, vigilantes, uniformed officers, reward seekers, all and more were scouring the

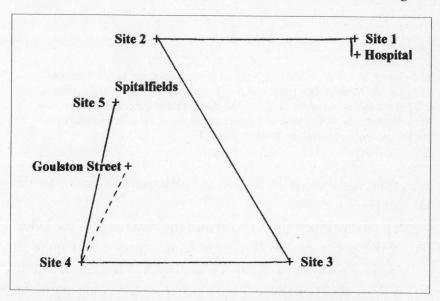

The trail the killer left from the first murder site in the locality of his address at the London Hospital. Note how the trail leads away from the area of the London Hospital and finally leads to 13, Millers Court, 26, Dorset Street, Spitalfields. Another trail (marked as -----) was left from Site 4 to Goulston Street which led in the direction of Dorset Street. The killer wanted the police to believe that he was heading to a lair in Spitalfields. He was in fact heading back to the hospital after leaving the message (and false trail) at Goulston Street

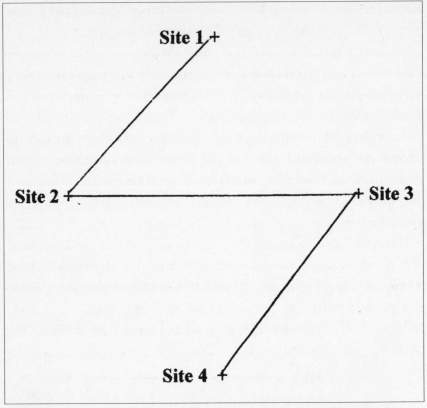

When sites 1, 2, 3, 4 are joined they make an occult symbol. This occult symbol was utilised by the Nazis as their symbol for the SS. The plan called for four prostitutes to be killed at the four points of the cross. I believe that Kelly was the odd one out in more ways than one. She was in some way separate from the first four victims and was possibly more of a personal matter to the killer

pubs, dens, passageways, back alleys and back streets searching for the invisible killer at night.

Many various types also flooded into the area to catch the killer. Didn't the police realise that their hunted prey could quite as easily have altered his appearance as they had done? And quite simply move about on the four busy main roads, keeping out of the pubs, etc.

A Reconstruction of the Killer's Routes

I travelled the routes several times at a quick pace and at a normal pace. The routes were busy day and night when I walked them.

Sites	Timed at a quick pace with a stopwatch
Centre to Court Street (and hospital)	8 minutes, 38.22 seconds
Centre to site of 29, Hanbury Street.	7 minutes, 41.82 seconds
Centre to Berner Street	4 minutes, 5.18 seconds
Top of Berner Street to site	1 minute, 5.22 seconds
Centre to Site 3 total time	5 minutes, 10.4 seconds
Centre to Dukes Street	3 minutes, 51.03 seconds
Duke Street to St James Passage	32.09 seconds
Top of St James passage to site	29.78 seconds
Centre to site 4, total time	4 minutes, 52.99 seconds
*Centre to Dorset Street	4 minutes, 36.04 seconds

*Timed to the original street line of 1888 which was 4m shorter than the present corner.

Distances between the centre and murder sites were measured, using a surveyor's wheel, as follows:

Sites	Distances (m)
Centre to Court Street (and hospital)	881.01
Centre to 29, Hanbury Street	745.17
Centre to Site 3	555.11
Centre to Dukes Street	371.08
Corner of Dukes Street to the entrance to St James Passage	61.4
Entrance to St James Passage to victim	51.3
Centre to victim four	483.15
*Centre to Dorset Street	440.08

*Taken to the original 1888 street corner. Routes were taken as they would have been taken in 1888. No subways were used and barriers were climbed over to keep the routes as straight as possible.

Sites	Timed at normal pace with wristwatch
Centre to site of 29, Hanbury Street	8 minutes, 30 seconds
Centre to Court Street and the hospital	10 minutes, 30 seconds
Centre to site 3	6 minutes, 27 seconds
Centre to site 4	6 minutes, 05 seconds
Centre to Dorset Street	5 minutes, 18 seconds

Gardner's Corner is the main junction for the area and is a hub of activity. After murders two, three, four and five the killer headed in this direction. The routes used by the killer and the times given to walk them have all been reconstructed. On two occasions I timed myself from the centre point marked on my map to the original south corner of Dorset Street walking at a military pace. There was only a difference of one second over a distance of 440.08m. This fact gives an indication as to the accuracy which can be achieved when timing is of the essence.

Jack's chosen routes to and from the sites had to be very efficient, thus he made them as straight as possible. When one views the photo (page 109) of the 500-yard view taken from Dorset Street to the centre point, one can appreciate how busy, open and straight the killer's chosen routes were. Access to all side streets (from the centre point) in which a murder was committed are as efficient as shown in this photo.

The killer had no need to move through the labyrinths and back streets of the area when he had such efficient routes to move on. One will note that of the five main roads leading from the centre only one did not have a murder committed off it. This was Leman Street where Kelly frequented and the direction in which she was seen to go just hours prior to her murder.

My suspect signed himself into the London Hospital as a private patient prior to the murders. But due to the evidence, including certain unexplained missing times, the layout of the sites, a link by association between my suspect and a lodging house owner in Leman

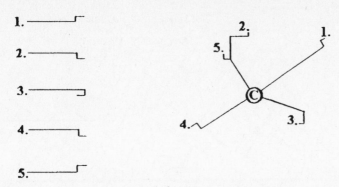

Shown above is the layout of each site from Gardeners Corner at the main junction. We have five victims off four main roads.

Shown right is how the layout of the murders should have appeared without the necessity of elaborate planning if the killer had decided in principle to take each victim (in any order) off a main road down a side road, and kill them off the side road. This would give us five victims killed off five main roads. Because he was following a plan with certain objectives and considerations in mind he could not commit the murders in the simple logical pattern shown below.

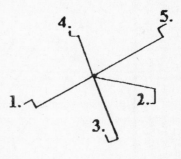

Street, and the fact that this killer was devious and smart, I believe that Jack did the unexpected and chose a site to go to ground as soon as possible near the centre.

My suspect was known to wear a wide-brimmed soft felt hat and a long overcoat, and a suspect at Berner Street was seen in such attire. It is feasible that the suspect left the hospital and went straight to Berner Street in his own attire, knowing that no mutilations were to take place on Stride. He just cut her throat once knowing that the chances of blood getting on his person were minimal.

He then went in the direction of Mitre Square stopping halfway there, at his bolthole in Leman Street. He then changed his attire, as he knew his next murder was to be a relatively messy affair. More to the point, such action would alter his appearance, which would help

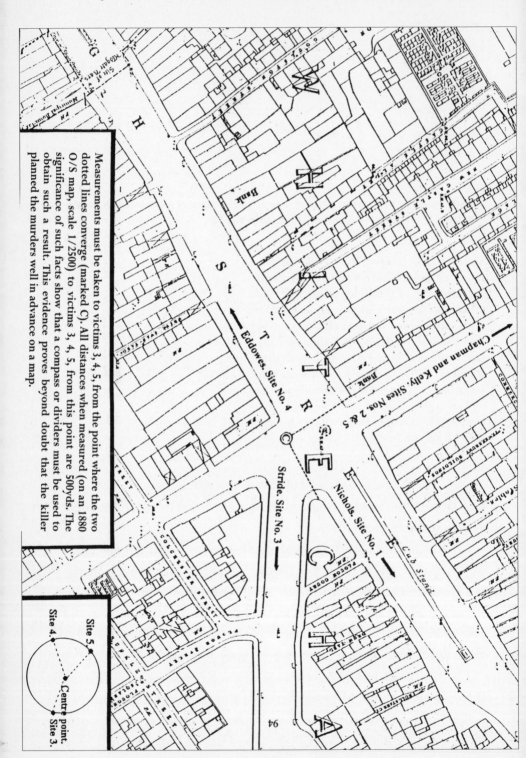

Measurements must be taken to victims 3, 4, 5, from the point where the two dotted lines converge (marked C). All distances when measured (on an 1880 O/S map, scale 1/2500) to victims 3, 4, 5, from this point are 500yds. The significance of such facts show that a compass or dividers must be used to obtain such a result. This evidence proves beyond doubt that the killer planned the murders well in advance on a map.

Eddowes. Site No. 4

Chapman and Kelly. Sites Nos. 2 & 5

Stride. Site No. 3

Nichols. Site No. 1

Site 5.

Centre point.
Site 3.

Site 4.

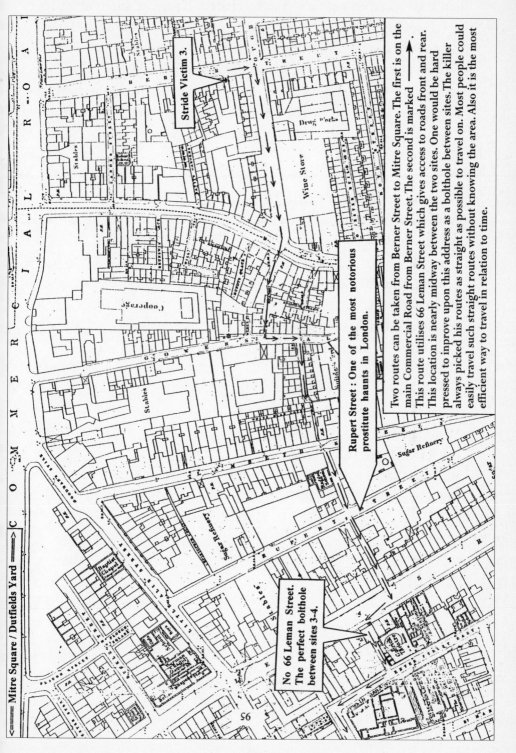

Stride Victim 3.

Rupert Street : One of the most notorious prostitute haunts in London.

No 66 Leman Street. The perfect bolthole between sites 3-4.

Two routes can be taken from Berner Street to Mitre Square. The first is on the main Commercial Road from Berner Street. The second is marked ———➤. This route utilises 66 Leman Street which gives access to roads front and rear. This location is nearly midway between the two sites. One would be hard pressed to improve upon this address as a bolthole between sites. The killer always picked his routes as straight as possible to travel on. Most people could easily travel such straight routes without knowing the area. Also it is the most efficient way to travel in relation to time.

Mitre Square / Dutfields Yard ➤

him if he was seen with a victim by chance. If seen in different attire at various sites it would confuse the issue and the police would be looking for several people instead of one.

Note how easy it is to reach all the side roads which contain the murder sites by simply walking in a straight line from the centre point. Common sense dictates that the killer used these routes.

From looking at the maps, the ease of access to sites is clearly illustrated.

From the centre point to site 1:
Walk up the Whitechapel Road, a left turn gives access
into Bucks Row.
From the centre point to site 2:
Walk up Commercial Street, a right turn gives access into
Hanbury Street.
From the centre point to site 3:
Walk down Commercial Road, a right turn gives access into
Berner Street.
From the centre point to site 4:
Walk down the High Street, a right turn gives access into
Mitre Square.
From the centre point to site 5:
Walk up Commercial Street, a left turn gives access into
Dorset Street.

JACK THE RIPPER'S OCCULT PLANS FOR THE WHITECHAPEL MURDERS

31 AUGUST – 9 NOVEMBER 1888

EVEN WITHOUT THE introduction of occult symbols there is already much material here to suggest an occult element to the mystery.

The killer always got his victims into a position from which they could not escape. His MO was to place his victims in a corner and asphyxiate them from behind. He would then lay them down on their left side (Kelly was on her right side when her throat was cut) at which point he would proceed to cut their throats, from left to right while kneeling behind them. He would then lay them on to their backs to mutilate them.

The Pattern

Victim one. Found on her back with her left side parallel with the stable door.

Victim two. Found on her back with her left side parallel with a wooden fence.

Victim three. Found on her left side parallel with wall. (Only victim not mutilated.)

Victim four. Found on her back with her left side parallel with a wall.

Victim five. Found on her back with her right side parallel with a wall.

The Differences

Victim one. Found with her feet in the corner, which one would expect if attacked from behind in a corner then laid down.

Victim two. Found with her head in the corner instead of her feet. Witness Mr Cadosch said that he heard a woman's voice cry, 'No', and shortly after he heard a bump against the fence. It is feasible that this victim was aware of the killer's intention and cried, 'No', before he had time to place her in the corner and manoeuvre behind her. Therefore, this victim was attacked close to the corner. Rendering the victim unconscious the killer bumped her against the fence whilst laying her down.

Victim three. Found as one would expect with her feet facing a corner.

Victim four. Found with her head facing a corner. Either the same scenario applied with this victim as with victim two or she was killed in the passage with her feet in the corner, as one would expect, and then pulled out feet first which would place her head in the corner of Mitre Square, where it was positioned.

Victim five. The initial attack by the killer was made easier by this victim prior to her death. She was murdered while already lying down on her bed with her head near the corner.

Certain points in relation to these crimes have never been satisfactorily explained, in fact many have been ignored. For example, it is taken for granted by many that the killer was a local man, yet it is most unusual for any serial killer to take his victims from his own neighbourhood! A simple dictum, for any criminal, is don't crap on your own doorstep.

The question of why Jack the Ripper took the missing body parts has never been properly addressed. It is most obvious that the killer had a use for the stolen body parts otherwise he would not have taken

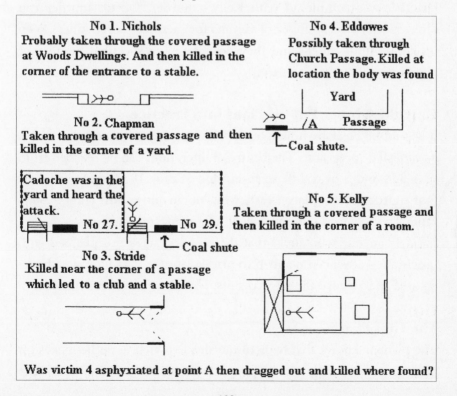

No 1. Nichols
Probably taken through the covered passage at Woods Dwellings. And then killed in the corner of the entrance to a stable.

No 4. Eddowes
Possibly taken through Church Passage. Killed at location the body was found

Yard

Passage

Coal shute.

No 2. Chapman
Taken through a covered passage and then killed in the corner of a yard.

Cadoche was in the yard and heard the attack.

No 27.   No 29.

Coal shute

No 5. Kelly
Taken through a covered passage and then killed in the corner of a room.

No 3. Stride
Killed near the corner of a passage which led to a club and a stable.

Was victim 4 asphyxiated at point A then dragged out and killed where found?

them. There are not many reasons why the killer would need to take the missing parts so this considerably narrows the field in assisting to find the true motive for the murders. One such reason can be found in occult murder.

Other Evidence for the Occult

The first four victims were killed at the four points of the compass

Occult murder decrees in some instances that the victims must be placed at the points of the compass.

Heinous mutilation of the dead occurred

The occult dictates that uteri, or wombs, taken from mutilated victims are to be used in the manufacture of holy candles.

The killer had a set number of victims, five in total

His task was completed with Kelly's murder. Occult murder can often specify a set number of victims for sacrifice. Serial killers keep on killing until caught and they do not pick a specified number of victims to kill and then cease.

How the Ripper Put his Plans into Practice

It should be clear by now that the Ripper planned his crimes with a great deal of precision. The centre of operations can be reached from sites 3, 4 and 5 by a difference in time of only 18 seconds. The first four murders were placed east, west, north and south. These results cannot be achieved without the aid of a map, and a compass.

I defy anyone who states that the murders were not planned with precision in advance on a map to place five sites at random in a built-up area and achieve the same results. This was a man on a mission.

The First Phase

The planner knows that he is to murder five victims so he makes his plans accordingly. He starts his plan at the main cross-roads. A line is run down the left-hand side of Commercial Street. Then a line is taken along the bottom of Whitechapel High Street until it converges with the line from Commercial Street.

The point where both lines converge is used as the starting point for his plan.

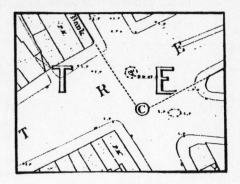

Example

A line is then taken from the point at the junction where the two previous lines converge. The line is taken to Room 13, No. 26, Millers Court a distance of exactly 500 yards.

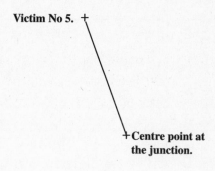

The Second Phase

Now the planner picks site 4 on the map. Using a square he uses the centre point for his vertical line and a spot he has chosen for his horizontal line. The 500-yard line from the centre to Kelly's abode is then moved until it converges with the horizontal line. The exact point at which the two lines converge is site 4.

The planner then reverses the square and swings the line from site 5 until it meets with the horizontal line from site 4.

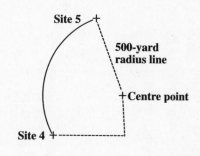

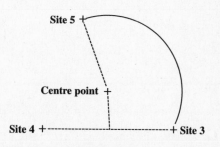

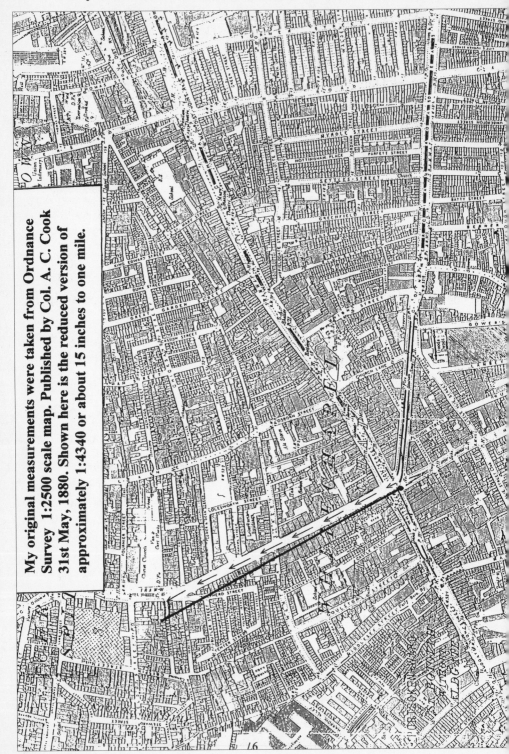

My original measurements were taken from Ordnance Survey 1:2500 scale map. Published by Col. A. C. Cook 31st May, 1880. Shown here is the reduced version of approximately 1:4340 or about 15 inches to one mile.

Example

We have a 500-yard radius from the centre which cuts through the exact spots on which victims five, four and three were found.

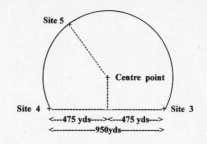

The Third Phase

The killer now has his base line (the line from site 3 to site 4) from which he is to determine the location of site 2. To achieve this objective both ends of the base line are arced. At the point of convergence site 2 is chosen.

We now have a triangle the base and sides of which are 950yds. These three lines are of importance and are drawn into the plan. Note on page 146 how site 2 became located in the middle of a crossroad, which was not viable for the killer. It was when he checked out this site on foot for suitability he decided to move it 63yds to afford himself greater privacy and cover.

Centre to site 2. (29 Hanbury St.) Up Commercial Street, turn right, then left.

To locate site 2, two lines are arced out and the point at which the two lines converge is site 2. The line from site 2 to site 4 is arced and then the line from site 3 to site 4 is also arced.

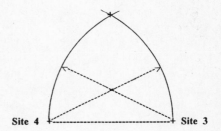

Example

The two equilateral triangles joined on page 145 are sacred symbols, which can refer to the moon representing the parturient energy of women. They also have a darker side. In

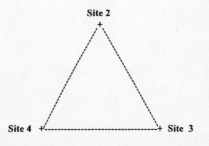

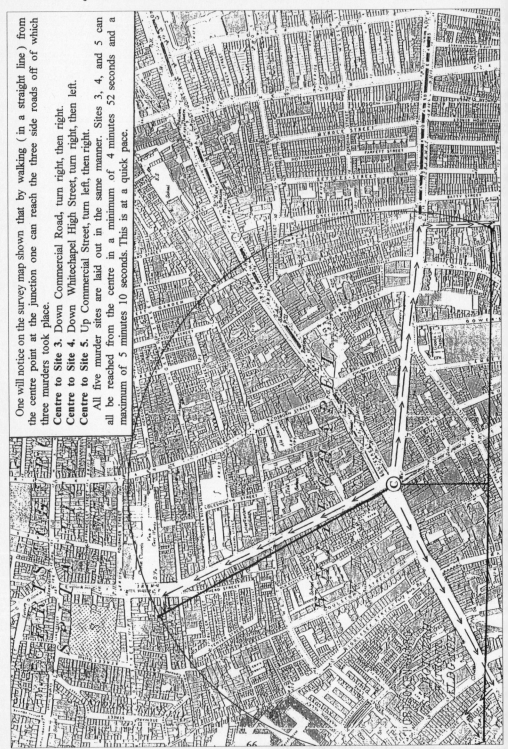

One will notice on the survey map shown that by walking (in a straight line) from the centre point at the junction one can reach the three side roads off of which three murders took place.

Centre to **Site 3.** Down Commercial Road, turn right, then right.
Centre to **Site 4.** Down Whitechapel High Street, turn right, then left.
Centre to **Site 5.** Up Commercial Street, turn left, then right.

All five murder sites are laid out in the same manner. Sites 3, 4, and 5 can all be reached from the centre in a minimum of 4 minutes 52 seconds and a maximum of 5 minutes 10 seconds. This is at a quick pace.

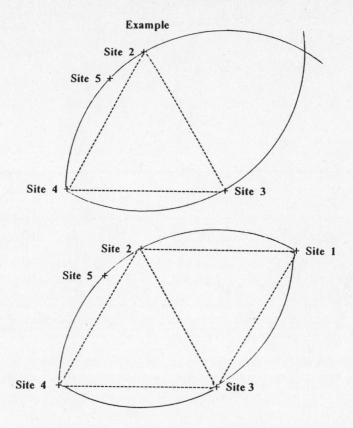

Example

occult doctrine Satan, the master counterfeiter, devised this symbol to be used in worship of him. The next symbol to be incorporated into the plan by placing a line east to west (sites 1 and 4) was the Christian cross. The cross is significant because it was to be profaned by the killer.

When all the sites were chosen on the map the killer checked them out (on foot) for suitability, adequate cover being his main concern. Site 1 did not afford the required cover. So the site was moved slightly further west. The site was moved to afford the killer greater cover in a stable alcove in Bucks Row. However, the site still remained due east.

Basic plans, without certain symbols, incorporated are shown. This stage was as far as I could go without seeking help, for I had no idea if the plan so far was complete, although I thought at the time that it was some type of occult plan. During further

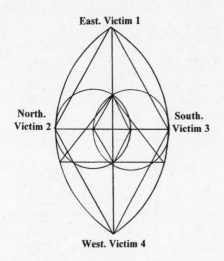

East. Victim 1

North.
Victim 2

South.
Victim 3

West. Victim 4

investigations into certain symbols and their meaning I made contact with a member of the Anthroposophical Society from Rudolf Steiner Press in London.

After I had informed him that I was looking into matters relating to sacred geometry and the occult he put me in touch with another gentleman who he thought could assist me, Mr Sidney Foster. Luck would have it

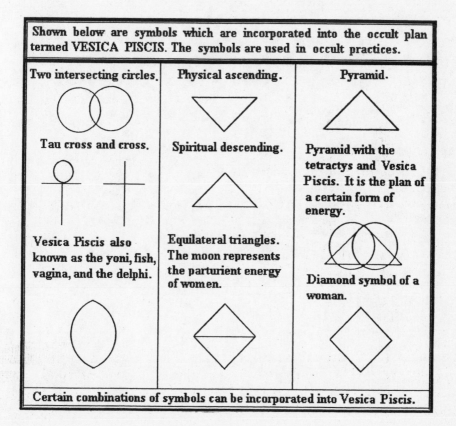

Shown below are symbols which are incorporated into the occult plan termed VESICA PISCIS. The symbols are used in occult practices.

Two intersecting circles.

Tau cross and cross.

Vesica Piscis also known as the yoni, fish, vagina, and the delphi.

Physical ascending.

Spiritual descending.

Equilateral triangles. The moon represents the parturient energy of women.

Pyramid.

Pyramid with the tetractys and Vesica Piscis. It is the plan of a certain form of energy.

Diamond symbol of a woman.

Certain combinations of symbols can be incorporated into Vesica Piscis.

that Mr Foster lived in my locality. A meeting was arranged at his home, where I showed him details of my research.

Mr Foster is a local politician, writer and Chairman of the Cody (aviator) Society. He is also involved in a great deal of charity work. He has been a member of the Masonic Society for 50 years. Over a period of several years Sidney gave me a wealth of private information and many works on various subjects which related to my research. We became good friends, but when asked if I would like to become a Freemason I graciously declined the offer.

Among other things Sidney supplied me with was a full set of plans, which included the remaining symbols I lacked. The picture was now complete. The plans I received are shown in their entirety on the top of page 147 and 150.

The Completed Plan of Vesica Piscis

If sites 1 and 2 had not been moved to afford better cover then the distances between sites 1, 2, 3 and 4 (the four sides of the parallelogram) would have been the same, 950 yards. Note the distance of 500yds from sites 3, 4 and 5 to the centre point. Considering that the murders were planned in such a manner, the distances that were involved and the built-up nature of the area the killer was as accurate as the situation would allow. I tried to improve upon the plan without moving two sites. I could not.

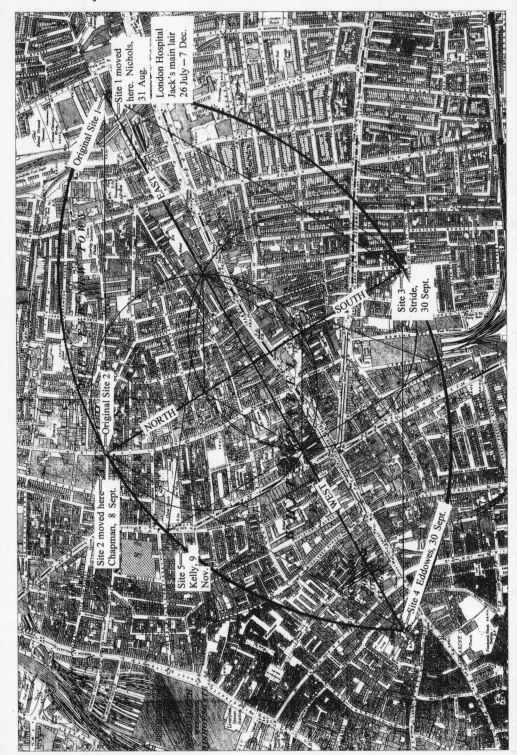

Original Site 1

Site 1 moved here. Nichols, 31 Aug.

London Hospital Jack's main lair 26 July — 7 Dec.

EAST

TO W

SOUTH

Site 3 Stride, 30 Sept.

Original Site 2

NORTH

WEST

Site 2 moved here Chapman, 8 Sept.

Site 5 Kelly, 9 Nov.

Site 4 Eddowes, 30 Sept.

RIPPER MYTH AND INACCURACY

SEVERAL MYTHS PERSIST about the nature of Jack the Ripper and his crimes. Below are some of the most common:

The Ripper Committed Two Other Murders

Period press reports give credence to the possibility that Emma Smith (attacked 4 April 1888) and Martha Tabram (died 7 August 1888) are victims of Jack the Ripper. Articles and political cartoons during the Reign of Terror list these two murders as the first and second victims thus making the first canonical (generally accepted) victim, Polly Nichols, the third victim. The implication of this is discussed in some depth later.

In the case of Emma Smith press accounts stated she was attacked by a gang of youths. After Nichols's murder her death was attributed to Jack the Ripper. She was 45 years old, the correct age for four of the five Ripper victims, and she plied her trade in the small hours of the morning. On Bank Holiday Monday, 3 April, she left her lodgings in George Street to look for clients.

By her own account she was stopped at the corner of Wentworth Street and Brick Lane, sexually assaulted and robbed by three or four youths. A blunt object had been forced into her vagina, tearing the

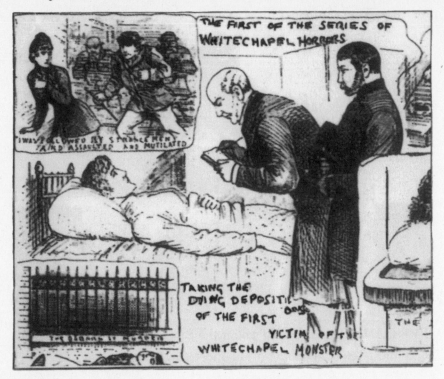

Emma Smith, Jack's first alleged victim, is shown being attacked by three men, while being described as the first victim of the Whitechapel monster

perineum. She managed to walk back to her lodgings where she was taken to hospital (apparently against her wishes). She told witnesses about the attack and succumbed to her injuries several days later at the London Hospital, Whitechapel.

Martha Tabram was a 39-year-old prostitute whose last known address was 19, George Street, Spitalfields. On Bank Holiday Monday, 6 August 1888, Martha, in company with Pearly Poll (Mary Ann Connely), was seen in several pubs with a soldier or soldiers. At around 11.45pm, the two women, with their respective customers, separated. Martha went into George Yard with a private and Pearly Poll went into Angel Alley with a corporal.

At 1.50am on 7 August Elizabeth Mahoney returned to her lodging in George Yard Buildings. She noticed nothing unusual. At 2am PC Thomas Barrett saw a Grenadier guardsman in Wentworth Street. Barrett questioned him and the guardsman said he was waiting for a

Mortuary photograph of Martha Tabram, Jack's second alleged victim

'chum who went off with a girl'.

George Crow saw what he thought was a homeless person asleep on the first floor landing (an apparently common occurrence in George Yard Buildings) and went on to bed. When John Saunders Reeves left his lodgings in George Yard Buildings at 4.45am he saw a body on the landing, but also the pool of blood it was lying in. Reeves returned with PC Barrett.

George Collier, the deputy coroner for the south-eastern division of Middlesex, noted that the clothes 'were turned up as far as the centre of the body, leaving the lower part of the body exposed, legs open and altogether her position was such as to suggest in my mind that recent intimacy had taken place'.

Dr Timothy Robert Killeen estimated Tabram's time of death as 2.30–45am. There were 39 stab wounds, focusing mainly on the breasts, belly and groin area. Killeen seemed to believe the attacker was right-handed and used a penknife. Only one wound seemed to have been caused by a sword or bayonet.

Certain other murders were also attributed to Jack the Ripper after he had killed his fifth and final victim of the Whitechapel series. Annie Farmer, Rose Mylett, Elizabeth Jackson, Alice McKenzie, the Pinchin Street murder and Francis Coles are listed. It would appear that there are nearly as many Ripper victims as there are Ripper suspects! Many prostitutes killed during the next two to three years would appear to be suspected Ripper victims. This extends to New York where the murder of Carrie Brown on 24 April 1891 has been attributed to Jack the Ripper! The Whitechapel murders committed by the killer dubbed Jack the Ripper numbered five, no more no less.

The Ripper Tried, Unsuccessfully, to Decapitate his Victims

It has been stated that the killer had tried to decapitate his victims without success. This is not true. We are dealing with a most determined killer here. If this man had the slightest intention of decapitating them then he would have done so. And he would have used the correct tool to achieve his aims.

He would have known that a surgical knife would not be up to the task. He would also have known that to walk about with a kidney or heart hidden on his person is one thing, but to walk around with a head tucked under your arm is quite another, if he in fact meant to take a head away from the crime scene.

The Use of Chloroform

The question has been asked, 'Were the victims chloroformed?' None of the victims were chloroformed. Trichloromethane, as it was also known, was first prepared in 1831. The Scottish physician Sir James Simpson of Edinburgh was the first to use it as an anaesthetic in 1847. It was in general use by 1853. The medical evidence given stated that no drug or poison had been administered to the victims.

Chloroform can leave traces of burning to skin tissue if brought directly into contact with the mouth or nose. Hence the open drop method. This was a cloth mask placed over the nose and mouth area but not making contact with either. Droplets of chloroform were then placed on the cloth. The fumes rendered the patient unconscious within minutes.

The inhaler method (invented later by Dr John Snow) and open drop method were both adopted in hospitals during the 19th century. The killer did not get his victims into the desired position only to produce a bottle of chloroform, take out the stopper, pour the liquid on to a cloth, replace the stopper and then place the bottle back into his pocket while the victim waited patiently. Chloroform is not a feasible method when one looks properly at Jack the Ripper's MO.

Jack the Ripper Made Himself Invisible

Occultist Aliester Crowley wrote in an article entitled 'Jack the

Ripper' that the killer had obtained the gift of invisibility through magic. No notice should be given to Crowley in relation to his rantings that he was personally acquainted with my suspect. *He heard a story and twisted it to suit his own ego.* However, the term invisible killer must be viewed in its correct content and should not be taken literally.

I know of professional criminals who succeeded in committing various crimes, not only because they dressed the part and were to all intents and purposes invisible, but also because they used criminal psychology to confuse and manipulate the opposition. Any professional criminal worth his salt will be well acquainted with many aspects of human psychology. Jack the Ripper knew all about police procedures and psychology. He knew how the police worked, which was to his advantage. He counteracted those procedures and played the game by his rules using psychological warfare in the process.

Many criminals have become invisible in the pursuit of crime. How many times have we heard of a crime committed in broad daylight in a busy public place, and no one has seen a thing? I can think of several straight off the top of my head. One took place in the high street of a provincial town on the busiest day of the week, a Saturday afternoon. Jewellery thieves stood on a busy pavement bold as brass (while hundreds of shoppers passed by) and cut through the window of a jewellery shop. They then stole the contents of the window display. No one in the shop saw a thing, neither did any of the shoppers passing by.

I once knew a professional criminal who was a shoplifter. He started when he was 14 years of age and finished in his 40s and he was never convicted for shoplifting. He would dress in a certain manner (for psychological effect) and would heist for several months after which he would cease and go on to other crimes.

He would alternate the times spent on various crimes lessening the chance of detection. On one occasion he was talking to the manager of a shop and while doing so he picked up an item which took his fancy. The pair talked while walking to the front of the shop. The criminal then said his goodbye to the manager, thanking him for his help, and walked out of the main door with the stolen item in full view. The manager was oblivious to what had happened. Why was this? Well, he did not expect it to happen. He was not looking for the unexpected. Just like the shoppers passing by the jeweller's shop and the staff inside.

Jack the Ripper's Bloodlust Increased Over Time

It has been suggested that the increase in number of multilations performed on victims as the murders progressed was due to an increase in the bloodlust and insanity of the killer. This is supposed to be a sign that he was becoming more unhinged with each murder, leading to an eventual tendency towards suicide. In fact, the degree of mutilation was due to the amount of time and cover which each site afforded. Time and cover went together with this killer. Further, the killer needed a specific number of organs.

The Whitechapel Murders were Examples of the Perfect Crime

The murders are thought by some to be the perfect crime simply because the killer evaded justice. This assumption is incorrect, for a perfect crime is a crime which goes undetected. Jack the Ripper had no such intention. In fact, he gave the powers that be more than a fair chance of catching him.

Jack the Ripper was a Local Man

Imagine you are back in time (November 1888) and living next door to Crossinghams lodging house in Dorset Street. A woman who had been living 90 yards away in Flower and Dean Street (homeless at the time of the murder) is murdered on a Friday morning. Eight days later, on a Saturday morning, a woman living next door to you in Crossinghams is murdered.

Then a woman who had resided a few doors away from you on and off for the past three years, who is living temporarily at Flower and Dean Street for a few days, is also found murdered three weeks later, on a Sunday morning! Then you find out that less than one hour after this victim was killed another woman from Flower and Dean Street (who had once lived in Dorset Street) had also been found murdered! Then about six weeks later on a Friday morning you find that another victim is found in her room opposite your address in Dorset Street. You are informed that all were killed by the same hand.

What is the first conclusion to come into your mind? If you believe that the killer must be a local man then you are wrong, for this is precisely what the killer intended both the public and the police to believe. I would conclude that only a fool would kill five victims under such circumstances on his own doorstep, and this killer showed no signs of being such a fool.

The Ripper manipulated the police into believing that he was from the area. He went to great lengths to achieve this objective. He knew the area well, because he spent time with the prostitutes who resided in the locality. I do not know of any serial killer who picked all of his victims from a 100-yard radius and in the process of doing so left his victims (apart from one, Kelly) in full view of the public, knowing that the victims could be found at once. Serial killers tend to try and hide their victims. They do not as a rule leave them to be found at once on a public pavement.

Jack the Ripper Killed Silently
It is incorrect to have stated that Jack was never heard when killing a victim.

Victim one: Mrs Lilley heard the attack at 3.30am.

Victim two: Mr Cadosch heard the attack at about 5.30am and if he had put his head over the fence he would have seen the killer at work.

Victim five: Two women heard a scream of 'Murder' come from the victim's room at 3.30-4.00am.

Witnesses are Unreliable Because they Disagree about the Ripper's Age
Witness testimony in relation to a suspect's age must be taken with caution. The suspect seen with Chapman was in his 40s. The age of the suspect seen at Mitre Square was given as about 30. The suspect who

picked up Kelly was put at 35. (We should do well to remember that the four victims killed at the points of the compass were all in their 40s. I put the age of the killer in the same age bracket as the first four victims, in his 40s.)

I refer to the following case on file to illustrate why caution should be shown in relation to the age of any suspect. A crime was committed in the dark hours, and near the scene were two witnesses who claimed to have seen what had transpired. The suspect, after leaving the scene of the crime, walked towards the two witnesses and upon drawing level with them he stopped. Standing no more than 18 inches from them he stated, 'Take a good look.' To which one witness replied, 'I will.' In a statement to police the witnesses stated that the suspect was 21 years of age. In fact, he was 35! From our modern perspective some witness testimony can be notorious for inaccuracy. Many an innocent man has been hanged or imprisoned on faulty witness evidence.

Jack the Ripper was Picked Up by his Victims

The Jack the Ripper A to Z states that Kelly picked up the suspect. This is not true. Hutchinson said of the suspect, 'He tapped her on the shoulder, then the man said something to her.' Prostitutes are often picked up by their customers. The killer we are dealing with picked his victims; they did not pick him. The Yorkshire Ripper picked his victims they did not pick him.

Jack the Ripper's Motive was Sexual

The greatest myth of all was that Jack the Ripper was a sexual serial killer. How he could be termed a sexual serial killer when the true motive was never proven is beyond me. I have yet to see such opinions corroborated with hard facts. His true motive was to kill four prostitutes as the occult decreed, and in so doing profane the cross. My evidence for this is factual.

The first four victims were indeed killed at the four points of the compass. The murders were not committed at random. Those that cry 'coincidence' have no idea of the statistical probabilities involved if four murders are committed at random and end up placed at the four points of a compass. The victims had to be killed at the points of the compass in a certain order. Certain organs had to be removed for use in an occult ritual. That is not the work of a sexual serial killer.

The only reason that Jack was ever termed a sexual serial killer was because his attention was drawn to the vagina and his victims were prostitutes. He also took a heart and a kidney. Is that the work of a sexual serial killer?

Many years ago in London I was introduced to a pimp who had killed his prostitute's client. It transpired that the client had aggrieved her. The client was murdered and buried in a forest on the fringes of London. Time passed and the girl went about her business. While on the streets she was arrested and taken to the police station where she was asked to empty the contents of her bag on a desk. She complied with the request and a penis fell out of her bag on to the desk. It was then a case of 'hello, hello, hello, what have we got here, then?'

Out of revenge, the victim's penis had been removed and the prostitute had kept it as a souvenir to commemorate the event. If the body had been found minus penis, before any arrest was made, would it have been assumed that it was a sexual murder? I believe so. But the truth of the matter was that it was not. It was a murder based on revenge, and the penis was cut off in revenge. The point I'm trying to make is that because a victim's genital area is mutilated it does not mean that the murder is sexually motivated.

Jack the Ripper Ate Kelly's Heart

It has been asked, Did the killer eat Mary Kelly's heart? No evidence exists to suggest that the killer was a cannibal. It has not been proven that the Lusk kidney was the kidney taken from Eddowes. The letter sent with the kidney (stating that the sender had eaten half the kidney) has never been proven to be sent by the killer. So let us look at why any killer would wish to take the heart of his victim. There exists a number of reasons why the killer could have eaten Kelly's heart but no evidence exists to show that he did.

Some 19th-century tribes worldwide held certain religious beliefs which encouraged them to eat the heart of their adversaries. They also held religious beliefs in relation to the mutilation of the dead. Some superstitious occult societies also held similar beliefs, rites and practices. The occult encourages this behaviour, unacceptable by normal standards.

My suspect held occultist beliefs which included the doctrine that certain degrading, degenerating and obscene acts are acceptable. Certain body parts, for example, can be utilised in the preparation of potions for various uses in the occult. These points are covered later by my suspect in his own words.

Some years ago I saw a slightly built, inoffensive, wimpish-looking young man in his 20s wearing small metal-rimmed glasses. He had killed his girlfriend, and after the deed was done he cut out the girl's heart and placed it in a small box. Then for revenge, and presumably out of cruelty, he sent the heart to the girl's mother. So did Jack take Kelly's heart for revenge?

It is possible that the heart was taken as a trophy. It is not unknown for killers to take souvenirs.

Many other misconceptions and untruths exist in the aftermath of the Ripper murders. Coins were alleged to have been found placed by Chapman's body. Kelly was alleged to have been attacked with an axe but the medical evidence makes no mention of such a weapon.

It was only assumed that the killer had sex with the victims on site. The medical evidence does not support such an assumption. The killer was alleged to have attacked his victims while facing them. It has been incorrectly assumed that the victims picked up the killer. The list is endless.

Those who are indoctrinated with such beliefs either get their information from incorrect sources or they misinterpret the true facts of the case when faced with them. Murders are not solved by misconceptions, false opinions or incorrect assumptions, yet this case has often been based on nothing more.

CHAPTER ELEVEN

WHO WAS JACK THE RIPPER?

The Evidence

After dealing with how and why the only remaining question is who? The killer must satisfy several criteria.

No. 1

The trail left by Jack started east from Bucks Row, north to Hanbury Street, south to Berner Street, west to Mitre Square and then on to Dorset Street. A false trail led from Mitre Square to Goulston Street. To find the direction the killer was coming from we simply follow the trail in the direction from which it originated. This leads us back to Bucks Row. So I believe the killer lived in the vicinity of Bucks Row.

No. 2

Working from all the available evidence and from my own experiences I believe the killer had a great deal of anatomical experience. Taking into consideration the adverse conditions in which he was working, the speed at which he was working, the obvious planning, precision, timing, the boldness shown, the attention given to detail, and believing that the killer was no stranger to personal danger, I believe military experience was in evidence. Thus I believe he was indeed a surgeon with possibly some military background.

No. 3

Working on the theory that many serial killers pick their victims from the same ethnic group as themselves and that the first four victims were in their 40s; I believe he was an older men who relied on his experiences to some extent. Another reason therefore to place Jack the Ripper in his 40s.

No. 4

Believing that the killer was possibly seen in the doorway of the Nelson Beer House in Berner Street it was decided it was feasible that the killer may have been about 5ft 11in in height with light brown hair. It is also likely that he smoked a pipe. He wore a dark overcoat and a wide-brimmed felt hat. However, the man in the doorway was placed at about 35 years of age. As already explained in relation to a suspect's age, witness testimony is sometimes unreliable.

No. 5

Because of the nature of the plans and certain evidence in the case, it was more than evident to myself that the killer was an occultist. He may have contracted VD at some stage because he was prostitute-oriented. Also, it was possible that he had been brought in for questioning at some point and then released due to lack of evidence, as in the case of Peter Sutcliffe (questioned nine times and released!) and many other well-known killers.

It was evident from my research that the killer (as with many other serial killers) had a very high IQ. From my research I also concluded that Jack the Ripper was not a local man and that he had planned the murders in such a way as to give the false impression that he was. He had knowledge of the area and of prostitutes living within that area.

So who did live in the vicinity of the first murder at Bucks Row during 31 August 1888 and 9 November 1888, and who fitted all of the criteria?

The Verdict

Crime journalist Bernard O'Donnell wrote a 365-page manuscript. The manuscript in question, and several other important discoveries made by author Melvyn Harris, relate to a suspect named Robert Donston

Stephenson, alias Roslyn D'Onston, who was a patient at the London Hospital during the murders. During my research into the identity of the killer, the name D'Onston came into the picture and he fitted the criteria.

D'Onston had been an occultist and a military surgeon; he had resided near Bucks Row during the murders, was aged 47 in 1888, wore a soft felt hat and a long overcoat, was 5ft 11in in height, caught VD from a prostitute prior to the murders and was arrested at least twice for the murders. Many such facts emerged which showed D'Onston as fitting all the criteria. This cannot be said of any other suspect placed in the frame.

I then started to research D'Onston over a period of several years. During the first of many subsequent visits to various London archives and the London Hospital, I saw records relating to R. Stephenson who had been a police suspect during 1888. During further research, which included visiting a few of D'Onston's old haunts, I did not find one piece of evidence or one valid point that could be raised to cast any serious doubt over his guilt.

All other suspects when placed in the frame have always lacked this one essential requirement. A wealth of information on D'Onston is still to be found. Now we go into the final stage, the devious life and times of Robert Donston Stephenson.

Name: Robert Donston Stephenson.
Known aliases: Dr Roslyn D'Onston.
Wrote under the names of 'Tautriadelta'
and 'One Who Knows'.
Born: Parish of Sculcoates, Hull, 1842.
Address: Willow House, No. 60,
Church Street, Hull.
Marital status: Married Anne Deary
on 14 February 1876, at St James
Church, Holloway. Anne Deary,
childless, disappeared in 1887 prior to
the murders. No record of her death has
ever been traced. Similarities with a

murder victim found (May–June 1887) dismembered and dumped in the Regents Canal. Victim (childless and in the same age group as Anne Deary) was cut up by a murderer with the experience of a surgeon. D'Onston resided at several addresses near the Regents Canal, including Salmon Lane and Burdett Road.

Hair: Light brown, fair, greying, thinning at the sides, full moustache which was mouse or fair-coloured and occasionally waxed, turned up at the ends. Could be manipulated to give various styles.

Eyes: Pale blue.

Complexion: Pale, sallow, queer, no colour. Bottom lip pink, upper lip hidden by fair moustache.

Height: 5ft 11in.

Build: Lean and slim, military bearing showing strength and power.

Voice: Pleasant and cultured.

Face: Full.

Appearance: Military; known to observe strangers with an eyeglass; on occasions carried a short military-style cane. Wore a brown wide-brimmed, soft, felt hat; wore a long overcoat. Clothes worn through brushing rather than wear, respectable shabby appearance.

Habits: Pipe smoker, took drugs, considered a 'soaker' (not a drunk) with alcohol use. Bathed every day and was known to be clean and tidy.

Hobbies: Sought the company of prostitutes, was a known gambler.

IQ: Exceptional.

D'Onston: The Facts

D'Onston was a self-professed magician who travelled the world in search of occult knowledge. He was a man of many experiences and parts. D'Onston utilised this knowledge and his experiences to devastating effect in the planning and execution of the murders. We would do well to remember that he was a proficient and devious magician. He was very good at deception and causing organised aggravation.

He gave full attention to projects. For example, when he decided to write a book he applied a great deal to the project over a 10 year period. He collated Bible texts from 120 of the Greek and Latin fathers from the 2nd to the 10th century, from the 26 old Latin versions of the 2nd century, from 24 Greek uncials and some cursive, from the vulgate, Syriac, the Egyptian and other ancient versions, all the Greek text from 1550 to 1881, plus all English versions from Wicliff to the American Baptist version of 1883. If D'Onston put all this effort into writing one book then what effort would he apply to a situation which could well have cost him his life if caught?

Work experience: Customs officer, army surgeon, writer, reporter, occultist, magician, doctor, soldier, self-confessed murderer, prospector, businessman. Well travelled (France, USA, Africa, India, Germany). Worked with the London Cottage mission in Salmon Lane and Burdett Road.

Address during the murders: The London Hospital, Whitechapel. Believed to have had a second bolthole, possibly at 66, Leman Street.

Income: Grey area. Used women as a convenience and was known to have been a kept man. He also wrote articles for cash. The Stephenson family were very wealthy, but D'Onston was an outcast.

Other: Contracted VD from a prostitute in Hull and was dismissed from the Customs Service because of his association with prostitutes. Known to have spent his whole life associating with prostitutes in Hull, Brighton, London and, possibly, Paris. Lived a Bohemian lifestyle. Known to have fasted for great lengths of time due to his occultist beliefs. He was a gameplayer and enjoyed playing mind games. Arrogant and filled with his own self-importance, he showed scant regard for the lives and feelings of others and was somewhat contemptuous of people in general.

Many negative comments have been made in relation to D'Onston by those who have not bothered to check the known facts. One self-styled psychic and author wrote that D'Onston was a magician and meddler but not a murderer. This unfounded statement was made despite the fact that Stephenson publicly confessed to killing at least two individuals abroad. D'Onston has been greatly underestimated by those who have not bothered to check the facts for themselves. They have instead relied on various unreliable sources.

D'Onston went on a journey to India in 1878 in search of the occult and magic illusions; he wrote a full account of his experiences in the

66, Leman Street marked 'B'. Mr Cullingford was the landlord of this property. He was also the landlord of the property off St Martin's Lane where D'Onston moved when leaving the London Hospital on 7 December 1888, after his murder spree

country. One illusion seen by D'Onston and one in which he was a participator culminated in a sword being thrust through his body. He felt no pain during the act. The sword was driven through at a safe spot, only after much pinching had left the flesh numb and bloodless.

I have seen a man lifted from the ground and suspended by the use of hooks placed through his flesh, the flesh being pinched beforehand. It is a trick used in India today. The act I refer to was filmed by Arthur

C. Clarke in India. This act was also practised by Native American Indians; it was part of a ritual tradition which turned them into warriors. In fact, it was demonstrated in the film *A Man Called Horse* by actor Richard Harris.

One such ritual was the o-kee-pa of the Mandans. The emphasis in the o-kee-pa was on placating the spirits. George Catlin's paintings detailing some aspects of the o-kee-pa were so shocking to Victorian eyes that they were attacked as morbid fantasies, and yet at this moment in time gentleman Jack with his upper-class breeding was performing acts on the streets of London which were more savage than the o-kee-pa. He reverted back to behaviour that is as old as man himself — human sacrifice — which is nothing more than ignorant superstition and basic animal instinct.

When he saw the futility of his beliefs and actions he decided to give up on the occult. Magic is nothing more than an illusion created by those who believe in their own superiority and the ignorance of others. D'Onston was misguided in his beliefs on the occult and his practices in the field of magic. He brainwashed himself while trying to brainwash others.

In July 1886 the Secretaryship of the Metropolitan and City Police Orphanage became vacant. D'Onston was a candidate for the post but was not shortlisted. The position was taken by Arthur Kestin. If successful in his application D'Onston would have come face to face with Commissioner Warren who chaired the board.

D'Onston may well have felt slighted and held a grudge against the Metropolitan and City police. It is interesting to note that the victims of Jack the Ripper were murdered on both City police and Metropolitan police areas. There is no denying that the murders did nothing to help the reputation of the Metropolitan and City police forces. Commissioner Warren resigned the day before the last murder, due to internal conflicts.

D'Onston was plotting, when an obstacle became apparent to him, an obstacle, which he did not intend to let interfere with the work at hand. The obstacle was his wife, and she had to go. Many serial killers have murdered members of their own families or close associates because they had become a liability to the wellbeing of the killer.

Serial killer Archibald Hall murdered his brother and his own girlfriend for similar reasons. Christie killed his wife because she knew too much. Fred West and his wife murdered in the family for the same reasons. The well being of the killer is the number one priority; everyone else is expendable when it comes to the killer's own safety. With a man such as D'Onston, a self-confessed killer, it would not surprise me to find that he murdered his wife in the circumstances.

Anne Deary, Stephenson's wife, was known to be alive in 1886, but after this year nothing was ever heard of her again. There is no record of her death; she vanished, and I believe it was her husband, the magician, who performed the vanishing act.

In May 1887, parts of a woman's body were found in the Thames and in the Regents Canal. The victim was a childless woman aged upwards of 29. The trunk of a human body was found floating near the Thames ferry landing at Rainham in Essex, and in June 1887 five more pieces were found. A thigh was found in the Thames, near Temple Steps and two arms and two legs were found at the St Mary's Lock section of the Regents Canal.

Dr Edwin Calloway supposed the body had been dissected with a knife and a saw and by someone with knowledge of the human body. The head of the victim was never found. If it had been, I believe the police would have been led to the murderer. This body I believe was once Anne Deary and the murderer was her husband. The point was that he could not afford to carry on his work in Whitechapel if he was suspected of dissecting his wife.

Leaving yourself open to such suspicion is termed 'putting yourself on offer'. And D'Onston wasn't about to compromise himself over his mother's serving girl, who also happened to be his wife. D'Onston lodged only yards away from the Regents Canal in 1860. He visited two mission houses on the very edge of the canal. The canal was the ideal dumping place, a place he could visit with different human parts at a time. The canal fed south into the Regents Dock, which opened up into the Thames.

After the inquest on this victim, in August 1887, D'Onston referred to himself as 'unmarried'. Of course he was unmarried; it was he who had achieved the 'unmarrying'. Now D'Onston was a free agent with no one to snoop into his habits, no one close enough to cause him problems. Not yet anyway.

The murder of his wife was, I believe, a milk run for D'Onston. He was getting his hand in for what was to come in August 1888. This was the date he set for the commencement of the murders. He had one year in which to prepare.

During 1888, D'Onston turned up at The Cricketers Inn, Black Lion Square, Brighton. This public house is located in the lanes area known as 'little London'. It reminds one of the area of Spitalfields. The pub was a well-known haunt for prostitutes and it was here that D'Onston spent his time planning the murders while enjoying the pleasures of the flesh.

While D'Onston was in Brighton, a gentleman named Edmund Gurney was found dead in his bed under strange circumstances at The Royal Albion Hotel. The day after the inquest on Gurney, D'Onston decided to leave Brighton to sign in as a private patient at the London Hospital, Whitechapel, on 26 July 1888.

On admission to the hospital a complaint of neurosthenia (not neurasthenia as often assumed) was entered in the register. This complaint was easy to fake. Treatment consisted of plenty of rest, fresh air, light diet and no stimulants. Brighton at the time was a famous health resort so we must ask ourselves the question, 'Why would a man suffering with a complaint that requires nothing more than a rest cure move from a renowned health resort by the sea to a dirty acrid, polluted, smog-ridden, rat-infested area like Whitechapel?' Because the illness was faked by D'Onston for the sole purpose of gaining entry into the London Hospital.

The chances are that D'Onston, being a doctor, diagnosed his own complaint and his case physician went along with it. It has been suggested that D'Onston was admitted with the DTs. Nothing could be further from the truth. This complaint does not take 134 days to cure, which was the duration of D'Onston's stay in the hospital.

I went to the London Hospital and viewed the patients register and

Above: The Cricketers Inn, Black Lion Square, Brighton. It is the oldest pub in Brighton and was well-known as being frequented by prostitutes in D'Onston's day. The cubicle still exists where the prostitutes entertained their clients. The pub is a fine example of a 19th-century London-to-Brighton coaching establishment, retaining all of its original features including the stables.

The Cricketers Inn houses a Jack the Ripper exhibition based on my work, which I was asked to supply by the owner. The famous Lanes shopping precinct and alleyways of Bohemian Brighton remind one of 19th-century Spitalfields, remnants of which can be seen around Artillery Lane

Opposite: The cubicle where the prostitutes entertained their clients. It could be curtained off to give greater privacy. Resident customers such as D'Onston could entertain prostitutes in the solitude of their own rooms if they so desired

D'Onston was admitted with neurosthenia. Symptoms are sleeplessness, tension and excitability. If one was to state that D'Onston's complaint of neurosthenia entered in the hospital register was a mistake then all entries in all hospital registers of the period could be considered a mistake.

Some researchers on the subject failed to find a source for neurosthenia and questioned its very existence. It transpired that it was their research abilities that were at fault and not the entry in the hospital register.

D'Onston had until 30 August to set a pattern and to adjust himself to his surroundings. Once settled in and confident that all possible measures had been taken to secure his success he made his move.

We are dealing with a thinker and when this thinker made a move he made it with more than one aim in view. When D'Onston plumped to use the hospital as his base he took a great deal into consideration. To understand the type of location chosen by D'Onston it is imperative to view all the necessary advantages and requirements which suited his needs.

There was only one location in Whitechapel that would meet with all his requirements, the London Hospital. He had to locate a base where the police were least likely to look for a killer. As a private patient in the hospital he would be in a position to create a very good alibi which could be substantially backed up by staff.

The gates of the London Hospital were locked at night in 1888. This fact, coupled with his feigned illness, would enforce the belief by staff and others that it would be most unlikely for a sick patient to climb railings and to perform the murders. Creating such an impression would be child's play to D'Onston.

As a private patient he could reconnoitre the hospital prior to the murders. He gave himself over a month to assess the situation and to devise a means to come and go without arousing suspicion. Once in the hospital, booked in as a private patient, D'Onston would be in a position to blend in and mix with many of his own class. As a private patient, with his alleged illness, he would have access to outside areas at all times. Unlike today hospital patients in 1888 wore their own clothes.

The hospital needed to be as close as possible to the first murder, for D'Onston intended to leave a trail which would lead away from him to Dorset Street and his last victim Mary Kelly. The plan is laid out so that D'Onston would be moving for the most part on the four major roads (apart from slipping down four side roads) which all converge at the centre on the Whitechapel Road. Ideally, he needed his lair on the Whitechapel Road if possible.

A sick man in a hospital bed would not be suspected of being the killer. As far as I am concerned, D'Onston picked very good cover. The London Hospital fits all the requirements and the location is perfect. He was a doctor, a surgeon and a con man and as such he would have no problems in conning the hospital staff with symptoms of an illness which would fit in with his plans.

After all, if he could fool Inspector Roots at Scotland Yard, along with other contacts on the police force, I see no reason why a problem should arise with a few medical people. Many cases exist where criminals have fooled members of the medical profession simply by doing their homework on their alleged complaint.

The London Hospital in 1888 held one of the most extensive collections of preserved body parts and bodies in the country and D'Onston would have known that. Every part of the human body in all shapes, sizes, conditions and age groups were in evidence. A man such as D'Onston would have had little or no trouble in gaining access to them had he needed them.

At the time it was possible to buy body parts for a small fee or a complete body for four pounds. D'Onston could have either stolen parts from the hospital or purchased a body for the organs he required if the motive was not occult. He never did so because the organs had to be taken from murdered prostitutes in a ritual manner at certain locations.

Many war criminals on the run after the Second World War and many other murderers have used hospitals as cover. The commandant of the concentration camp portrayed in the film *Schindler's List* was found posing as a patient in a hospital. It's a trick that has been used before.

The London Hospital of 1888 had extensive grounds, which were covered with trees, plants, scrub and empty builders' sheds, where it would be easy to conceal any item. The railings around the hospital were of the same type and height (5ft) which were used at D'Onston's home in Hull when he was a boy. D'Onston was nearly 6ft tall and he would have had no trouble getting over the railings at the hospital, so they did not constitute a problem to D'Onston. He may have had another means of coming and going at his leisure.

Far too much has been taken for granted in relation to D'Onston's age and faked illness. Many killers were far older and in frailer health than

D'Onston. The oldest killer I ever met was aged in his 60s, while the youngest were still at school. They both strangled a man who had befriended them. One of the boys was 14 years of age and blond, a lookalike for the children in the film *Village of the Damned*.

I remember the blond boy because, when I looked at him, the hair on the back of my neck stood up. This was the only occasion when I reacted in such a manner on coming face to face with a killer. It was partly due to his eyes, his look. There was something about this boy, he radiated evil, despite the fact that many killers I spoke to did not mince words and were more than forthright in stating all the finer details. Killing for some is no more than a means to an end.

While having a great deal of experience with most types of killers I did not view every killer I met as dangerous. Many domestic murders are committed on the spur of the moment. With others it is simply a case of 'there but for the grace of God go I'. At the other end of the spectrum we have the most obnoxious type of killer which I refer to as evil. D'Onston was such a killer.

As for his fitness, I wish to make the point clear that many men in their 40s and 50s are very fit. Some months ago my brother came to visit for a few days. On the evening of his arrival he popped out for a while and forgot to take his key. Thinking I would be home before him I locked the premises, but left one bedroom window open upstairs. When I returned home I found him indoors.

He had climbed 9ft, to the top of a bay window, and then a further 5ft to climb through a window 11in wide. My brother is lean and over 50. D'Onston was lean and in his 40s in 1888. Being a pipe-smoker with a complaint that made him stay awake at night, he could leave the ward at any time for a smoke in his own clothes in the grounds.

D'Onston, as always, created a situation which he could manipulate. This was how he worked. Taking everything into consideration, D'Onston planned very well, giving thought to the finer details and placing a great deal of thought into each move he was to make. He also made sure he had all the answers to the questions the police were likely to ask him.

I have made it apparent that I believe the perpetrator of the murders to be a Satanic killer, that he had medical knowledge, that he checked out the five murder sites and police beat times beforehand and that he picked his times when the main roads were very busy on weekends. I have already stated that it was essential to understand two murders which were to distort the true situation and influence events at a later date.

I refer of course to the murders of Emma Smith and Martha Tabram. One misconception, which had far-reaching consequences, was that Jack the Ripper murdered from five to 14 victims in relation to the Whitechapel murders. Shortly after midnight on 3 April 1888 Emma Smith was found murdered. On 7 August 1888 Martha Tabram was found murdered. Police officers, Dr Robert Anderson and Inspector Abberline endorsed the belief that Tabram was also a Ripper victim.

When D'Onston signed in at the London Hospital from Brighton, lady luck was on his side. For these two murders were considered to be the first two of the series. So when D'Onston committed his first murder in the series by killing Nichols in Bucks Row on 31 August 1888 it was listed as the third in the series. No one in the hospital (or elsewhere) would ever dream that D'Onston was the killer, because he was not in Whitechapel when the first two murders took place. So, one would reason, if he was not the killer of the first two victims then he could not possibly be the killer of the third victim.

This state of affairs was not to end there. For after D'Onston had killed his fifth victim on 9 November 1888, various other murders took place which were also attributed to the Ripper. On Wednesday, 17 July 1889, Alice McKenzie of 54, Gun Street, Spitalfields was murdered. Her body was found by PC Andrews in Castle Alley. The victim's throat had been cut. McKenzie was considered by many to be a Ripper victim. So now we have seven Ripper victims instead of five.

This meant that anyone who suspected D'Onston of being the Ripper was on a sticky wicket. They may have concluded that they were wrong when in fact they were right. W. T. Stead of the *Pall Mall Gazette* thought D'Onston was the killer but at a later date he had second thoughts on the matter, which is hardly surprising under the circumstances.

What we do know is that Stead thought him more than capable of committing the murders. D'Onston is on record as stating that the killer used the Whitechapel Road as a 'sort of base'. He also gave the motive for the murders and other information. His comments are shown to be true in relation to my research. My beliefs were also shared by the press of the period as shown here.

The special Sunday edition of the *News of the World*, London, 7 October 1888, printed a front-page story which concluded that the killer had peculiar surgical knowledge and some experience (however obtained) which should make it easier to hunt the criminal down. The article went on to add that the killer was:

> ... cool, cautious, confident, cunning and daring, being previously familiar with the murder sites on which he had checked out the police beat times and that the need to change police beat times is essential as it is a friendly arrangement for burglars and assassins. Nobody noticed him, the reason being that the two neighbourhoods are so thickly populated, especially about midnight on a Saturday, and every man and woman, being intent either upon their market purchases or the last drop at the closing public houses, as to be regardless of anything else.

The killer is also referred to as 'a Satanic death dealer'. The article goes on to add that the killer kept to the main Whitechapel Road. The article voices the opinion that a better detective force is required and reform of the system essential. It also adds, 'It is a general belief among the police that should they catch the assassin he will endeavour to make "short work of them".' They believe him to be a strong and powerful man. Vittoria Cremers who was D'Onston's business partner did indeed refer to him as being 'strong and powerful'.

I have heard several reasons given why the killer only killed at the weekends. The favourite seems to be that he had a job during the week. I believe that D'Onston had several reasons for choosing the weekend to commit the murders. Staff reductions on the wards at the hospital took place on the weekends.

It was a very busy time in the area so the killer would blend in as 'invisible'; he would be just another tree in the forest. Sailors from the shipping in the local docks would be on weekend shore leave. All had money in their pockets with the intention of spending it on a good time.

The *Star*, 19th December 1888 printed the following story: 'Nurses and doctors were going in and out of a Croydon infirmary at night by scaling gates and walls. They were getting the night watchman to place false information in the official records.' The Star of 4th October 1888 printed a story that police investigating hospitals were being obstructed in their duty by hospital staff and it is on record that night staff were going to sleep on the job.

The prostitutes in the area would have known that the weekends were a very lucrative time for them. Therefore the maximum number would have been out and about on weekends. The killer would have known that more potential victims would be on offer. I now intend to cover the only piece of constructive comment I have heard to date by critics of D'Onston which casts doubt as to whether he was the killer. Some doubt has been raised as to how D'Onston managed to leave the hospital to commit murder and then return without being missed. This would be child's play to a man such as D'Onston. From my own experiences in hospital I know that it is possible. On one occasion, while in hospital due to a very painful nerve injury to my arm, morphine was refused. The pain caused many sleepless nights and I often went for walks around the grounds. When the doctor and matron came on their rounds in the mornings I was never in my bed or in the ward and no questions were ever asked. In fact, I would moonlight for hours from the ward for a smoke and a drink, during both the day and the night. This was probably the method used by D'Onston in relation to his fake illness. Once I had set a pattern the staff became accustomed to it and never once questioned it. The security in a modern hospital is far tighter than in the Whitechapel hospital of 1888. The killer worked on Friday, Saturday or Sunday mornings and staff reductions took place on these days. During the day the ratio was one sister, two nurses and two probationers for every 30 patients. During the night the ratio was one staff nurse and two probationers for every 30 patients. These are the figures for the maximum number of patients. There was fewer staff still if there was a minimum number of patients. These figures are for weekdays only.

John Merrick, the Elephant Man, was in the London Hospital at the same time as D'Onston. The curious would gain entry to the hospital grounds at night, after closing, to obtain a sight of Merrick. This became a problem. In fact, nothing could be done to stop people gaining access to the hospital grounds. So bars had to be placed on the window of Merrick's private bedroom, not to stop him getting out but to stop others from getting in. If people were getting in to the hospital to view the Elephant Man after hours then D'Onston would have had no trouble getting out of the hospital. A friend, Mr Nicholas Way, enforces this point. 'During 1997 I was involved in a discussion with Ivor Edwards concerning hospital security in the 1880s. I felt compelled to tell of two exploits involving patients at the Surrey County Hospital in Guildford. The first incident occurred in the mid-1980s.

'A friend of mine, Martin Edwards, was involved in a motorcycle accident resulting in a few broken bones. It was midsummer and the patient was very hot and bothered in his ward. To cheer him up we smuggled him out in a wheelchair and went into Guildford for a few hours. After we had returned the patient to the ward we were very surprised that no one had even noticed him to be missing. We planned another trip for a later date.

'The second incident happened about 1990 and could have resulted in dire consequences. Another friend, Ian Taylor, had been diagnosed with a very serious and rare disorder. He had been placed on a type of drip-fed machinery with digital counters and tubes. He had been placed in a ward full of very sick people. While visiting Ian, who loves the odd pint or two, he talked me into taking him to his local pub, The Royal, in Stoughton, Guildford.

'This seemed like a bit of a task due to all the machinery he was hooked up to, but we soon set about our task of sneaking him out of the hospital. We left unnoticed, complete with machinery, and enjoyed a few pints, much to the amusement of the pub regulars. Upon our return to the ward we were amazed that our antics had gone undetected.

'In my opinion this strengthens Mr Edwards's case that someone could easily enjoy relative freedom whilst residing in a hospital in the 1880s as the security couldn't possibly match a modern general hospital with CCTV, security guards, etc.'

Mr Way had only minutes to make a decision and to move the patient, and all was done on speculation. The situation demanded it be done on the spur of the moment. In spite of this fact, the objective was achieved on several counts; getting the patient out and back again without being seen on either occasion or without him being missed in the process.

D'Onston had planned and plotted for over a month in the hospital before making his move. This man did not debunk on speculation. Dozens of cases exist where certain individuals have debunked from secure buildings at one place or another only to commit a crime and then return while not being missed. Many men have escaped from prison camps and other secure places and were gone for days or longer unnoticed. All it takes is some imagination and boldness.

To even contemplate that such a thing could not be achieved by D'Onston shows a lack of imagination. It also shows that his abilities have been too easily discounted. *Pall Mall Gazette* editor W. T. Stead described D'Onston as the most amazing man he had ever met. Stead was the confidant of presidents and he was far from being a fool, so what exactly was it that made D'Onston so amazing in his eyes?

D'Onston has not been satisfactorily researched by his critics. Usually I find that they have obtained what little information they have fromunreliable sources such as Aleister Crowley. Also human nature being unfortunately what it is I would not expect all Ripperologists considered experts to agree with me, for most have suspects of their own.

After the Kelly murder D'Onston wrote to W. T. Stead asking for funds to catch Jack the Ripper. Note that as soon as the last murder was committed D'Onston was well enough to inject himself into the search and make an attempt to con money out of Stead. The latter wrote to D'Onston on 30 November 1888, declining the offer and refusing funds. On 1 December 1888, an article written by D'Onston appeared on the front page of the *Pall Mall Gazette*. It would appear by the title of the article that even D'Onston saw himself for what he truly was.

The Whitechapel Demon's Nationality and Why He Committed the Murders

by D'Onston

In calmly reviewing the whole chain of facts connected with these daring and bloodthirsty atrocities, the first thing which strikes one is the fact that the murderer was kind enough (so to speak) to leave his card with the Mitre Square victim. But this most important clue to his identity which 'he who runs may read', seems to have baffled the combined intellects of all grades of the police. This admits of no question, because we find in all the journals a note from Sir Charles Warren to the effect that no language or dialogue is known in which the word 'Jews' is spelt 'Juwes'.

O! Most sapient conclusion! Let us see what we can make of the word. It will be remembered that a chalk inscription (which is not denied was written by the murderer) was found on the wall in Mitre-square, just above the body of the murdered woman. It ran as follows: 'The Juwes are the men who will not be blamed for nothing' and was evidently intended to throw suspicion on the Jews. This writing was only seen by the police by means of artificial light, and was unfortunately obliterated by them before daylight. *Hinc illae lachrymae!* Why did the murderer spell the word Jews 'Juwes'? Was it that he was an uneducated Englishman who did not know how to spell the word; was he in reality an ignorant Jew, reckless of consequences and glorying in his deeds, or was he a foreigner, well accustomed to the English language, but who in the tremendous hurry of the moment unconsciously wrote the fatal word in his native tongue? The answers to these three queries, on which the whole matter rests, are easy. Juwes is a much too difficult word for an uneducated man to evolve on the spur of the moment, as any philologist will allow. Any ignorant Jew capable of spelling the rest of the sentence as correctly as he did, would know, certainly, how to spell the name of his own people. Therefore, only the last proposition remains, which we shall now show, in the most conclusive manner, to be the truth. To critically examine an inscription of this kind, the first thing we naturally do is not to rest satisfied with reading it in print, but to make, as nearly as we can, a facsimile of it in script, thus:-

Juives   Juwes

Inspection at once shows us, then, that a dot has been overlooked by the constable who copied it, as might easily occur, especially if it were placed at some distance, after the manner of foreigners.

Therefore we place a dot above the third upstroke in the word Juwes, and we find it to be Juives, which is the French word for Jews. Strictly, Juives and grammatically speaking, of course, it is the feminine form of Juifs and means 'Jewesses'. But in practice it will be found that Frenchmen who are not either litterateurs or men of science are very inaccurate as to their genders. And almost all the ouvrier and a large majority of the bourgeois class use the feminine where the word should be masculine. Even the Emperor Napoleon III was a great sinner in this respect, as his voluminous correspondence amply shows. Therefore, it is evident that the native language, or to be more accurate, the language in which this murderer thinks, is French. The murderer is, therefore, a Frenchman.

It may be here argued that both Swiss and Belgians make French almost their mother tongue; but Flemish is the natural and usual vehicle for the latter, while the idiosyncrasy of both those nationalities is adverse to this class of crime. On the contrary, in France, the murdering of prostitutes has long been practised, and has been considered to be almost peculiarly a French crime.

Again, the grammatical construction of the sentence under examination is distinctly French in two points—first, in the double negative contained; and secondly, in the employment of the definite article before the second noun. An Englishman or an American would have said, 'The Jews are men who, etc.' but the murderer followed his native idiom 'Les Juifs sont des hommes' in his thoughts, and when putting it into English rendered des hommes 'the men'.

Again, neither Belgians nor Swiss entertain any animosity to the Jews, whereas the hatred of the French proletarian to them is notorious.

The grounds for research being thus cleared and narrowed, the next question is what is the motive? Speculation has been rife the cries are many; almost every man one meets, who is competent to form an opinion, having a different one. And in endeavouring to sift a mystery like this one cannot afford to throw aside any theory, however extravagant, without careful examination, because the truth might, after all, lie in the most unlikely one.

There seems to be no doubt that the murderer, whether mad or not, had a distinct motive in his mutilations; but one possible theory of that motive has never been suggested. In the 19th century, with all its enlightenment, it would seem absurd, were it not that superstition dies hard, and some of its votaries do undoubtedly to this day practise unholy rites. Now, in one of the books by the great modern occultist who wrote under the non de plume of 'Eliphaz Levi', 'Le Dogme et Rituel de la Haute Magie', we find the most elaborate directions for working magical spells of all kinds. The second volume has a chapter on Necromancy, or Black Magic, which the author justly denounces as a profanation. Black Magic employs the agencies of evil spirits and demons, instead of the beneficent spirits directed by adepts of *la haute magie*. At the same time he gives the clearest and fullest details of the necessary steps for evocation by this means, and it is in the list of substances prescribed as absolutely necessary to success that we find the link which joins modern French necromancy with the quest of the East End murderer. These substances are in themselves horrible, and difficult to procure. They can only be obtained by means of the most appalling crimes, of which murder and mutilation of the dead are the least heinous. Among them are strips of the skin of a suicide, nails from a murderer's gallows, candles made from human fat, the head of a black cat which has been fed forty days on human flesh, the horns of a goat which have been made the instrument of a infamous capital crime, and a preparation made from a certain portion of the body of a harlot. This last point is insisted upon as essential and it was this extra-ordinary fact that first drew my attention to the possible connection of the murderer with the black art. Further, in the practise of evocation the sacrifice of human victims was a necessary part of the process, and the profanation of the cross and other emblems usually considered sacred was also enjoined. In this connection it will be well to remember one most extraordinary and unparalleled circumstance in the commission of the Whitechapel murders, and a thing which could not by any possibility have been brought about fortuitously. Leaving out of the last murder, committed indoors, which was most probably not committed by the fiend of whom we speak, we find the sites for the murders, six in number, form a perfect cross. That is to say, a line ruled from No. 3 to No. 6 on a map having the murder sites marked and numbered, passes exactly through Nos. 1 and 2, while the cross arms are accurately formed by a line from No. 4 to 5. The seventh, or Dorset Street murder, does not fall within either of these lines, and there is nothing to connect it with the others except the mutilations. But the mutilations in this latter case were evidently not made by anyone having the practical knowledge of the knife and the position of the respective organs which was exhibited in the other six cases, and also in the mutilated trunk found in the new police buildings, which was probably the first of the series of murders, and was committed somewhere on the lines of the cross, the body being removed at the time. Did the Murderer, then, designing to offer the mystic number of seven human sacrifices in the form of a cross — a form he intended to profane — deliberately pick out beforehand on a map the places in which he would offer them to his infernal deity of murder? If not, surely these six coincidences (?) are the most marvellous event of our time.

To those persons to whom this theory may seem somewhat far-fetched, we would merely remark that the French book referred to was only published a few years ago; that thousands of copies were sold; that societies have been formed for the study and practice of its teachings and philosophy; and finally, that within the last twelve months an English edition has been issued. In all things history repeats itself, and the superstitions of yesterday become the creeds of today.

In his letter, D'Onston wrote that the profanation of the cross and other emblems usually considered sacred was also enjoined. This statement stands to condemn D'Onston. We know that four sites are located at the four points of the compass thus forming the symbol of the Christian cross. But D'Onston went on to add that there were other sacred emblems (symbols) enjoined with the cross, which must also be profaned.

There are indeed other sacred emblems enjoined with the cross and I have produced them on my plan of the murders. Only two people have ever connected these sacred symbols to the murders since 1888 – myself and D'Onston. Also I find it more than coincidence that two symbols incorporated into the plan are used in the worship of Satan.

Stead paid D'Onston four pounds for the article of 1 December 1888. It is clear to see that he was playing a devious game by writing this letter, just as he played a devious game with the letter sent to the City police on 16 October 1888. He played ignorant to certain facts relating to the case so that he could give himself an 'out' should the need arise if the heat became intense. It would not do for him to appear to know too much. So he threw in some red herrings to confuse the issue.

He wrote with the purpose in mind that anyone reading about his opinions would know that he was incorrect in some instances and therefore could not possibly be the killer. He wrote: the writing on the wall was in Mitre Square, the mutilations to Kelly were not made by anyone having practical knowledge of the knife or the position of the organs exhibited in the other six cases. The trunk found in the new police buildings (New Scotland Yard), which was probably the first in the series, was committed somewhere on the lines of the cross and then moved. All such statements were untrue and intended to deceive.

D'Onston is the only journalist since 1888 (to my knowledge) who has ever stated that the writing on the wall was at Mitre Square above the body and not at Goulston Street. He did not wish anyone to know that he knew 100 per cent about the case. It is clear to see that D'Onston was playing a psychological game. Psychology played a great part in the devious way he was thinking. If ever brought before a court or even questioned by police his defence would have been that he could not possibly have been the killer because certain things he wrote were known not to be fact. He was playing it safe.

Pleading ignorant to certain known facts is a method adopted by many criminals to give a false impression. He stated there were seven killings but he told a business associate, Vittoria Cremers, that the murders numbered five and five only. He wrote the Dorset Street murder is not connected to the others. Yet he told Cremers that the killing at Millers Court was the last murder the killer would commit in the series. He was right. Only the killer himself would know this.

He hoped to give the impression that he was not the killer by purposely mis-stating certain facts of the case. He informed the *Pall Mall Gazette* of the mistake made by the police in copying the message on the wall at Goulston Street, going on to add, 'And in endeavouring to sift a mystery like this, one cannot afford to throw aside any theory, however extravagant, without careful examination, because the truth might, after all, lie in the most unlikely one.'

When I read this advice I thought D'Onston was quoting Sir Arthur Conan Doyle, who had a piece published in the *Pall Mall Gazette* on the same day as D'Onston (1 December 1888). It is more than likely they read each other's work. The nearest quote from Sir Arthur Conan Doyle that I could match with D'Onston's reads, 'When you have excluded the impossible, whatever remains, however improbable, must be the truth.'

This quote can be found in two books by Conan Doyle, *Beryl Coronet* (1892) and *The Sign of the Four* (1890). I have spent a great deal of time in researching D'Onston and he was certainly not a 'Walter Mitty' character, although he may have appeared to give such an impression to those who have underestimated his intentions or abilities. Although he told lies he did not tell them just for the sake of doing so. There was a purpose behind the lies he told. He lied to create false impressions for his own benefit. He was very devious and very dangerous.

When we are dealing with such people we must expect them to lie for they are generally out to deceive others by using whatever means they have at their disposal. Thus the wheat must be sorted from the chaff. Only then can we hope to understand the true situation rather than the situation such people wish to impose upon us.

D'Onston wrote, 'Did the murderer deliberately pick out beforehand on a map the places in which he would offer them to his infernal deity … of murder? If not, surely these six coincidences (?) are the most marvellous event of our time.' Before I had ever heard of D'Onston I had conclusive proof that the murders were indeed planned in advance on a map.

D'Onston again knew of 'facts' which have only come to light since my research. Again he is proven correct in stating that all sites were prearranged and picked from a map. Common sense dictates that the sites would have been checked out on foot by D'Onston for suitability once he had picked out the sites on his map.

He is correct in every aspect on the killings apart from the intentional 'outs', which he leaves to cover himself. As for four victims found at the points of a cross, is this coincidence or was it intended on the part of the killer? It is very easy to dismiss such an assertion with a cry of 'coincidence', but my evidence is powerful and conclusive.

An independent study in Canada brings confirmation. The Canadian lawyers Jay Clarke and John Banks looked at these murders. They have been involved in more than 60 murder cases and specialise in the field of criminal insanity. They considered the possibility of preplanning and took this problem to a professor of Statistics at Columbia University. They asked, 'How do you calculate the probability of finding four bodies randomly distributed in a city so that they form the points of a cross?'

The answer was simple. Put a grid over a map of the area – eight squares by eight will do – and work from that. But the odds at the end of the calculations were 1 in 15,249,024! If the grid squares were made smaller, and this would be quite legitimate, then the odds would soar enormously. This is also without the exact distances being taken into account.

Distance from victim 1 to victim 2 = 930 yards.
Distance from victim 2 to victim 4 = 930 yards.
Distance from victim 3 to victim 4 = 950 yards.
Distance from victim 3 to victim 5 = 950 yards.
Distance from the centre point at junction to site 3 = 500 yards.
Distance from the centre point at junction to site 4 = 500 yards.
Distance from the centre point at junction to site 5 = 500 yards.

I would not even try to contemplate the odds against the figures shown above as being by chance. Now consider another vital point of the murders. Four points of this cross are placed east, north, south and west. Victim two was placed 63 yards off due north (over a total distance of nearly 1,000 yards is not worth concern under such circumstances), because the original site chosen was located slap bang at a busy crossroad.

The killer wanted a second site which afforded more cover and he did extremely well by getting a second site so near to the first, especially when one takes into consideration the nature of the immediate area which consisted of nothing more than house and shop fronts.

What was the Method in D'Onston's Occult Practices?

Mrs P. Stephens, from California, who has extensively studied the occult informed me, 'When D'Onston took organs from women for a ritualistic purpose, it is more likely that he devised the ritual on his own rather than using something from the grimoires that were available at that time, unless he was adept at reading Latin, French or German.' (Which he was.)

It is unlikely (but possible) that he got his hands on a 'secret manuscript' that hadn't already been translated into English. For example, you get rituals that use different circles and different implements, and they often specify things that are nearly impossible for the magician to do. And trying to tie D'Onston into a specific ritual might be a bit tricky.

All rituals have some commonalities and some differences with regard to certain details. D'Onston, in his letter of 1 December 1888, wrote about certain points made above in relation to rituals. D'Onston also stated that the killer's intentions were to profane the Christian cross and other such sacred symbols.

We know that the first four victims were murdered at the points of a cross. So that leaves Kelly and other symbols to be profaned. What other evidence is there of other Christian symbols? Another Christian symbol, which shows up on my plan, is Vesica Piscis, also known as the 'fish' or 'yoni'. This symbol was a secret symbol used by the early Christians. This symbol is still used today and resembles a fish in shape.

Kelly was murdered to profane this symbol and her murder was committed on the line of Vesica Piscis. See the full plan with symbols and location of sites. Stride, Eddowes and Kelly were all murdered on the line of Vesica Piscis and all three were found on the line of the 500-yard radius.

D'Onston could not have come out with the whole truth or he would have been caught, so he came out with the next best thing – 'half-truths'. To understand D'Onston one must first and foremost comprehend the many games which are played by criminals and also have the ability to comprehend the working mind of a very devious gameplayer.

It has been suggested that D'Onston could have been admitted to the London Hospital with the DTs or a number of other complaints. Firstly, the DTs did not take 134 days to relieve in 1888. Secondly, D'Onston carried his own treatment, which dealt with the DTs.

The prescribed remedy for the DTs was a dose of spirits of chloroform mixed with alcohol. This could be one part of chloroform mixed with nine parts alcohol. The alcohol could be gin, brandy and suchlike. A doctor would usually prescribe nine parts pure alcohol to one part chloroform. D'Onston most likely mixed his own.

I have seen the entry for D'Onston in the London Hospital register and he was admitted with neurosthenia. D'Onston has been referred to as a drunk, which is quite untrue. We have witness testimony that he could drink all day and evening and remain sober. He controlled the drink it did not control him.

Many ill-founded comments have been made about D'Onston for varying reasons. Being familiar with the subject he is a far better candidate for the Ripper than most suspects in the frame. He has been dismissed out of hand only too readily by the ignorant and those involved in inter-Ripper rivalries.

On 7 December 1888, D'Onston left the London Hospital while all his fellow journalists were staying put waiting for another murder. He moved away from Whitechapel and rented lodgings in Castle Street, off Upper St Martin's Lane. His landlord at this address was also the landlord at 66, Leman Street. His lack of interest to the murder area showed that no more murders were planned by him for Whitechapel. His actions indicated that he knew the truth of the situation.

Now one should always expect the unexpected and in relation to D'Onston at this period in time the unexpected did indeed raise its head. A postal worker intercepted a letter sent by a patient at the London Hospital. The writing was said to resemble that of the original Ripper letters. The sender was a man said to be well acquainted with the East End, with contacts among the rescue and mission workers there. The police became interested and kept a lookout for the man.

The facts of the case fitted D'Onston. His contacts among the mission workers began when he edited sermons for Rev. Alex McAuslane. He decided to play another of his devious games and deliberately court suspicion. His plan was to inject himself into the investigation so that the police would not take him seriously. His plan was to find and con a person who would take what he said hook, line and sinker and then report D'Onston to the police as the killer. D'Onston found such a man in the form of George Marsh.

Marsh was an unemployed man who wanted to become a private detective. D'Onston manipulated Marsh as he did with most people he came into contact with. Marsh was no match for D'Onston and his devious ways. D'Onston fed Marsh a cock-and-bull story about a Dr

Davies being the killer. He informed Marsh that he knew the killer well, then he described facts relating to the case with the intention of letting Marsh believe that he was talking to the killer himself. The trick worked and Marsh soon rejected the idea of Dr Davies being the killer and decided that D'Onston was the culprit.

Within three weeks of meeting D'Onston he went to Scotland Yard and fingered D'Onston as the Ripper. This went along with D'Onston's plans exactly. Marsh's statement, dictated to Inspector J. Roots on Christmas Eve 1888 read:

About a month ago at Prince Albert public house, Upper St Martin's Lane, I met a man named Stephenson and casually discussed the murders in Whitechapel with him. From that time to the present we have met two or three times a week and we have on each occasion discussed the murders in a confidential manner. He has tried to tell me how I could catch the man if I went to work his way. I simply told him I was an amateur detective and that I had been for weeks looking for the culprit. He explained to me how the murders were committed. He said they were committed by a woman-hater after the forthcoming manner:

The murderer would induce a woman to go up a back street or room and to excite his passion would 'bugger' her and cut her throat at the same time with his right hand, holding on by the left.

He illustrated the action. From his manner I am of the opinion he is the murderer in the first six cases, if not the last one.

Today Stephenson told me that Dr Davies of Houndsditch (I don't know the address, although I have been there and could point it out) was the murderer and he wished me to see him. He drew up an agreement to share the reward on the conviction of Dr Davies. I know that this agreement is valueless, but it secured his handwriting. I made him under the influence of drink, thinking that I should get some further statement, but in this I failed as he left to see Dr Davies and also to go to Mr Stead of the *Pall Mall Gazette*, from which he expected two pounds. He wrote the article in the *Pall Mall Gazette* in relation to the writing on the wall about the

Jews. He had four pounds for that. I have seen letters from Mr Stead in his possession about it; also a letter from Mr Stead refusing to allow him money to find out the Whitechapel Murderer.

Stephenson has shown me a discharge from the London Hospital. The name Stephenson had been obliterated and that of Davies is marked in red ink. I do not know the date.

Stephenson is now at the common lodging house No. 29, Castle St, St Martin's Lane, WC, and has been there three weeks. His description is age 48, height 5ft, 10ins, full face, sallow complexion, moustache heavy-mouse-coloured, waxed and turned up, hair brown turning grey, eyes sunken. When looking at a stranger generally has an eyeglass. Dress, grey suit and light brown felt hat – all well-worn; military appearance; says he has been in 42 battles. Well educated.

The agreement he gave me I will leave with you and will render any assistance the Police may require.

Stephenson is not a drunkard; he is what I call a soaker – can drink from 8 o'clock in the morning until closing time but keep a clear head.

The 'agreement' referred to by Marsh, written by Stephenson reads, 'I hereby agree to pay Dr R. D'O. Stephenson (also known as "Sudden Death") one half of any or all the rewards or monies received by me on a/c of the conviction of Dr Davies for wilful murder.'

Knowing full well that this note would land on the desk of his good friend Inspector Roots, Stephenson used his correct name. He also showed how devious he in fact was by using the name 'Sudden Death', a term used in gambling.

When I first saw this gambling term used by D'Onston I became rather amused and laughed aloud for it was like a joke. I believe that two reasons lay behind the use of the term. The first being that many like myself would not really take the story seriously after reading 'Sudden Death' and would see it as something of a joke to be dismissed.

The other reason is far more sinister. D'Onston is in fact placing a hidden meaning behind the term. He is saying that he is indeed the killer and that he kills in a very sudden manner. Sudden Death is just as appropriate as Jack the Ripper. The police, however, took him seriously at a later date because they arrested him on suspicion of the murders.

Two days after Marsh went to Scotland Yard and made his statement to Roots Stephenson followed suit. He went straight to his old friend Roots and tried to fit up the unfortunate Dr Davies. Let us not forget that Stephenson had already written a letter to the police from the hospital accusing Dr Davies. He stated that he would visit the police when well enough. True to his word, he did just that. This proves that he was thinking well ahead of the game.

He made the following statement to Roots:

I beg to draw your attention to the attitude of Dr Morgan Davies of ... Houndsditch, E. with respect to these murders. But my suspicions attach to him principally in connection with the last one committed indoors.

Three weeks ago I was a patient in the London Hospital, in a private ward ... with a Dr Evans, suffering from typhoid, who used to be visited almost nightly by Dr Davies, when the murders were our usual subject of conversation. Dr Davies always insisted on the fact that the murderer was a man of sexual powers almost effete, which could only be brought into action by some strong stimulus, such as sodomy. He was very positive on this point that the murderer performed on the women from behind – in fact, per ano. At that time he could have no information, any more than myself, about the fact that the post-mortem examination revealed that semen was found up the woman's rectum, mixed with her faeces. [I must add at this point that even if this were true it would not necessarily mean that it was the killer's semen. For example, Kelly could well have been sodomised by a client before she was murdered by Stephenson.] Many things, which would seem trivial in writing, seemed to me to connect him with the affair – for instance, he is himself a woman hater. Although a man of powerful frame, and (according to the lines on his sallow face) of strong sexual passion. He is supposed, however, by his intimates to never touch a woman. One night, when five medicos were present, quietly discussing the subject and combating his argument that the murderer did not do these things to obtain specimens of uteri (wombs) but that – in his case – it was the lust of murder developed from sexual lust – a thing not unknown to medicos, he acted (in a way which fairly terrified those five doctors) the whole scene. He took a knife, 'buggered' an imaginary woman, cut her throat from behind; then when she was apparently laid prostrate, ripped and slashed her in all directions in a perfect frenzy.

Previously to this performance I had said, 'After a man had done a thing like this, reaction would take place and he would collapse and be taken at once to the police, or would attract the attention of the bystanders by his exhausted condition?' Dr D said, 'No! He would recover himself when the fit was over and be as calm as a lamb. I will show you!' Then he began his performance. At the end of it he stopped, buttoned up his coat, put on his hat, and walked down the room with the most perfect calmness. Certainly, his face was pale as death, but that was all. It was only a few days ago, after I was positively informed by the Editor of the *Pall Mall Gazette* that the murdered woman last operated on had been sodomised that I thought, 'How did he know?' His acting was the most vivid I ever saw. Henry Irving was a fool to it. Another point. He argued that the murderer did not want specimens of uteri, but grasped them and slashed them off in his madness as being the only hard substance that met his grasp, when his hands were madly plunging into the abdomen of his victims.

I may say that Dr Davies was for some time House Physician at the London Hospital Whitechapel, that he has lately taken this house in Castle St, Houndsditch; that he has lived in the locality of the murders for some years and that he professes his intention of going to Australia shortly should he not quickly make a success in his new house.

Roslyn D'O Stephenson

P.S. I have mentioned this matter to a pseudo-detective named

George Marsh of 24, Pratt St., Camden Town NW, with whom I have made an agreement (enclosed herewith) to share any reward he may derive from my information.

The exact nature of the enquiries directed towards Dr Davies remains unknown.

Inspector Roots made a report in relation to the visit to Scotland Yard by Stephenson, which read:

> With reference to the statement of Mr George Marsh of 24th inst., regarding the probable association of Dr Davies and Stephenson with the murders in Whitechapel. I beg to report that Dr Stephenson came here this evening and wrote the attached statement of his suspicions of Dr Morgan Davies, Castle St, Houndsditch; and also left me with his agreement with Marsh as to the reward. I attach it. When Marsh came here on 24th I was under the impression that Stephenson was a man I had known 20 years, I now find that impression was correct.
>
> He is a travelled man of education and ability, a doctor of medicine upon diplomas of Paris and New York; a major from the Italian Army – he fought under Garibaldi; and a newspaper writer. He says that he wrote the article about Jews in the *Pall Mall Gazette*, that he occasionally writes for that paper, and that he offered his services to Mr Stead to track the murderer.
>
> He showed me a letter from Mr Stead, dated 30th November 1888 about this and said that the result was that the proprietor declined to engage upon it. He has lead a Bohemian life, drinks very heavily, and always carries drugs to sober him and stave off delirium tremors. He was an applicant for the Orphanage Secretaryship at the last election.

(Note: D'Onston's military rank in the army of Garibaldi was Surgeon Major with the rank of lieutenant. He could therefore refer to himself quite legitimately as Major Stephenson if he so wished.)

On 30 December 1888, *The Sunday Times* produced some of the details of the investigation that had spooked and alarmed D'Onston. As published by the *Pall Mall Gazette*, this story ran:

... a gentleman who has for some time been engaged in philanthropic work in the East End recently received a letter, the handwriting of which had previously attracted the attention of the Post Office authorities on account of its similarity to that of the writer of some of the letters signed 'Jack the Ripper'. The police made inquiries, and ascertained that the writer was known to his correspondent as a person intimately acquainted with East End life, and that he was then a patient in a metropolitan hospital. It is stated that on an inquiry at the hospital it was discovered that the person sought had left without the knowledge or consent of the hospital authorities, but that he had been subsequently seen, and is now under observation. The police are of the opinion that the last five murders were a series and that the first two were independently perpetrated.

Whether D'Onston ever wrote any such letters is open to debate. We do know however, that D'Onston was arrested and taken in for questioning on two occasions. It has been suggested that his arrest took place because of the statement Marsh made accusing him of being the killer. Nothing could be further from the truth.

D'Onston would not have been arrested on the strength of the statement made by Marsh any more than Dr Davies would have been arrested on the strength of the statement made by D'Onston. No evidence exists that Dr Davies was even questioned, let alone arrested. Also D'Onston went to see Inspector Roots of his own free will. He was not taken to see him under arrest. He was, however, more than a match for the police. He was so bold that he had placed his head into the lion's den. Inspector Roots had not known D'Onston for a period of 20 years solely because D'Onston was a criminal and always in trouble with the law. There was far more to it than that.

The only evidence to show that D'Onston ever had a 'run in' with the police was when he was arrested over the Whitechapel murders. He knew Roots in a professional capacity rather than a criminal one. I would be interested to know the exact method used by D'Onston to steer Marsh in the direction of his old friend Roots. Marsh could have gone to any local police station, to any policeman, but he went to a specific station to speak to a specific person who had known D'Onston for many years.

It is interesting to note that Marsh said Stephenson had told him that the killer induced his victims to go up a back street or to a room. The victims did not take the killer to the sites; he took them.

CHAPTER TWELVE

A CLASSIC CASE OF MISHANDLING BY POLICE AND PRESS

SIR ROBERT ANDERSON, Assistant Commissioner, Metropolitan Police, CID stated that unsolved murders in London at the time were rare. In the East End of London alone, between 1888 and 1891, the following murders went unsolved.

Emma Smith. Attacked in Spitalfields, April 1888, died in hospital.

Martha Tabram. Found in George Yard Building, Whitechapel, August 1888.

Mary Ann Nichols. Found in Bucks Row, Whitechapel, August 1888.

Annie Chapman. Found at 29, Hanbury Street, Spitalfields, September 1888.

Elizabeth Stride. Found in Berner Street, Whitechapel, September 1888.

Catherine Eddowes. Found in Mitre Square, Aldgate, September 1888.

Mary Kelly. Found in Dorset Street, Spitalfields, November 1888.

Alice 'Clay Pipe' McKenzie. Found in Castle Alley, Whitechapel, July 1889.

Pinchin Street torso. East End, September 1889.

Frances Coles. Found in Swallow Gardens, East End, February 1891.

Mrs Squires and her daughter. Found murdered in their shop, Hoxton, 1872.

Harriet Buswell. Found murdered in her room, Great Coram Street, 1872.

Mary Anne Yates. Prostitute murdered in a house at Burton Crescent, 1884.

Rachel Samuels. Found murdered in her home at Burton Crescent, 1878.

Mathilda Hacker. Her remains were found at 4, Euston Square, 1879.

Napoleon Stranger. Mysteriously disappeared from his bakery, St Lukes, 1881.

Cannon Street case. 1888.

Unknown childless woman. Found in the River Thames and Regents Canal, minus head, cut into pieces and dumped, 1887. Possibly the wife of Robert D'Onston Stephenson.

The Whitehall Mystery. The torso of a woman's body was dumped at the building site of New Scotland Yard, 1888.

The previous list does not include all unsolved murders. Furthermore I would not like to contemplate the number of murders that went undetected. Police Commissioner Sir Charles Warren stated on 15 September 1888, 'I am convinced that the Whitechapel murder case is one which can be successfully grappled with if it is systematically taken in hand. I go so far as to say that I could myself in a few days unravel the mystery, provided I could spare the time to give undivided attention to it!.'

At a later date, Anderson stated that he had spent a day and a half examining the evidence, which proved correct in every respect. This man gave the impression that he knew who the killer was. Then on 23 October 1888 Anderson wrote to the Home Office, 'That five successive murders should have been committed without our having the slightest clue of any kind is extraordinary if not unique in the annals of crime.'

Note how this man has fallen into the old trap by stating in this letter that there had been five murders to date, 23 October 1888, when in fact there were only four murders up to this date. One recommendation made by this man was to arrest every prostitute found on the streets after midnight! This remark in itself should have set the alarm bells ringing. He then went on to state of the killer, 'In saying that he was a Polish Jew, I am merely stating a definitely ascertained fact.' This man's idea of the facts invites scrutiny.

When Anderson related to the murders, he made the most elementary mistakes. He confused witness information by putting the wrong witnesses on site and he would put one situation from one site on to another. Sir Charles Warren was just as bad in many respects. They knew very little when it came to crime and criminal methods. They knew far less when it came to the criminal mind. I have rarely seen so many conflicting statements by men of such so-called stature. The pair should have been released from the police force for aiding and abetting the killer, because between them they destroyed vital evidence, told blatant untruths and had little or no understanding of the true situation.

Sir Charles Warren consistently made great mistakes. His judgement came into question in Africa during the Boer War where he was involved in a 'lions led by donkeys disaster'. He failed in his duty to silence Boer artillery bombarding British troops. From a force of over 1,700 men, 1,500 were killed or wounded. This action eventually led to a British retreat.

The rantings of Warren in respect of what he thought he could achieve and his policing and military incompetence stand to remind me of Captain William J. Fetterman, US Army. This officer tempted fate by stating that he 'could ride through the Sioux nation with 80 men'. Unfortunately for Fetterman he spoke too loudly. The Great Planner himself must have heard Fetterman's utterings for his 'dream' was soon turned into reality when fate took a hand.

Fetterman found himself with the desired number of men he required (exactly 80) when he decided to put his plan to the test on 21 December 1866, near Fort Phil Kearny. He attacked a band of Sioux put at 1,000–2,000 strong. Suffice to say, not one man survived. The 80 men were scalped and mutilated. Ears, noses, fingers, hands and other body parts were severed. Eyes were gouged out, brains bashed out and entrails torn from the bodies and placed on rocks. The mutilations were due to the superstitious religious beliefs held by the tribes that the enemy soldiers would remain helpless in the spirit world and would therefore be unable to seek retribution.

As to the press, when one compares the Victorian press of the Ripper's day to the tabloids of today one can clearly see that certain aspects have not changed. In fact it could be said they have worsened. A certain reporting mentality existed which has now grown out of all reasonable control. The murder of James Bulger is one such example of reporting for sensationalism purposes. James was abducted by John Venables and Robert Thompson from a shopping mall in Liverpool.

The nature of the crime enraged the British public. But the press, not content with the public outcry, added fuel to the fire by printing unjust and outrageous lies about the actions perpetrated on young James by Venables and Thompson. Those members of the press, lacking in morals, who were responsible for such blatant lies in their propaganda campaign, should themselves have faced court under the Public Order Act for causing further distress, suffering and pain to the relations of the poor hapless victim.

The tabloids of 1888 have much to answer for, because sensationalism overcame scruples. An assortment of underhand tricks were employed by many journalists to fan the fire and blow the case out of all proportion to push up sales. Sheer mischief also contributed to the situation. According to the police, hoax letters were sent by members of the press.

The Dear Boss letter, one of the most famous of these correspondences, sent to the Central News Agency on 27 September 1888, from London, is still under debate today! The envelope was addressed to: The Boss, Central News Office, London City, and was postmarked SP 27 88 and posted in London EC. The letter itself was headed with the date 25 Sept, 1888.

Tom Bullen, of Central News Limited, sent the letter to the police on 29 September. The Assistant Commissioner Metropolitan Police CID Sir Robert Anderson wrote that the Dear Boss letter was the work of a reporter whom he could identify. The only police officer known to have named the writer was Chief Inspector John George Littlechild of the Special Branch. He named Tom Bullen as the perpetrator of the hoax. In the Littlechild letter (dealt with later) he wrote:

> With regard to the term 'Jack the Ripper' it was generally believed at the Yard that Tom Bullen of the Central News was the originator but it is probable Moore, who was his who chief, who was the inventor.
>
> It was a smart piece of journalistic work. No journalist of my time got such privileges from Scotland Yard as Bullen.

The press were on to a good thing and they milked it for all it was worth. Even my suspect was writing articles on the murders in his own name for the *Pall Mall Gazette* and was paid in the process. He explained the motive for the missing body organs, the meaning of the Goulston Street graffito and much more. The known mail that he wrote to both police and press during the murders was sent under his own name.

There is no evidence to date which conclusively proves that the killer sent a single letter signed Jack the Ripper. Anderson stated that he could identify the journalist who wrote the Dear Boss letter but refused to do so. Apparently there was a law for one class and a law for another. A poor young woman was prosecuted for sending such a letter. Yet the police, having knowledge of a crime committed by a journalist, swept the facts under the carpet and refused to identify the sender.

I find it intolerable that such men as Anderson were content to let these matters go unchecked. We know that such hoaxes can have a devastating effect on any murder inquiry. The case of Sutcliffe is only one such example.

In relation to Jack, I have never known a murder case on which more money, manpower and effort has been expended with no result for a period exceeding 100 years. Another thing that surprises me is the amazement shown at the time by the police that the killer was able to do his work undisturbed, free of any inconvenience, after all the precautions they had taken to make it appear otherwise. They could not believe that they let this man slip through their clutches.

The term 'invisible killer' was being coined yet the true explanation of the situation could not be simpler. He knew what steps were being taken to catch him, therefore he made his plans accordingly. For every move produced to catch him he produced a counter move. He must have known that to be seen with a woman after midnight would invite police scrutiny. He simply overcame this problem by not being seen by police with the women.

The fact of the matter is no one can say for certain if Jack the Ripper was ever seen with a victim. The men seen with the victims were no more than suspects. The man seen by Lawende and company at Mitre Square could have just been leaving the scene after being serviced by Eddowes. Jack could have been waiting in the shadows. I concede that while it remains possible that the man seen with Eddowes was her killer it is not conclusive that he was.

It is absolutely absurd and ridiculous that so many suspects exist. It comes as no surprise that this case was never solved with so many suspects. Many of the suspects named weren't even in Whitechapel when the murders were committed. So much rubbish has been accumulated that it has obliterated the true situation.

Even today investigations of serial killers can prove to be just as negative as they were in 1888. Many lessons exist which are still to be learned.

If Jack the Ripper had been caught, then we may not have had so many copycat killings of prostitutes. It is a case of 'If he could do it and get away with it and make a name for himself in the process, then so can I.' Some serial killers have admitted to seeking notoriety as a motive for their actions. Even the Yorkshire Ripper was influenced to a certain degree by Jack the Ripper.

While viewing mug shots on a murder hunt, one officer stated to another, 'Look at him, he looks like a killer.' Any individual who follows such a doctrine should give up detective work and seek other employment. A killer looks like anyone else on the street. Many survivors of serial killer attacks report that they did not think the attacker looked like a killer. This error makes them drop their guard.

Perhaps someone can inform me what a killer is supposed to look like. I have met and conversed with dozens of killers, including many serial killers, and I have never seen a killer who looked like a stereotypical killer. A serial killer's problem is in his brain and not his appearance. I have however seen one or two with very peculiar (dodgy) eyes, which unsettled me.

In the case of the Yorkshire Ripper, hoax letters and a tape were received purporting to have come from the killer. No evidence existed on the tape to prove that the voice was that of the killer. It was only assumed it was. Yet this mistake was to cost more lives and many more incorrect assumptions were to take place before the killer was apprehended by chance.

This particular case is worth reading up on if only to know how *not* to investigate a series of murders. The hoaxer who sent the tape phoned the police to explain that the tape was a hoax. No credence was given to the call by those in charge of the inquiry. The number of mistakes made in this particular case are wholly unacceptable. The nature of the mistakes is beyond comprehension. The list is endless.

A book could be written about the number of mistakes made and their ramifications which cost innocent lives. One excuse put forward by an officer on the case was, 'we are only human we all make mistakes'. Making a mistake is one thing but being consistent in persisting to make them when lives are on the line is quite another matter.

Sutcliffe and Jack the Ripper did not kill in a blind frenzy. They were in control of the situation and thought of the next move they were going to make. They placed items on the crime scene in a deliberate fashion and worked in a cool and deliberate manner. These killers enjoyed their killing spree and looked upon it as a game.

The motive put forward by Sutcliffe, that 'God told me to do it' was a load of rubbish; he was simply trying to be sectioned off as insane. This, in turn, would mean that he would serve his time in a 'comfortable hospital' rather than under threat in prison. Sutcliffe knew that if sent to prison it would be in his interest to be segregated under Rule 43 for his own protection.

Paedophiles and men such as Sutcliffe are considered by the majority of criminals in prison as 'jail bait' and are seen as no more than targets to be attacked. In fact, Sutcliffe was attacked in custody and lost an eye. Eventually he obtained his objective by manipulating incompetent and naive people and was sent to Broadmoor. It was not in his interests to tell the truth for he would not wish others to know how inadequate he really was.

If Jack the Ripper had been caught, his excuse would probably have been, 'God told me to do it'. He would never have given the true reasons which lay behind his actions. The simple and prolific mistakes made by the police investigating Sutcliffe, the Yorkshire Ripper, stand to remind us that there are always lessons to be learned.

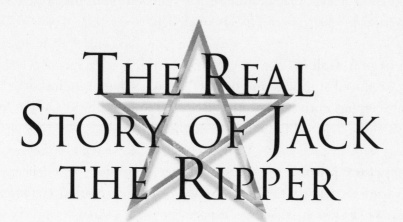

THE REAL STORY OF JACK THE RIPPER

Cast of players in the drama of 1888

Dr Robert Donston Stephenson, alias Roslyn D'Onston
Jack of all trades, murder being but one.

Mabel Collins
D'Onston's mistress and business partner, spiritualist medium, writer. This woman had as many secrets to hide as D'Onston. Believed D'Onston to be Jack the Ripper.

Baroness Vittoria Cremers
Collins's friend and business partner, Theosophist, infatuated by Collins. Believed D'Onston to be Jack the Ripper.

W. T. Stead
Editor of the *Pall Mall Gazette*. Considered by some to be the greatest man on board R.M.S. *Titanic* when it sank. Believed D'Onston to be Jack the Ripper.

Bulwer Lytton

Founder of the Lodge of Alexandria and writer. Taught D'Onston tenets of black magic. Initiated D'Onston into the Lodge of Alexandria which was *not* a Masonic lodge.

George Marsh

Unemployed at time of murders, D'Onston's dupe who had dreams of becoming a private detective. Referred to Roots by D'Onston for statement. Believed D'Onston to be the Ripper.

Inspector J. Roots

Scotland Yard, knew D'Onston for 20 years, took Marsh's testimony naming D'Onston as Jack the Ripper.

Madame Helena Blavatsky

Theosophical Society head, writer, friend of Collins, Cremers and D'Onston. Subject of fraud investigation by Edmund Gurney.

On 3 January 1889, Stead published a piece on black magic written by D'Onston for the *Pall Mall Gazette*. It concerned the magical cults of the West Coast of Africa. In January 1889 D'Onston's father died and showed his utter contempt for his son by leaving him nothing. Then, on 15 February, Stead commissioned a second piece in which D'Onston admitted to the murder of a woman witch-doctor in the Cameroons.

On Monday, 13 May 1889, D'Onston was admitted into the London Hospital seriously ill with a bout of 'Chloralism'. At this moment in time he was living in Burdett Road at the headquarters of the London Cottage Mission. Whether this was a suicide attempt or an accident is not known. It was during this second stay at the hospital that he was contacted by Mabel Collins.

Chloralism is a paralysing condition caused by over-indulgence of Chloral Hydrate ('Mickey Finn'). Overdoses can cause coma, cardiac failure, delirium and hallucinations. We know that D'Onston (according to the evidence from Marsh and Roots) fasted, was a heavy drinker and took drugs to sober him and stave off delirium tremens. These facts alone show that D'Onston was not in a normal state of mind.

During this period in his life D'Onston was in fact very ill. He was to spend 74 days in the London Hospital in Whitechapel, his main lair during the Whitechapel murders of 1888. It was during this period that he wrote his piece on African Magic and it was due to the publishing of this piece that Mabel Collins wrote to him at the hospital.

On his discharge the two became confidantes and lovers. W. T. Stead had been known to D'Onston for many years and he had published many of his articles. In 1896, Stead published more articles by D'Onston and then made the most amazing statement about the man:

> He has been known to me for many years. He is one of the most remarkable persons I have ever met. For more than a year I was under the impression that he was the veritable Jack the Ripper; an impression that I believe was shared by the police, who at least once had him under arrest; although, as he completely satisfied them, they liberated him without bringing him to court.

D'Onston knew too much and he could not keep his mouth shut. His ego got the better of him. He stated that the killer planned the murders in advance on a map, picked the sites in advance and then checked them out on foot. He stated that the killer used the Whitechapel Road as a sort of base. He went on to add that sacred emblems were profaned in the process of committing the murders. Everything this man stated about the planning and execution of the murders was true, because all of these facts and much more show up in my material.

It would appear that many who knew this man believed him to be the killer. He was out to impress, was self-opinionated and very dangerous. He was the only man who ever gave the true meaning about the Goulston Street graffito. He was the only man, in fact, to give many true fine details of the five murders. He knew why and he knew how, and most important of all he knew who.

JACK THE RIPPER'S BLACK MAGIC RITUALS

It is worth noting that D'Onston had a history of associating with prostitutes from his youth in the red light district in the Port of Hull to his days in the Port of London. D'Onston contracted VD from a prostitute in Hull while he was a customs officer and it was while he was off sick with this complaint that he was shot in the thigh on board a boat while shooting seabirds. D'Onston's associate on this expedition was a known smuggler named Thomas Piles.

Two questions arise from the shooting incident. What was D'Onston doing in the company of a smuggler? Was the shooting a genuine accident or a bungled attempt at murder? On return to work in 1868, he was sacked. The official customs report on his condition states, 'There is little or no doubt that the illness from which he is now suffering is the result of the discreditable life he leads.' The official wording of his dismissal was 'Struck off the establishment'.

It was soon after this affair that he moved to London. He applied for the Government Post 'Orphanage Secretaryship' without success. D'Onston now had a motive to hate both prostitutes and the establishment. He planned to advance himself in the world of the occult, and in so doing could kill two birds with one stone. He could wreak his revenge on prostitutes and the establishment at the same time.

D'Onston's Interest in the Occult Deepens

D'Onston's hero was the great Magist Sir Edward Bulwer Lytton. After a chance meeting in Paris during 1859 he met his great hero's son. It was now only a matter of time before D'Onston met with his hero. The pair were to meet in London during the spring. Sir Arthur Conan Doyle was moving in the same Theosophical, occult and Masonic circles and may well have known D'Onston.

Once Sir Edward was introduced to D'Onston the two talked at some length on many occasions. After a short period of time D'Onston became the pupil of Lytton. Sir Edward arranged to teach D'Onston his craft and of his first lesson D'Onston wrote:

I entered, he was standing in the middle of the sacred pentagon, which had been drawn on the floor with red chalk, and holding in his extended right arm the baguette, which was pointing towards me, Standing thus, he asked me if I had duly considered the matter and had decided to enter upon the course. I replied that my mind was made up. He then and there administered to me the oaths of the neophyte of the Hermetic lodge of Alexandria – the oaths of obedience and secrecy.

D'Onston was now involved with a lodge from which he was to learn the foul side involved in such teachings.

It would appear that more than one player in this game belonged to one secret society or another. D'Onston would have remained lost in the mists of time if Vittoria Cremers had not told her story to Fleet Street journalist Bernard O'Donnell. He had received information from Hayter Preston, editor of the *Sunday Referee*.

Preston was a friend of the poet Victor Neuburg, and Neuburg had once been a dupe of Aleister Crowley's. The latter was a professional occultist and writer on the subject, and he had stated that he once knew the Ripper. It is likely that Vittoria Cremers informed Crowley that she had known the killer and that Crowley had jumped on to the band-wagon.

Neuburg was suffering in health due to Crowley's demands. Crowley's business manager, Vittoria Cremers, intervened and helped him to break away from Crowley. Cremers was a citizen of the USA and the widow of Baron Louis Cremers, at one time attached to the US Embassy.

This lady had information on the Whitechapel murders. Neuburg had been informed by Cremers of facts relating to the murders. O'Donnell however did not receive enough information from Neuburg to warrant a story so he decided to track down Cremers.

O'Donnell traced the lady to 34, Marias Road, Balham, south-west London. From 1930 until 1934 Cremers wrote pieces for O'Donnell after which time he had in his possession the complete memoirs of Cremers for the years 1888–91. Cremers did not receive any reward or gain for her reminiscences. It is said of this woman that she was almost fatalistic in her beliefs. Her contribution to the story of Jack the Ripper should not be dismissed.

O'Donnell was never to trace the man that Cremers had detailed. Cremers had only known him as Roslyn D'Onston when his true name was Robert Donston Stephenson. Cremers spent over 18 months with Jack the Ripper.

Her story begins in a New York bookshop in 1886. While browsing, she found a book entitled *Light on the Path*, by Mabel Collins. This book related to the Theosophical movement. The book made such an impression upon her that she joined the society. In 1888, on her arrival into Britain she went to the British Society to enrol and met Madam Helena Blavatsky, the greatest name in Theosophy.

Once Blavatsky found that Cremers had been involved in publishing, she asked her to take over the society's monthly magazine *Lucifer*. Cremers agreed and worked from the society's headquarters at 17, Lansdowne Road, Holland Park. She knew that Mabel Collins was a well-known novelist and spiritualist medium. She also knew that Collins lived nearby, so she concluded that it would only be a matter of time before the two met. I have found no reason to doubt the story Cremers told in her memoirs.

Vittoria Cremers recalled that she met Mabel Collins when Dr Archibald Keightley, his cousin Bertram and Collins visited the *Lucifer* office at 17, Landsdowne Road, which backed on to the garden of 34, Clarendon Road – Collins's address. In addition to her Theosophical work and the novels she wrote, Mabel Collins was also a fashion writer on Edmund Yates's periodical *The World*. Cremers told Collins that *Light on the Path* had been the direct cause of her joining the Theosophical movement. The pair became very good friends.

In 1888 Cremers went to America on business and did not return until February–March 1890. She spent a few weeks in Paris before returning to England. She moved into lodgings at 21, Montague Street, off London's Russell Square. On this same day she decided to look up Mabel Collins so she proceeded to Collins's address at York Terrace, just behind Madame Tussaud's in Marylebone Road.

On her arrival, the maid informed her that Collins was away in

Southsea writing a new novel. The maid gave Cremers the address and the very next day she took a train to Southsea. On arrival she was appalled at the shabby state of the road in which the address was situated and also by the address itself.

It would appear by the evidence that both D'Onston and Collins had a seamier side to their lives, which they tried to keep hidden from many of their associates. One can only imagine the depths of degradation to which they would sink. Their sexual exploits knew no bounds. And in relation to D'Onston, it would appear that his lust for power and sexual gratification would make Collins's pale into insignificance.

On enquiring as to the whereabouts of Mabel Collins, Cremers was led by an unkempt woman to the room Collins had acquired. Cremers said the room was sparsely decorated and was not a comfortable place in which to be. She was amazed that someone like Collins would inhabit, let alone pay to stay in, such a place. It was on this first visit that Cremers was introduced to the man she would come to know as Roslyn D'Onston.

Collins questioned Cremers about her recollection of a *Pall Mall Gazette* article about Rider Haggard's 'She' written by D'Onston. Cremers remembered that Collins had mentioned the article in early 1889 but had not read it herself. Collins admitted to writing to the author of the article, D'Onston, who had been ill in hospital. D'Onston had promised to meet with Collins as soon as he was better.

Collins said D'Onston had finally contacted her and was described as a great magician who had wonderful magical secrets. Her excitement at meeting this man was evident and she admitted that he was with her in Southsea. She also suggested that the three of them go into business together.

D'Onston finally arrived and Cremers was introduced to Collins's lover. Cremers said he entered the room so quietly that she was surprised to find him there. She noticed afterwards that there was an uncanny absence of sound in all his movements, describing him as 'the most soundless human being she ever knew'.

Collins had informed Cremers that D'Onston never ate and would refuse an offer of tea. This statement struck her as most peculiar, but she was to recall it later when she knew more about D'Onston. Cremers said her first sight of D'Onston was of a tall, fair man of unassuming appearance, at whom no one would look twice. She admitted she was impressed, but could not really say why – saying it was an 'indefinable something'.

D'Onston had a pleasant and cultured voice and a military bearing, suggesting power and strength. He was pale; his face had a queer pallor – not a particle of colour anywhere; his bottom lip was pink, his upper lip hidden by a fair moustache. His teeth appeared to be discoloured from pipe smoking. D'Onston's eyes were pale blue and 'there was not a vestige of life or sparkle in them'. He also appeared to be extremely well groomed.

Collins and D'Onston moved back to London 14 days after their encounter with Cremers. Collins wished, for the time being, to keep her affair with D'Onston very discreet; after all was said and done she had her reputation to consider. Cremers came to the rescue by persuading her own landlady, Mrs Heilman, to take D'Onston in as a lodger. This state of affairs lasted for a very short period of time because he never appeared to eat anything. Mrs Heilman expressed her fears that he might die on her property and asked him to find other accommodation, but the situation soon straightened itself out.

The trio engaged in discussing a business project. D'Onston was possessed of little-known recipes for beauty products. Collins and Cremers put up the money and D'Onston provided the recipes from which the various concoctions were prepared. They formed a company, the Pompadour Cosmetique Company, and took premises in Baker Street on the site where Baker Street Underground Station now stands. It was then a street of houses and the office must have been just opposite the fictional residence of Sherlock Holmes.

It consisted of a large office on the first floor, where all the business was conducted and the 'concoctions' made up, and a smaller room immediately behind it. The second floor was occupied by a private family. Cremers had a flat on the third floor. The problem of D'Onston's accommodation was solved by letting him live in the small back room on the first floor. This was Mabel Collins's suggestion and it certainly was a way out of the difficulty. It was she who had furnished it for him with just a bed, table, washstand, chair and a huge zinc bath.

The trademark of The Pompadour Cosmetique Company designed by D'Onston was a naked woman cut off at the genitals. This veiled clue must have appealed to his ego. D'Onston's fixation for naked women seems to have occupied a considerable amount of his time. He chose the colour red for his trademark. D'Onston liked to write with red ink. Imagine how those Victorian women would have reacted if they had known what they were smearing on their faces!

D'Onston was responsible for the manufacture and packaging of the products, the development of the logo and the naming of the company. D'Onston took full advantage of Collins and milked her for all she was worth. For D'Onston, women were no more than a means to an end. Collins was to go bankrupt shortly after her association with D'Onston came to such a sour end.

Cremers now persuaded Blavatsky to commission an article from D'Onston as she knew that he was always strapped for cash. The piece which he wrote for the November 1890 issue of *Lucifer* was entitled 'African Magic' and it contained chilling revelations.

Cremers said she did not see the article until it was brought to her notice in 1931. She stated that she would not have fully understood it at the time and certainly would not have associated the writer with the Ripper crimes.

African Magic
by Tau-Tria-Delta

article by Roslyn D'Onston

Before we enter into the subject of the occult art as practised on the West Coast of Africa, it will be well to clear the ground by first considering for a moment what we mean by the much-abused term 'Magic'.

There are many definitions of this word; and in bygone ages, it was simply used to designate anything and everything, which was 'not understood of the vulgar'. It will be sufficient for our purpose to define it as the knowledge of certain natural laws which are not merely unknown but absolutely unsuspected by the scientists of Europe and America.

It is a recognised fact that no law of nature can be – even for a single moment – abrogated. When, therefore, this appears to us to be the case – when for instance, such a universally known law as that of the attraction of gravitation seems to be annihilated, we must recognise the fact that there may be other laws at present unknown to Western science which have the power of overriding and suspending for the time being the action of the known law.

The knowledge of these hidden laws is what we understand by the term occult science, or magic. *And there is no other magic than this,* and never has been, at any period of the world's history. All the so-called 'miracles' of ancient times can be and are reproduced at the present day by magists when occasion requires. An act of magic is a pure scientific feat, and must not be confounded with legerdemain or trickery of any kind.

There are several schools of magism, all proceeding and operating on entirely different lines. The principal of these, and on whose philosophy all others are founded, are the Hindu; the Tibetan, the Egyptian (including the Arab) and the Obeeyan or Voodoo. The last named is entirely and fundamentally opposed to the other three; it having its root and foundation in necromancy or 'black magic', while the others all operate either by means of what is known to experts as 'white magic', or in other cases by 'psychologising' the spectator. And, a whole crowd of spectators can be psychologised and made at the will of the operator to see and feel whatever things he chooses, all the time being in full possession of their ordinary faculties. Thus, perhaps a couple of travelling fakirs give their performance in your own compound or in the garden of your bungalow. They erect a small tent and tell you to choose any animal, which you wish to see emerge therefrom. Many different animals are named in rotation by the bystanders, and in every case the desired quadruped, be he tiger or terrier dog, comes out of the opening of the canvas and slowly marches off until he disappears round some adjacent corner. Well, this is done simply by 'psychologising', as are all the other great Indian feats, such as 'the basket trick', 'the mango tree', throwing a rope in the air and climbing up it, pulling it up and disappearing in space, and the thousand and one other similar performances which are 'familiar as household words' to almost every Anglo-Indian.

The difference between these schools and that of the Voodoo or Obeeyah is very great, because in them there is deception or want of reality in the performance. The spectator does not *really* see what he fancies he sees: his mind is simply impressed by the operator and the effect is produced. But in African magic, on the contrary, there is no will impression; the observer does really and actually see what is taking place. The force employed by the African necromancers is not psychological action by demonosophy.

White magists have frequently dominated and employed inferior spirits to do their bidding, as well as invoked the aid of powerful and beneficient ones to carry out their purposes. But this is an entirely different thing: The spirits which are naturally maleficient become the slaves of the magist, or votary of black magic, is, on the contrary, the slave of the evil spirit to whom he has given himself up.

While the philosophy of the magist demands a life of the greatest purity and the practice of every virtue, while he must utterly subdue and have in perfect control all his desires and appetites, mental and physical, and must become simply an embodied intellect, absolutely purged from all human weakness and pusillanimity, the necromancer must outrage and degrade human nature in every way conceivable. The very least of the crimes necessary for him (or her) to commit to attain the power sought is actual murder, by which the human victim essential to the sacrifice is provided. The human mind can scarcely realise or even imagine one tithe of the horrors and atrocities actually performed by the Obeeyah women.

Yet, though the price is awful, horrible, unutterable, the power is real. There is no possibility of mistake about that. Every petty king on the West Coast has his 'rain-maker'. It is the fashion among travellers, and the business of the missionaries, to ridicule and deny the powers of these people. But they do possess and do actually use the power of causing storms of rain, wind and lightning. When one considers that however ignorant and brutal a savage may be, yet that he has an immense amount of natural cunning and his very ignorance makes him believe nothing that cannot be proven to him, no 'rain-maker' could live for one year unless he gave repeated instances of his powers when required by the king. Failure would simply mean death. And the hypothesis that they only work their conjurations when the weather is on the point of change is only an invention of the missionaries. The native chiefs are, like all savages, able to detect an approaching change of weather many hours before it takes place. And is it at all likely that they would send for the rain-maker and give him sufficient cattle to last him for twelve months, besides wives and other luxuries, if there were the slightest appearance of approaching rain?

I remember well my first experience of these wizards. For weeks and weeks there had been no rain, although it was the rainy season. The mealies were all dying for want of water; the cattle were being slaughtered in all directions; women and children had died by scores, and the fighting men were beginning to do the same, being themselves scarcely more than skeletons. Day after day, the sun glared down on the parched earth, without one intervening cloud, like a globe of glowing copper, and all Nature languished in that awful furnace. Suddenly, the king ordered the great war drum to be beaten, and the warriors all gathered hurriedly. He announced the arrival of two celebrated rain-makers, who would forthwith proceed to relieve the prevailing distress. The elder of the two was a stunted, bow-legged little man, with wool which would have been white had it not been messed up with grease, filth and feathers. The second man was rather a fine specimen of the Soosoo race, but with a very sinister expression. A large ring being formed by the squatting Negroes, who came – for some unknown reason – all armed to the teeth, the king being in the centre, and the rain-makers in front of him, they commenced their incantations. The zenith and the horizon were eagerly examined from time to time, but not a vestige of a cloud appeared. Presently the elder man rolled on the ground in convulsions, apparently epileptic, and his comrade started to his feet pointing with both hands to the copper-coloured sky. All eyes followed his gesture, and looked at the spot to which his hands pointed, but nothing was visible. Motionless as a stone statue he stood with gaze riveted on the sky. In about the space of a minute a darker shade was observable in the copper tint, in another minute it grew darker and darker, and, in a few more seconds developed into a black cloud, which soon overspread the heavens. In a moment, a vivid flash was seen, and the deluge that fell from that cloud, which had now spread completely overhead, was something to be remembered. For two days and nights that torrent poured down, and seemed as if it would wash everything out of the ground.

After the king had dismissed the rain-makers, and they had deposited the cattle and presents under guard, I entered the hut in which they were lodged, and spent the night with them, discussing the magical art. The hut was about fourteen feet in diameter, strongly built of posts driven firmly into the ground, and having a strong thatched conical roof. I eventually persuaded them to give me one or two examples of their skill. They began singing, or rather crooning, a long invocation, after a few minutes of which the younger man appeared to rise in the air about three feet from the ground and remain there suspended, and floating about. There was a brilliant light in the hut from a large fire in the centre, so that the smallest detail could be distinctly observed. I got up and went to feel the man in the air, and there was no doubt about his levitation. He then floated close to the wall and passed through it to the outside. I made a dash for the doorway, which was on the opposite side of the hut, and looked round for him. I saw a luminous figure, which appeared like a man rubbed with phosphorised oil; but I was glad to rapidly take shelter from the torrents of rain. When I re-entered the hut, there was only the old man present. I examined the logs carefully but there was no aperture whatever. The old man continued his chant, and in another moment his comrade re-appeared floating in the air. He sat down on the ground, and I saw his black skin glistening with rain, and the few rags he wore were wet as if he had been dipped in a river.

The next feat was performed by the older man and consisted in several instantaneous disappearances and reappearances. The curious point about this was that the old man was dripping wet.

Following this was a very interesting exhibition. By the old man's directions we arranged ourselves round the fire at the three points of an imaginary triangle. The men waved their hands over the fire in rhythm with their chant when dozens of tic-polongas, the most deadly serpent in Africa, slowly crawled from the burning embers, and interlacing themselves together whirled in a mad dance on their tails round the fire, making all the while a continuous hissing. The young man then came round to me, and, kneeling down, opened his mouth, out of which the head of a tic-polonga was quickly protruded. He snatched it out, pulling a serpent nearly three feet long out of his throat, and threw it also into the fire. In rapid succession he drew seven serpents from his throat, and consigned them all to the same fiery end.

But I wanted to know what they could do in the way of evocation of spirits. The incantation this time lasted nearly twenty minutes, when, rising slowly from the fire, appeared a human figure, a man of great age, a white man too, but absolutely nude. I put several questions to him, but obtained no reply. I arose and walked round the fire, and particularly noticed a livid scar on his back. I could get no satisfactory explanation of who he was, but they seemed rather afraid of him, and had evidently – from the remarks they interchanged – expected to see a black man.

After the appearance of this white man, I could not persuade them that night to attempt anything more, although the next night I had no difficulty with them. A most impressive feat, which they on a subsequent occasion performed, was the old custom of the priests of Baal. Commencing a lugubrious chant they slowly began circling around the fire (which said fire always is an essential part of the proceedings), keeping a certain amount of rhythm in both their movements and cadences. Presently, the movement grew faster and faster till they whirled round dancing like dervishes. There were two distinct movements; all the time during which they were gyrating round the circle, they were rapidly spinning on their own axies. With the rapidity of their revolutions their voices were raised higher and higher until the din was terrific. Then, by a simultaneous movement, each began slashing his naked body on arms, chest and thighs, until they were streaming with blood and covered with deep gashes. Then the old man stopped his erratic course and sitting down on the ground narrowly watched the younger one with apparent solicitude. The young man continued his frantic exertions until exhausted. Nature could bear no more and he fell panting and helpless on the ground. The old man took both the knives and anointed the blades with some evil smelling grease from a calabash, and then stroked the young man's body all over with the blade that had done the injuries and finished the operation by rubbing him vigorously with the palms of the hands smeared with the unguent. In a few minutes time the young man arose and there was not the slightest trace of wound or scar in his ebony skin. He then performed the same good offices on the old man with the same effect. Within ten minutes afterwards they were both laid on their mats in a sweet and quiet sleep. In this performance there were many invocations, gestures, the circular fire and other things which satisfied me that some portion, at all events, of the magical processes of West Africa had been handed down from the days of Baal and he was an actual God, and mighty in the land.

Lucifer, November 1890

Once in business with Collins and D'Onston, Cremers found herself both confidante and friend to D'Onston. If D'Onston was Jack the Ripper then Cremers was now in a position to notice any signs, including actions or comments. She did not have long to wait before a true picture began to emerge of this seemingly inoffensive man. A strange confrontation took place between the two which marked the start of her doubts.

One evening, when Cremers returned to Baker Street, she saw D'Onston standing outside the door of his room. He appeared to be drawing some sort of sign upon it with his thumb. She noticed the figure he traced was the outline of an inverted triangle on the door.

D'Onston asked Cremers if she had noticed the figure he had traced. She acknowledged seeing the figure and D'Onston told her a story about sensing a horrible presence outside his door several years before. He said he knew how to guard against its intrusion by making the sign of the triangle on the door of his room before entering.

Cremers said she did not know there was any magical significance, either black or white. As for his story of the 'horrible presence', it faintly recalled the awe-inspiring description of the Presence which figured in Bulwer Lytton's *Zanoni*. This work partially describes the return of an evil spirit inadvertently summoned. Much of Lytton's work contains occultist doctrine thinly veiled as fiction. D'Onston held strong beliefs in a presence which had scared him.

Some may consider that such beliefs hold no place in the realms of reality, and there are those that believe such writings do indeed play a part in the Great Plan of Life. D'Onston firmly believed in such things. It is well worth taking note that D'Onston thought that he could control the presence simply by making the outline of a triangle on his door, a sign which he thought could control what he believed were demons and spirits. This shows it was all in his mind.

D'Onston explained his signature, Tautriadelta, by saying that the Hebrew Tau was always shown in the form of a cross; it is the last letter of the sacred alphabet. Tria is Greek for three, while Delta is the Greek letter D, written in the form of a triangle. The completed word signifies 'Cross three Triangles'. The plan does include three triangles.

By using the word Tautriadelta D'Onston was on another game-playing ego trip. He was simply stating, 'I'm so clever and everyone else is so stupid, because only I know the true meaning of the word.' Tau is also the first letter in the Greek word for cut, and some writers and mathematicians use this letter to represent the Golden Ratio which will be dealt with later.

The truth of the matter is that D'Onston's ego got the better of him and he wanted to come out and tell the world what he had done. But he knew he would end up on the end of a rope if he did. The hidden meaning behind the name relates to hidden secrets and it was a dangerous game, but not for those who knew the stakes. Throughout time those in possession of secret knowledge have always put themselves above others. When all is said and done, it's all a matter of deception.

From earliest times certain men possessed the ancient mysteries of life and they knew about the astronomical cycles and much more. To keep such information to themselves they simply used secret codes and symbols. This concealed their knowledge from others. As time passed the codes became more complicated and harder to break.

Cremers and a lot of other people would not have the slightest idea what Tautriadelta meant. We know that Cremers saw D'Onston with foul candles, possibly made of human fat. He had informed her that he had made the candles but did not inform her how. D'Onston wrote of the use of human fat in various black magic rituals. The symbols on the plan Vesica Pisces, and the missing uterus from two victims, all relate to the same thing, the vagina or yoni.

D'Onston wrote that the purpose of such studies was to obtain power, it would appear that this man would go to the darkest depths of human degradation to obtain it. Such things still exist today, unfortunately.

A friend of mine, just back from the West Coast of Africa and in hospital with a bout of malaria, told me of several cases of black magic which took place in a village near where he was located. One case involved a female victim murdered and with certain body parts missing. These parts were believed to have been stolen for use in black magic rituals.

This killing was nearly identical to the Millers Court murder. I was also informed that it was not an uncommon occurrence for children to become victims of the occult. During my research I have concluded that the occult practised on the West Coast of Africa is linked with the occult of the Egyptians.

The old Egyptian religion was no more than an occult religion, which involved the use of magic in everyday life. Black and white magic were not separate at this time. The cult of Isis appears to have been centred at Abydos near the Delta in lower Egypt. She is in fact the archetype of a cult that continues in the Christian churches to the present day. She is also known as the Black Virgin. Her image was revived during the late 19th century. Many occult traditions equate her with the Virgin Mary.

Helen Blavatsky stated, 'Cyril, the bishop of Alexandria, had openly embraced the cause of Isis, the Egyptian goddess and had anthropomorphised her into Mary, the mother of God. The black virgins, so highly reverenced in certain French cathedrals ... proved, when at last critically examined, they were indeed basalt figures of Isis. She is also possibly the archetype for the high priestess of the Tarot.'

Blavatsky's first book was called *Isis Unveiled*. Occult religion came into being to manipulate the masses by using fear on the ignorant; fear of death and the unknown. Control over the many by the few was essential religion and is still used for the same purpose today.

The Story of Isis

The Egyptian sun god Ra, depicted as ram-headed, was the creator of everything that existed in the known world of the ancient Egyptians, including man himself. By speaking the name of something Ra created it, and ultimately controlled it. He sailed his sun boat across the sky by day and through the underworld by night.

Isis, wife of Osiris, mother of Horus and sister of Seth, was a god in her own right. She possessed the art of magic and healing. However, she soon became envious of the powers of Ra. The key to his magical powers lay in his secret name. Isis, wanting greater powers, devised a method of obtaining Ra's secret.

When Ra drooled Isis collected his spit and, by mixing it with soil, created a snake. The snake was then turned into dart form and placed in the path of Ra's daily route across the sky. When Ra passed the snake it rose up and bit him. The venom from the snake then took effect on Ra and he became increasingly ill.

Because Ra had not made the snake he had no control over it. Isis offered to work her magic on Ra to cure him but only on the condition that he reveal his secret name. He offered several names but Isis, not to be outdone, was not taken in by such subterfuge. Owing to the increasing deterioration to his life Ra finally gave Isis his secret name.

Thus Isis learned of Ra's all-powerful magic and knew the secrets of immortality. Seth the god of evil quarrelled with his brother, Osiris, killed him and cut his body into pieces, spreading the remains throughout Egypt so that he could never be restored to life.

The tears of Isis at the death of Osiris were said to cause the rising of the Nile. Isis travelled throughout the land collecting the remains of Osiris. The only part of Osiris that she failed to find was his penis. The remains of Osiris were put together and wrapped in bandages.

Isis fashioned a substitute penis and placed it on the body and through her magical power brought him back to life.

Osirus, god of the dead, is depicted as a mummified man wearing a feathered crown and bearing the crook and flail of a king. Isis hid her son, Horus, from Seth, until Horus was fully grown and was in a position to avenge his father. Horus is depicted as a falcon-headed man with a solar disc on his head.

The chief aspect of Isis was that of a great magician, whose power was far greater than all other deities. The Egyptians were the master magicians of the ancient world. Master magicians were said to have turned sticks into snakes, and to have divided the waters of lakes.

Sound familiar?

Because D'Onston was in daily contact with Cremers over a period of 18 months, common sense dictates that he would loosen up to a certain degree. He would tell Collins far more than he ever told Cremers. So if Cremers thought he was Jack the Ripper, Collins would certainly know he was.

We know that Collins told Cremers that D'Onston was the Ripper. One afternoon he spoke to Cremers about an incident involving his favourite cousin. This cousin was in love with a girl who had rejected him as a suitor but had accepted him as a friend. One day the cousin came to D'Onston in great anguish. The girl he loved had been made pregnant by another man and this seducer had deserted her and left the country for America.

D'Onston asked for a handkerchief belonging to the girl, telling his cousin and the girl that they would not see nor hear from him until the girl had been avenged. His hunt for the seducer took all of 15 months but at last he caught up with him in California. On his return D'Onston bragged that he had dipped the handkerchief in the seducer's blood and returned it to the girl.

It is interesting to note that a similar story is related in *A Study in Scarlet* (1887) by Sir Arthur Conan Doyle. The story relates how Jefferson Hope, the hero, avenges Lucy Ferrier by killing two men who affronted her honour. After killing one victim in the USA, he returned to London to kill the other. During the second killing he suffers a nosebleed and writes the word 'Rache' upon the wall in his own blood. We know D'Onston more than likely used the graffito trick from the same book.

Cremers recalled thinking the story indicated what a braggart D'Onston was, yet the story was related to her in a very matter of fact way. Cremers was a born listener and prided herself on never asking questions or interrupting conversations; she let the speaker carry on 'to the bitter end'.

One story D'Onston related to Cremers involved his experiences during the California Gold Rush. He recalled prospecting a claim with a friend but the resulting settlement did not amount to a large sum. The friend and D'Onston decided to ask a Chinese man if he would be interested in selling his allegedly larger claim. The pair followed the man and at an opportune moment D'Onston claimed his friend's handgun 'accidentally' went off. No details were added to this story.

D'Onston's apparent callousness was evident in many such stories. During his stint as a surgeon in the Garibaldean army of 1860 he worked under ghastly conditions in the field. He stated he often had to perform amputations without anaesthetic and his patients suffered horribly. His only comment about the experience was that he could not have acquired the same experience in 20 years as a surgeon in England.

Cremers began to understand the indifferent attitude D'Onston had when he mentioned a brutal incident for which he was directly responsible. D'Onston said he had gone for several days without sleep when he was awakened by a subaltern who said a wounded prisoner had been brought in.

The subaltern wanted to know what to do with the prisoner and D'Onston, half awake and irritable, ordered the prisoner to be dispatched straight away. His directive was carried out to the letter. He commented that the man was an enemy and enemies are meant to be killed. These events show that D'Onston was a man who believed life had no value, apart from his own, of course

Cremers recalled that the association between Mabel Collins and

D'Onston was of the closest nature, adding that Collins was more involved than D'Onston appeared to be. Collins took D'Onston to Southsea to recuperate after his 'illness', provided him with his creature comforts and furnished a room for him in Baker Street, supplying him with money. Cremers said D'Onston was always polite and courteous but his actions never revealed any degree of pleasure when Collins was in his company.

A power struggle within the Theosophical Society began to take shape in which Blavatsky's position was challenged by Colonel Orcotott and A. P. Sinett. In true political style the mud-slinging came into play. Collins was accused of sexual perversions. She was revealed to be a woman with much to hide. Collins was accused of accepting Tantrism, teachings that included group sex, sodomy, incest, bestiality and necrophilia.

It was humiliating for Collins to know that members of the society were free to picture her in unbridled private ecstasies. Blavatsky decided to purge her staff of disloyal members by fair means or foul. The struggle was fought by devious means; the knives came out, and malicious charges were aired. Blavatsky eventually asked Cremers to break her ties with Collins; instead Cremers resigned from the society.

Collins started a libel suit against Blavatsky in July 1889, but it did not reach court until July 1890. It was a very short-lived action; in the opening moments Blavatsky's attorney showed the counsel for Collins a letter she had written. The action was stopped immediately and the contents of the letter never revealed. It appears she was stupid enough to actually record details of her sexual taboo-breaking. Her vulnerability in this area makes it clear to understand why D'Onston could exercise such control over her.

Mabel Collins entered the offices of the Pompadour Cosmetique Company in Baker Street and nervously told Cremers that she believed D'Onston to be Jack the Ripper. Cremers was understandably shocked by this revelation and pressed Collins for proof. Collins never informed Cremers why she was suspicious of D'Onston but her actions convinced Cremers that she was speaking the truth. She did say that D'Onston showed her something which convinced her that he was Jack the Ripper.

Cremers now started to investigate D'Onston by searching for incriminating evidence. He had a heavy, black-enamelled box in his room, which he kept locked. Cremers had located a key to his room in Baker Street and occasionally entered his room while he was out. The box contained some books on magic, both in English and French, and some old soiled ties. The ties drew her attention and she examined the stains on the backs of them. She did not identify the stains on them at the time but wondered why he would keep such relics under lock and key. That knowledge came later.

During a general conversation D'Onston mentioned his wife and Cremers pressed him for more information. He became agitated and began to pace the room. He stopped in front of Cremers's desk and drew a finger across his throat. D'Onston's apparent disregard for life, exhibited through the various stories he had related in the past, and Collins's accusation that D'Onston was Jack the Ripper came to her mind. Collins knew he had been married, but said D'Onston had told her his wife had disappeared without a trace some years before.

After this incident, Collins went to Scarborough with the instruction that D'Onston was not to be told of her whereabouts. It was no secret that Cremers was infatuated with Collins and the resulting triangle of Collins, Cremers and D'Onston was to be used to his advantage. D'Onston told Cremers of incidents that only she and Collins would have knowledge of, leading her to understand that Collins had breached their friendship and confidence.

Cremers confronted Collins, hoping she would justify her behaviour, but Collins did not apologise or excuse herself. It was a sad time for Cremers but she felt anger towards D'Onston. She told him what she thought of him for betraying Collins when she had been so kind to him. He only smiled. She decided then and there to discover whatever she could about him.

In July 1890, the *Westminster Gazette* printed information on Jack the Ripper. It claimed that the police had gained advance information about the killer's intentions. A new wave of fear was about to begin.

Cremers read this and decided to mention it to D'Onston to gauge his reaction. When she did so D'Onston told her there would be no more murders. He added that he knew Jack the Ripper.

D'Onston recalled that Mabel Collins had written to him after the 9 November murder of Mary Kelly in Millers Court. He admitted that he had been living in Whitechapel at the time and that he had met Jack the Ripper while in the London Hospital.

Cremers noted that D'Onston told her how the killer had taken away the uterus of two of the victims tucked into the space between his shirt and tie, acting it out as he told her. She recalled in a flash the black tin box in his room with the stained ties. She knew then that the 'doctor' friend was nothing more than D'Onston's imagination.

Cremers did attempt to find the motive but, when asked, D'Onston merely shrugged and told her she would not understand. He told Cremers he had been in for questioning on two occasions but had been released, as he was able to satisfy the authorities.

Cremers suggested that D'Onston write the story down and submit it to W. T. Stead, editor of the *Pall Mall Gazette*. D'Onston was extremely hesitant to do this but scribbled a few words on a sheet of paper. He left the room abruptly, taking the notes with him. Cremers had no knowledge that W. T. Stead already knew D'Onston's tale involving 'Dr Davies', and that he too suspected D'Onston of being Jack the Ripper.

D'Onston told Cremers the police could not see an inch before their noses, adding that the killer was right-handed, how he selected each site beforehand for a very special reason, how he would make several journeys before deciding on the spots best suited to fit in with his scheme, how having got the victim on site he would manoeuvre to get behind them, placing his left hand over their mouth and nose and how the killer used the Whitechapel Road as a sort of base. D'Onston went on to add that the only thing the doctors got right at the inquests was the fact that the victims did not fall but appeared to have been laid down by the killer and then the mutilations were performed.

D'Onston continued his narrative of what happened at the scenes of the crimes by saying the police were looking for a man with bloodstained clothes but that by killing the women from behind their bodies offered protection.

The Pompadour Cosmetique Company partnership ended on a sour note. Collins wanted to break from D'Onston because she now knew him to be what he truly was. Unfortunately Collins had written letters to D'Onston and she wanted the letters back in her possession before she terminated her association with him. She asked Cremers to assist her in the matter of retrieving the damning evidence before she could escape D'Onston's clutches.

In 1891, Vittoria Cremers took letters on behalf of Mabel Collins from D'Onston's room to deter any blackmail attempt and to break the hold D'Onston had over Collins.

D'Onston was then ordered from the premises and the company was disbanded. D'Onston demanded the return of the letters, resorting to the courts. The case was quickly dismissed when D'Onston appeared to be unable to testify in court. Cremers never saw Collins again but D'Onston wrote to her asking for money. She ignored his initial attempts but others followed and she finally agreed to allow him to meet with her at her lodgings. She took the precaution of having two male acquaintances to stand by to provide protection.

D'Onston simply took the money offered him and left without further words. After returning from abroad four years later a bundle of letters awaited her from D'Onston. She resisted the urge to open them and burned the lot.

Cremers said she did not go to the police because she was a Theosophist and believed that whatever is done in this life is rewarded or punished in the next. She clearly believed it was not up to any human being to interfere with another's destiny. She also indicated that D'Onston had assured her there would be no more murders after 9 November 1888. Since she believed he was the murderer he would know that no further harm would come to members of the public.

When Vittoria Cremers died in 1936 she did not know D'Onston's real name and background. She would never know how important her memoirs were to those interested in discovering the man known to history as Jack the Ripper.

D'Onston had now shot his bolt. He was disillusioned and a shadow of his former self. He had not obtained the power he had sought through his gross acts of murder. He had placed his life on the line for nothing. More to the point he had perpetrated a reign of terror by murdering five prostitutes needlessly, all to no avail.

He was involved with the occult from an early age for he was always fond of everything pertaining to mysticism, astrology and other occult sciences. He admitted reading every book or story he could get hold of having any relation to these subjects. In fact, D'Onston had much in common with Rasputin for both set out to gain power by controlling people and events by the use of devious means, including hypnotism. D'Onston recalled an encounter at the age of 14, when he practised hypnotism on his friends and his younger cousin. The incident with his cousin ended with the boy walking in his sleep, forcing D'Onston to stop his activities.

During the 1890s D'Onston wrote a book entitled *The Patristic Gospels*. It was published by Grant Richards in 1904. Richards stated that D'Onston was an odd, calm man, who would sit silently until he could be seen. Richards went on to say that he felt D'Onston was a pseudonym. It was soon after this event that D'Onston vanished without trace. A record of his death has yet to be found.

In relation to how many people D'Onston actually murdered we will never know but by his own admission he was responsible for more than the five Whitechapel victims. Prostitutes played a major role throughout D'Onston's life from the time of his youth in Hull through middle-age until his disappearance. It was a reformed prostitute who played a major part in D'Onston's later years.

Victoria Woodhull and her sister Tennie (Tennessee) were the most notorious harlots in the US. Victoria was known as Mrs Satan. The two women serviced men who attended their seances, one of which was Cornelius Vanderbilt. His friendship brought them wealth and fame. They started the *Woodhull & Caflins Weekly*, a radical feminist crusading newspaper.

The Woodhulls started a political organisation, which affiliated with the First International. In line with this new commitment, their paper published the first English translation of Karl Marx's 'Communist Manifesto'. Victoria ran for president of the US, sparked off the Ward Beecher scandal, went to prison on pornography charges and then found religion. After Vanderbilt's death, Victoria came to Britain and toured as an evangelist, preaching her new slant on Christianity.

At one of her rallies she captivated Roslyn D'Onston. At the time D'Onston was in a suicidal mood, and in January 1893 he said, 'None of these quack remedies (Spiritualism, Socialism, Theosophy) will ever avail to save the body politic, or to elevate the soul of man; we turn from them all weary, heartsick and disappointed with the haunting doubt hissing in our ears, "Is life worth living?"

'A calm serene and silver voice, having within it the thrill of ecstatic triumph, answers us "yes!" We turn and see before us the apostle and prophetess of the new faith – the new cult of 'Womanhood'... a new and sublime interpretation of Christian morality ... which shall purify and elevate all mankind ... in the fullest harmony with the divinely reviled religion of the Bible.'

D'Onston faded from the stage of life while still associating with prostitutes. I often wonder if he murdered other harlots in Brighton, Paris or any other prostitute haunts he frequented all over the world.

The evidence of Roots, Marsh, Stead, Collins and Cremers and the letters and comments of D'Onston cannot be ignored. Such people as these were in a far better position to judge D'Onston at the time than any of his critics today. Inter-Ripper rivalry which exists will undoubtedly do nothing for my work. It is not felt to be in the interests of many considered 'experts' to contradict their past opinions.

We know that four of the five individuals named above thought D'Onston was the Ripper, however, we do not know what Roots believed. When all the true facts are taken into consideration a very strong case emerges against D'Onston. Above all else, D'Onston was arrested at least twice for the murders, which is more than can be said for 98 per cent of the accepted list of suspects ranging from James Maybrick and Lewis Carroll to Queen Victoria.

Such suspects give an insight into the quality of research

undertaken by the blind who continuously lead the blind. The subject has become more confused with the passage of time as more and more suspects get heaped on to the pile as every year passes. If D'Onston is not to be seriously considered as a top suspect now then no one should be termed a likely suspect.

The Usual Suspects

A great deal of attention has been focused on the identity of the killer. In fact the first question I get asked by most people is 'Who was he?' rather than 'Why did he do it?' Most researchers and authors and members of the general public have not been interested in how and why the murders were committed; they have been far more interested and preoccupied in looking at the list of suspects and choosing a likely culprit from the list. The legacy accumulated since 1888 is one of dozens of lovely suspects all with stories woven around them.

I have researched various Ripper suspects and it can be proven that some were not in Whitechapel at the time of the murders. In fact there is no evidence against many of them to start with. There is no need for so many suspects to exist but it does give one an insight into the fact that anyone can nominate a suspect with little or no grounds for doing so.

Montague Druitt (1857–88), for example, has been placed as a suspect on the slightest of evidence. He committed suicide after the last murder and was pulled from the Thames on 31 December. He left a note explaining that because he felt that he was going to be like his mother (insane) it would be best for all concerned if he were to die. It was alleged (but never proven) by Sir Melville Macnaughton, Assistant Chief Constable, CID, Scotland Yard, that Druitt's own family thought he was the Ripper. Such then is the evidence to suggest Druitt was the killer.

Neill Cream (1850–92) is another example. Dr Cream poisoned four prostitutes between 1891 and 1892 and was convicted of the murders. It was alleged that while on the trap of the scaffold he was heard to say, 'I am Jack the …' before being launched into eternity. It has been proven without a shadow of a doubt that Cream was in prison in the United States in 1888.

It is beyond all logic that such suspects exist. Such facts only serve as an example to give an insight into the pitiful and prevailing circumstances which surround the case. We can be thankful that we do not have the names of every crank, publicity seeker and attention seeker who admitted committing the murders at the time otherwise we would also have them to contend with.

Ripper suspect Maybrick is the result of a hoax and no credence should be given to Maybrick as Jack the Ripper.

Aaron Kosminski (1864/65–1919) was a lunatic and was incarcerated as such. Author Paul Begg believes that Israel Schwartz might have been Anderson's witness, and might have seen Kosminski killing Stride though he did not kill the other Ripper victims.

I agree with this theory with one exception. Although Kosminski possibly attacked Stride, he did not kill her. This was achieved by the man seen in the doorway. The name Kosminski is quite legitimate to be placed in the suspects list because it is possible that he attacked Stride. The Royal Conspiracy is yet another hoax and nothing more than a con trick which deserves even less comment.

Unfortunately the subject has become the target for con men/women because it is such a soft target. This is partly due to the gullibility of some experts on the subject who do not have the ability to see a confidence trick when faced with one. The greatest crime was that when certain experts did see a 'con' when faced with one they were either ignored or not believed by the gullible when they gave their opinions based on fact.

Dr Thomas Bond, who was involved in the case, gave a profile of the killer. Profiling can be a very hit and miss affair and while Bond made misses he also made some hits. He wrote:

The murderer must have been a man of physical strength and of great coolness and daring. There is no evidence that he had an accomplice. The murderer in external appearance is quite likely to be a quiet inoffensive looking man, probably middle-aged and neatly and respectably dressed. Assuming the murderer to be such a person as I have just described he would probably be solitary and eccentric in his habits. Also, he is most likely to be a man without regular occupation, but with some income or pension. He is possibly living among respectable persons who have some knowledge of his character and habits and who may have grounds for suspicion that he is not quite right in his mind at times. Such persons would probably be unwilling to communicate suspicions to the police for fear of trouble or notoriety, whereas if there were a prospect of reward it might overcome their scruples.

Comparing D'Onston with this profile shows incredible similarities. D'Onston was a man of strength; he was cool and daring. He was not 'right in the head'. He was middle-aged, inoffensive looking, neatly and respectably dressed, was solitary and eccentric in his habits. He was living among respectable persons at the time of the murders. People who were known to this man suspected him of the killings. One did not reveal their suspicions to the police out of fear, the other (George Marsh) went to claim the reward.

We will never know the actual number of his victims beyond the Whitechapel murders or the flights of fancy that goaded him. The death of Anne Deary I certainly attribute to D'Onston. The premature death of Edmund Gurney (1847–88) has always had a question mark at the end of it. Could it possibly be attributed to D'Onston?

Did D'Onston Kill Gurney?

Gurney was the son of a clergyman and went to Trinity College, Cambridge. He obtained his fellowship in 1872. He was a member of musical, artistic and philosophical groups. His friends included Maitland and Pollock, two renowned authorities on English law.

Gurney had a reputation as being a man of great energy and persistence. He was honorary secretary for the Society of Psychical Research who investigated phenomena and fraudsters.

He investigated Blavatsky and became a very painful thorn in her side. D'Onston was far more than just an acquaintance of Blavatsky's. They had a lot in common. Both had fought under Garibaldi; both were sexual deviants; both were involved in the occult, etc. Gurney was rocking the boat and in a position to sink it. In fact Gurney became a threat to Blavatsky and those closely associated to her.

It is known that D'Onston knew Blavatsky after the death of Gurney, but it remains unknown if he knew Blavatsky prior to Gurney's death. While in London during June 1888 Gurney received a letter from an unknown source and left for Brighton booking into The Royal Albion Hotel at the seafront near the Palace Pier. Although Gurney was to die in the hotel sometime after 10pm on 22 June, he was not found until 2pm on 23 June. He apparently overdosed on chloroform.

More to the point the hotel was only several minutes walk from D'Onston's address at The Cricketers Inn. Of all the hotels, in all of the land, Gurney chose one that was only a stone's throw away from D'Onston's address. It is interesting that D'Onston left for Whitechapel to commence on his five planned murders the day after the inquest verdict on Gurney was given.

Did he stay in Brighton of his own accord until the inquest verdict was given thus waiting for the all clear? Or was he asked not to leave Brighton until the inquest verdict was announced? Or was it all a coincidence? Jeffrey Bloomfield, who is a most intrepid investigator, wrote the following:

THE END OF MR GURNEY
by Jeffrey Bloomfield

Brighton has had its seasons of scandal and rumour. This was especially true in the late 19th century. In 1871, Christiana Edmunds caused a panic, and committed one murder, by spreading poisoned candies throughout the town. She ended up in a criminal asylum for the insane. In 1881, a dishevelled young man left the train at nearby Preston Park, with a story about an attack on himself and an elderly man on the train he had come in on. Eventually, the young man, one Percy Lefroy, was tried for the murder of the elderly man and would be executed. And then, in June 1888, came the death of Mr Edmund Gurney at the old Royal Albion Hotel ... and the recurring question of what exactly happened to him.

Edmund Gurney was born in 1847 at Hersham, near Walton-on-Thames. He went to Blackheath and Cambridge University. He came from a wealthy family (his uncle being a Member of Parliament), and numbered among his friends the American philosopher and psychologist William James and the Philosopher Henry Sidgwick. Gurney originally pursued studies in music eventually writing 'The Power of Sound' (1880) in which he attempted to analyse the effect of melody on the individual. He began preparations for a career in medicine but gradually became interested in psychic studies.

The 19th century was one of intensive scientific examination of all natural phenomenon. It was the century of Maxwell and Faraday and Herz, of Pasteur and Koch, of Freud and Darwin and Wallace and Mendel. Much of our knowledge of electromagnetism, of microbes, of the psyche, of evolution and genetics was discovered in the 19th century. It was inevitable that the same cumulative drive for knowledge would turn its attention to the occult as well.

For the 19th century was when mediums like Daniel Douglas Home were important public figures. Seances were treated as serious social events, for in the heavy religiosity of the time was a desire to see if contact with the dead was possible. The scientific spirit of the time dictated the necessity of trying to apply the vigour of testing to all occult phenomenon so that the 'laws' (if any) which governed them could be discovered for man's improvement.

So, in 1882, the Society for Psychical Research was formed by Henry Sidgwick, Frederic Myers and several others. Myers and Sidgwick were both friends of Gurney and invited him to join. He soon became involved in the leading investigation of the new society: proving thought transference. Within a few months of the founding of the society Gurney became very much involved in investigating such phenomena, writing 'Phantasms of the Living' with Myers and Frank Podmore and 'Hallucinations'.

The issue of mental telepathy really became Gurney's main study in 1885 when he began a series of experiments regarding telepathy and hypnotism, to try to prove that some independent force worked within hypnotic phenomenon. These tests were conducted in Brighton from 1885 to 1888. Gurney was assisted on them by his private secretary, George Albert Smith, a former hypnotist. In June 1888 Smith was on his honeymoon.

On Thursday, 21 June 1888, Gurney received a letter (the contents of which remain unknown as the letter has never been accounted for). He was in London, and after dinner with a friend, he left London for Brighton, checking into a room at the Royal Albion Hotel on 22 June 1888. It was the first time he ever used the hotel. After dining alone he asked a waiter for a glass of water and went upstairs to bed at 10.00pm. When he failed to respond to knocking by 2.00pm the following day, the door was broken open. He was found in bed with a sponge saturated with chloroform on his face. A small bottle of some liquid was found next to him.

The official coroner's report is no longer in existence but from newspaper accounts we know what the official verdict was on the death of Gurney. He suffered from sleeplessness and neuralgia and frequently used chloroform or chloral to sleep. As he was alone this was a very dangerous thing to do as he might fall asleep with the rag or sponge on his face thus ensuring his death. The official view was death by misadventure. And so the official verdict of the coroner's court has remained accepted by most people. But was it correct?

Death by misadventure is a possibility. However, in 1888 chloroform had a sullied reputation in England. Two years earlier there had occurred the trial of Adelaide Bartlett for the murder of her husband, Edwin, by chloroform. With the assistance of a lover, who may or may not have known what the purpose of the drug was, the liquid chloroform was procured and ended up inside Mr Bartlett's stomach.

Due to several flaws in the prosecution's case (including the problem of anyone being forced to silently drink chloroform – it burns terribly), Mrs Bartlett was acquitted. One of the possible reasons the jury found in her favour was that Edwin Bartlett had supposedly spoken of his death on several occasions, suggesting a morbid, even suicidal, state of mind.

So, if not an accident, then what? Suicide perhaps? This was the theory of Trevor Hall in his book, *The Strange Case of Edmund Gurney*. Hall was concerned with those special, long series of tests that Gurney worked on for three years. With the assistance of his secretary, George Smith, Gurney hypnotised various working-class boys to perform a wide variety of different tests that would prove mental telepathy.

The results were used in many volumes of 'findings' that Gurney published with the Proceedings of the Society of Psychical Research, and had been (more than *The Power of Sound* or a recent volume of essays, *Tertium Quid*) the basis for Gurney's growing name and reputation. He was widely admired for the thoroughness and care of his experiments and seemed to be giving a respectable basis for psychic phenomenon. But, according to Hall, this was about to collapse in utter ruin.

George Smith had been a professional entertainer before he worked with Gurney. Hall showed that Smith, seeking to please both Gurney and the S.P.R., had fixed the experiments. As had been shown many times in our century by magicians like Harry Houdini or James Randi, frequently even the best minds are fooled by magicians especially when they are expecting to see certain results.

The key to this theory is that unknown letter Gurney received before he left London. Hall believes that while Smith was on his honeymoon Gurney found proof of the tampering while working at Smith's desk. The letter may have been from Smith's sister, Alice, verifying the truth. The collapse of his hard work, his reputation and the (perceived) probable collapse of the S.P.R. caused Gurney to kill himself.

Hall's view has been criticised by Gordon Eppeson in *The Mind of Edmund Gurney*. Eppeson points out that far from being suicidal or depressed on the day of his death, Gurney was cheerful and in good spirits. He was not known to be given to despair or self-pity. By temperament he was a fighter and would have continued to try to do his work (which Eppeson does not dismiss as Hall does).

Finally, Eppeson feels that Hall's conclusions are based too much on supposition and guesswork and lack a clear understanding of the subject's personality. Eppeson feels the coroner was right – death by tragic overdose, due to misadventure.

So accident or suicide? Well, what about a third possibility, which always lurks around the corner in mysterious deaths? Could Edmund Gurney have been murdered?

Murder is one possibility according to Mr Ivor Edwards. This theory has nothing to do with George Smith and the telepathy studies. It has to do with other matters at the S.P.R. which were occupying its leadership (such as Gurney) and some shadowy figures. One, Helena Blavatsky, is still remembered as a founder of the cult of Theosophy – still going strong at the end of the 20th century. The other, Dr Robert Donston Stephenson, is a far more sinister figure than Madam Blavatsky, and if the supposition about him is true he may be the most sinister figure of the 19th century.

Helena Blavatsky was born in 1831 in Ekatinoslav Russia. Her family was in the minor nobility. She married an elderly official in 1848 but deserted him after a few months. For the next 20 years she claimed to have travelled widely around the globe, including trips to India and two attempts to reach Tibet. Beginning in 1858, again in Russia, she became a medium.

Eventually, she went to the United States where she lived from 1870. While there she studied occult and kabbalah, as well as Hindu and Buddhist scripture. She eventually amalgamated many of the occult and spiritual notions, including the belief in Tibetan sages (mahatmas) who were guides through their 'astral bodies' to her giving her messages. They also told her to perform tricks to convince sceptics.

Initially, Blavatsky was working with a lawyer and occultist named Col. Henry Olcott, with whom she founded the Theosophical Society in 1875, to discover the laws of the universe and to enable mankind to used their latent powers. She and Olcott went to India, where Theosophy actually began, to get some ground support. Blavatksy encouraged a universal following; a mingling of all races. This was unusual in the 1870s.

Although the authorities were appalled that Blavatsky, a fat, foul-mouthed woman, was the group's spokesperson, the group prospered. It is interesting to note that Blavatsky was an avid follower of Lord Lytton. It was due in part to his work that she eventually became such a public figure.

In 1884, Helena Blavatsky returned to Europe to spread her message. However, two of her followers spread stories of her less attractive and more questionable activities. The S.P.R. sent Richard Hodgson to India to double-check the stories. His final report, in 1885, labelled Blavatsky one of the most successful impostors in history.

To save Theosophy, the followers convinced Blavatsky to step aside and allow Olcott to take over the movement. She was exhausted and agreed. She soon recovered her health and formed a new Theosophical group in England. Her success was ensured by the support of Annie Besant, a leading social reformer of the period and Blavatsky's greatest convert. Madam Blavatsky died in 1891.

During her career, Blavatsky managed to meet Dr Robert Donston Stephenson. Born in Hull in 1841, Stephenson had a questionable career. He had served with Garibaldi's forces in the 1860s but returned to England and a job in Hull in the civil service. He lost this job when a misadventure with a prostitute revealed he had lied to his superiors.

All through his life, Stephenson would skirt the edge of the criminal world. If he ever did enter it, he was careful to cover his own tracks. His wife disappeared about 1887 and no explanation as to her fate ever was made … least of all by her husband. He may have been involved in several deaths.

Stephenson made several trips abroad to study the occult in West Africa and India. He may have murdered a female witch doctor in West Africa (he certainly boasted of this and the death of a Chinese man, but in that age of Imperialism few English people would have cared). He was deeply interested in the Egyptian occult and this brought him into the orbit of Blavatsky, who had many Egyptian occult ideas in her philosophy.

In June 1888, Stephenson was staying at The Cricketers Inn, Brighton. He was putting together several plans for future activities. He was planning to check himself into the London Hospital, in the East End of London. A very fine hospital of the day, Stephenson was planning to study its scheduling, to note when it was possible to leave and re-enter without being noticed. For he had plans, deep and dark ones. But first, there were other matters. Blavatsky, was still being annoyed by the S.P.R., not so much her former enemy, Mr Hodgson, but the chief correspondence secretary, Mr Edmund Gurney. And Mr Gurney was coming to Brighton.

Within a few months of Gurney's death a series of horrible murders of prostitutes occurred in the East End of London. Jack the Ripper seemed able to come and go in the area without any problems. Everyone was suspected that summer and autumn of 1888. Once the police were even looking for a patient from a London Hospital who fitted Stephenson's working background.

Edmund Gurney arrived at Brighton's Royal Albion Hotel on Friday, 22 June 1888 and was found dead the next morning. The inquest was held on Monday, 25 July 1888. The next day Dr Robert Donston Stephenson left Brighton for London and infamy.

Misconceptions About D'Onston

Critics of D'Onston who place their own suspects in preference have made the point that the Whitechapel murders were more likely to have been committed by a younger and fitter man than D'Onston. Also, he has been referred to as a drunk. Besides if he was a drunk (which he was not) then that would not exclude him from having the ability to murder the prostitutes. Thousands of murders have been committed by those who were drunk at the time.

I would like to address the question of how old and fit a killer needs to be. Jack's victims were not strapping 6ft dockworkers. They were prostitutes who were, in the main, middle-aged, of small stature, one of which was undernourished and weak (and, in fact, dying). Jack was preying on weak and vulnerable targets.

A killer who uses the element of surprise on his victim has the advantage. In fact, many strong and fit people have been murdered by a weaker adversary. John Wayne Gacy was not fit; he was middle-aged, fat, drank a lot and smoked pot. He also took amyl nitrate and valium, yet his victims were boys and fit young men aged 17, 18 and 19. Gacy's victims are estimated to number at least 33. Four of the five Ripper victims were in the same age bracket as D'Onston.

Cremers met D'Onston after the murders had occurred and described him as 'a man with military bearing suggesting power and strength. Tall with not an ounce of superfluous flesh upon him'. Cremers never made mention of any connection in relation to D'Onston and drink in her memoirs. Marsh, who drank in the company of D'Onston, described him as a soaker and not a drunk.

Stead knew D'Onston very well before the murders were committed and never made one known comment in relation to D'Onston and drink. Even so, many murders have been committed by people in a drunken state. I met one middle-aged killer who had arrived home with his wife late at night after celebrating their wedding anniversary. He was the worse for drink.

In the bedroom his wife made a fatal mistake. She told him that she was leaving him. He went into the bathroom, which was undergoing renovation work, and picked up a hammer. He went back into the bedroom and beat his wife to death. Aileen Wuornos was a prostitute who killed seven of her male clients.

To state that D'Onston was not capable of committing the murders because of age, drink or a feigned illness would be to underestimate the situation. Even if he had neurosthenia (not to be confused with neurasthenia, its opposite) he could still commit murder. *The Mammoth Book of Jack the Ripper* edited by Maxim Jakubowski and Nathan Braund implies in the suspect section that D'Onston recounted that he had once held a commission in the British Army. This is quite untrue.

The conclusion is also drawn that physically D'Onston does not match the descriptions of Schwartz, Hutchinson or PC Long. Schwartz saw two men and as already stated the man seen to attack Stride did not kill her. The description of the other man seen in the doorway does fit with D'Onston in relation to height, hair colour and clothing. There is no evidence to suggest that the man seen by Hutchinson was Jack the Ripper; he could have been a client. As for PC Long he never saw any suspect! He was the policeman who found the graffito and piece of apron at Goulston Street.

More errors found in the book include that the sudden cessation of the murders was supposedly due to D'Onston's conversion, not least because he continued to lecture on the occult for years after and also enjoyed tormenting the likes of Cremers and Collins with hints which do not speak of remorse or of the sort of mental anguish which must have afflicted any such convert.

Such comments are wholly unfounded and far from the truth. D'Onston only planned five murders and with the demise of Kelly they stopped in November 1888. They certainly did not stop due to any conversion for he was not converted until 1893. Also, his association with Cremers and Collins came to an end in 1891. Furthermore there is no evidence to show that he continued to lecture on the occult years after the murders. As far as I am aware only three people have researched D'Onston in great depth for any number of years and these are Bernard O'Donnell (deceased), Melvin Harris and myself.

Yet untrue statements continue to be peddled by those who either rely on the faulty stories of others or do not research D'Onston or the subject matter as correctly as they should. I have yet to see one valid point or one piece of good evidence which seriously places doubt on D'Onston being the killer.

APPENDIX 1

D'Onston's Chronology and Official Records

1841: Born: Robert D'Onston Stephenson, 20 April, Sculcoates, Hull. Lives at Willow House, 60, Church Street. Mother's maiden name Dauber. Parents wealthy mill owners.

1859: Visits Paris where he meets Lord Lytton's son, who then introduces him to Lord Lytton.

1860: D'Onston's initiation into the Lodge of Alexandria is performed by Sir Bulwer Lytton.

1860: Lives in Islington with a friend.

1860–63: Fights with Garibaldi in Italy.

1863: Goes to the West Coast of Africa to study witchcraft. He murders a woman witch doctor while there and writes of the deed later.

March 1863: Takes a post at the Customs House in Hull.

1867: His father is a prominent manufacturer and holds the elected post of collector of Hull Corporation Dues. His brother, Richard, is a ship owner, partner in the firm of Rayner, Stephenson and Co., Vice-Consul for Uruguay and a Hull City councillor.

July 1868: Shot in the thigh by Thomas Piles under suspicious circumstances. Sacked from Customs because of his association with prostitutes, which led to him contracting VD.

1869: Living in London.

14 February 1876: Marries Anne Deary, his mother's serving girl, at St James Church, Holloway. Married under the name of Roslyn D'Onston Stephenson.

1878: Goes to India to study magic. It was at this time that Bulwer Lytton's son, Edward, was the Viceroy of India.

1881: On the 1881 Census is living at 10, Hollingsworth Street North with his wife, Annie. The Census states he is an MD, not practising but is a scientific writer for the London press. Age is given as 39, his wife's, 37.

1886: Vittoria Cremers comes across a copy of *Light on the Path* by Mabel Collins in a New York bookshop.

July 1886: D'Onston applies for the position of Secretaryship of the Metropolitan and City Police Orphanage. Is not short-listed.

1886: Anne Deary is known to be alive at this time.

May 11 1887: Six finds of portions of a woman's body in the Thames and the Regent's Canal. Possibly Anne Deary. Done by someone with medical knowledge. No death certificate for Anne Deary has ever been found.

1888: Vittoria Cremers arrives in the UK going to the HQ of the British Theosophical Society to enlist. It is at this time that she meets Madame Helena Petrova Blavatsky, the head figure associated with the Theosophical Society. She obtains work as an associate editor of *Lucifer*, a work printed by the movement. First contact with Mabel Collins.

1888: D'Onston moves to The Cricketers Inn, Brighton, to plan the murders. The Cricketers Inn was a well-known 18th-century inn frequented by prostitutes. When D'Onston is at The Cricketers, Edmund Gurney (founder member of the Society for Psychical Research and English spiritualist, who is also investigating psychical fraudsters including Madame Blavatsky, known to D'Onston) is found dead in his room at The Royal Albion Hotel, only a few minutes' walk from The Cricketers Inn. The day after the inquest, D'Onston moves from The Cricketers Inn into the London Hospital to execute his well-laid plans.

26 July 1888 to 31 August 1888: He sets a pattern in the hospital. He then strikes at 3.30am on 31 August 1888. The series of five murders ceases on 9 November 1888 and he moves from the hospital on 8 December 1888.

16 October 1888: D'Onston writes a letter to the City of London Police about the message left by the killer known as the Goulston Street Graffito.

1 December 1888: D'Onston writes a piece to the *Pall Mall Gazette* suggesting that Jack the Ripper was a black magician. Mabel Collins reads this article and writes to D'Onston. Later the two meet and become lovers, then business partners.

Friday 7 December 1888: Moves into a lodging house, St Martin's Chambers, 29, Castle Street, on discharge from the London Hospital. The landlord, Mr Cullingford, also owned the property at 66, Leman Street.

Christmas Eve 1888: George Marsh goes to Scotland Yard to make a statement to Inspector Roots (D'Onston's friend of 20 years) to the effect that D'Onston was Jack the Ripper.

Boxing Day 1888: D'Onston goes to Scotland Yard and makes a statement to his friend Inspector Roots that Jack the Ripper is Dr Davies.

3 January 1889: Article written by D'Onston for the *Pall Mall Gazette* dealing with the magical cults of the West Coast of Africa.

15 February 1889: D'Onston writes a second piece for the *Pall Mall Gazette*. It contains his own views on devil worship. He admits to the murder of a woman witch doctor in the article.

March 1889: Cremers visits Southsea to meet with Mabel Collins. She finds Cremers living with D'Onston. Collins and D'Onston return to London 14 days later. D'Onston moves to a lodging house run by Cremers's landlady for two weeks. Collins wants to be discreet about the affair.

13 May 1889: Moves from HQ London Cottage Mission, 304, Burdett Road, Mile End and admitted to the London Hospital with an acute case of 'Chloralism'.

25 July 1889: Discharged from hospital.

1889: D'Onston's father dies and leaves him nothing.

July 1890: Collins lodges a libel action against Blavatsky.

1890: D'Onston starts the Pompadour Cosmetique Company with Cremers and Collins. D'Onston lives in a small room at the back of the first floor.

November 1890: Blavatsky commissions an article from D'Onston entitled 'African Magic'. The piece appears in *Lucifer*.

D'Onston is arrested at least twice for the Whitechapel Murders prior to this time.

1891: Marks the end of the Pompadour Cosmetique Company.

1891: D'Onston takes Collins to court over stolen letters; the case is dismissed.

1893: D'Onston is converted to Christianity by the converted prostitute Victoria Woodhull.

1896: W. T. Stead, editor of the *Pall Mall Gazette*, introduces articles by D'Onston in his quarterly magazine *Borderland*. Stead adds that D'Onston is Jack the Ripper. D'Onston works on his book *The Patristic Gospels*.

1904: *The Patristic Gospels* is published.

1904: D'Onston disappears. May have gone abroad or stayed in England and changed his name. No record of his death has been discovered.

Official Records

This information was taken from the Mormon Surname Survey of 1881.

Surname: Stephenson **Forename:** Roslyn D. **Age:** 39 **Relationship to head:** Head **Marital status:** Married **County:** Middlesex, London Islington **Occupation:** MD, Not practising. Scientific writer for the London Press. **Name of head:** Self **Born:** Yorkshire **Parish:** Sculcoates

PRO Reference: Roll: 0242 Folio: 15 Page: 24 Film: 1341053

Surname: Stephenson **Forename:** Annie **Age:** 37 **Relationship**

to head: Wife **Marital status:** Married **County:** Middlesex, London Islington **Name of head:** Roslyn D. Stephenson **Born:** Yorkshire **Parish:** Thorn

PRO Reference: Roll: 0242 Folio: 15 Page: 24 Film: 1341053

D'Onston, Marsh, and Roots letters. Corporation of London Records Office. Ref. Police Box 3.23 No.390

London Hospital Register. Physicians' male patients.
Date. 26th July 88
General number. No. 1146
Without ticket. 5
Name. Roslyn Stephenson
Address. Cricketers Inn, Black Lion Sq, Brighton.
Age. 47
Civil state. U (unmarried)
Occupation. Journalist
Ward. Davis
Case. Neurosthenia
Physician. Dr Sutton
Days in Hospital. 134
Time of discharge. Dec. 7th 88
Condition on discharge. Relieve

London Hospital Register. Physicians' male patients.
Date. 13th May 89
General number. No. 713
Without ticket. 2
Name. Roslyn D'Onston
Address. Burdett Cottage, Burdett Road, Mile End
Age. 50
Civil state. S (single)
Occupation. Author
Ward. Davis
Case. Chloralism

Physician. Dr Sutton
Days in hospital. 73
Time of discharge. July 25th 89
Condition on discharge. Cured

Marriage of Roslyn D'Onston and Anne Deary was solemnised at St
James Church, in the Parish of Islington, in the county of
Middlesex, on 14th January 1876. D'Onston's father is on the
certificate as Richard Stephenson. **Profession** Gentleman. Anne
Deary's father is on the certificate as Charles Deary. **Profession**
Farmer. **Certificate No. 464.**

APPENDIX 2

Map-reading Madmen

It is not unusual for murderers, sexual perverts and other types of criminals to use maps to aid them. One multiple murderer who planned his killings with the aid of maps was Harvey Louis Carignan. This man was 47 at the time of his arrest (my suspect was the same age in 1888) in Minneapolis, Minnesota, in September 1974. Carignan was arrested for a string of rapes and rape murders. It transpired that he had spent more than half of his life in prison.

He marked remote areas on a map that he had first checked out during the course of travelling thousands of miles in his car. The Ripper also checked out his sites prior to the murders.

When Carignan was arrested quantities of maps were found at his home and in his car which covered the area of over five states and southern Canada. On these maps were found 180 red circles, each one denoted a suitable murder site in a remote area. Just like the Ripper sites, each site was accessible by a lonely side road where a victim could be lured or forcibly abducted.

While serving in the US Army in Anchorage, Alaska, he had escaped execution following a conviction for murder as far back as 1949. He denied attempted murder but admitted rape. He was convicted on the basis of a confession, which was subsequently challenged in the US Supreme Court.

The death sentence was commuted to 15 years imprisonment. While in prison he plotted and planned and studied cartography, sociology, psychology and journalism and like most serial killers he was of above average intelligence.

He was released on parole in 1960. Four months after his release he was arrested on two counts of burglary. The first in Duluth, Minnesota, the second in Seattle, Washington. In 1973, Carignan purchased a petrol and service business and advertised in the *Seattle Times* for a female assistant.

Kathy Miller, 15, applied for the part-time job. On 1 May 1973 she went to be interviewed for the job and was never seen alive again. Carignan was questioned by the police as being the last person to see her alive, but he denied that she had turned up for the interview. Days later her schoolbooks were found 26 miles away in a car park in Everett. Weeks later her decomposed body was found in a field near Everett by a man out walking his dog. She had been raped and strangled.

The police could not prove a case against him but, due to circumstances described by Carignan as police harassment, he sold up and moved first to Denver then to Minneapolis. It was in Minneapolis that he met Eileen Hunley, a blonde teenager who went missing from her home in August 1974. No trace of this girl has ever been found. Carignan cruised in an old Buick, picking up young girls.

Now we come to what I consider to be one of the most important factors concerning serial killers including Jack the Ripper. A pattern emerged in which young girls were being picked up and taken in the direction of their destination. The killer would then turn off the main road and down a quiet side street to a remote area. The victims were then ordered from the car at knifepoint, assaulted and raped. Four girls who survived their ordeal at the hands of Carignan had suffered severe blows to the head with a hammer.

They related why they had accepted a lift from the killer. And here we have it in a nutshell.

One victim stated, 'He looked harmless enough.'

Another said, 'He was old enough to be my father.'

Yet another said, 'I thought he looked as if I could trust him.'

Many people go on first impressions and doing so can have disastrous results.

On 24 September 1974, Carignan was pulled in by two alert policemen in Minneapolis who spotted him by the girls' description of their attacker. He was arrested as he was getting into his car, which had also been described. All four girls picked out Carignan and identified him as their assailant. His defence was mistaken identity. His downfall was forensic evidence. Many of the red circles, pinpointed on the maps, coincided with known sites of rapes and assaults on young women.

It is interesting to note that this killer's excuse was the same as the Yorkshire Ripper's. When in court, Carignan was asked why he had picked up a certain victim he replied, 'God told me to.' He said that he talked to God on a frequent basis and that God had told him to kill and humiliate women. Referring to the girl he had attempted to murder, the subject of the charge he was facing, he stated, 'I was sorry I did not kill her because I was supposed to.'

The jury found him guilty of aggravated sodomy and attempted murder. Further trials ensued on several charges of sexual assault and on a further two counts of murder of which he was found guilty. He accumulated sentences totalling more than 100 years plus life, which means he is to die in jail. It is interesting to note that Carignan studied psychology, cartography, sociology and journalism in his pursuit of rape and murder.

APPENDIX 3

General Information on Sacred Geometry and Vesica Piscis

It has been questioned by some doubting Thomases why a Mason would give me any information on this or any other matter. Mr Sidney Foster had two reasons for assisting me in this matter. While one reason remains a private matter between myself and Sidney he gave me permission to quote the other reason he had for assisting me which is as follows: 'I am proud to "come out" because freemasonry has become too secret and I and other members wish to do away with the old ways and make it more open. The general public should know about what goes on and I welcome such changes.'

Sidney informed me that he cannot tell me things about passwords. However, I do know where to locate them. When I placed certain information in the public domain I received a rather irate message from a police officer in the USA who also happened to be a freemason.

He said I was talking rubbish in stating that freemasonry is connected in any way to the temple in ancient Egypt. This individual then went on to refer to me as a troublemaker and accused me of being up to no good. It is amazing how some people react when faced with the truth. If searching for enlightenment and the truth is causing trouble in the eyes of such people then they should be seen for what they truly are.

Sidney Foster informed me that Freemasonry can indeed trace its roots back to ancient Egypt and that 30 to 40 years ago he was giving lectures on the subject. I know from my own research that this is true. Sidney has been a Mason for 50 years and he certainly knows what he is about as far as his craft is concerned.

I am not saying that Jack the Ripper was a Mason or that the crimes were directly connected to the Masons. And the sooner some people let this sink in the better it will be for all concerned. I am fed up with explaining that certain occult groups use the same symbols, etc. that are to be found in Freemasonry. *I have found no evidence to suggest that Jack the Ripper was a Freemason.*

Neither have I found any evidence to show that any Mason was directly or indirectly involved, or that any cover up has ever taken place. I have found no evidence to show that more than one man was involved in the murders. Furthermore the victims were killed where they were found. They were not murdered elsewhere in a carriage and then dumped where found.

The evidence which does exist has either been misinterpreted or ignored by many people otherwise they would not draw such ill-founded conclusions. This is also true when one looks at many other various murders including that of Jon Benet Ramsey, a six-year-old beauty Queen from Boulder, Colorado. The general consensus was that her devoted parents murdered her for a number of unfounded and ridiculous reasons.

Retired policeman Lou Smit who worked on over 200 murders (and who never lost a court case) was brought in to work on the murder several months after it had occurred. He got to the truth of the matter but many people who saw themselves as prosecutor, judge and jury had already made up their minds and nothing was going to change their views including concrete evidence. Also reputations were at stake and in such situations the truth comes a poor second best.

The authorities tried to suppress Lou's findings because it was not what they wanted to hear because it was not in their interests. Lou eventually dropped out of the case due to the bloody-minded behaviour of other people.

In the English judicial system the truth has been suppressed by those who represent the law in many criminal cases including murder. The Guildford Four and Birmingham Six are only two such examples. When the cry of 'injustice' was heard rather late in the day (as is usually the case) one obnoxious judge even went so far as to state, 'If we had retained hanging then that would have been the end of the matter.' I wonder if he would have stated the same if he had been unlawfully 'fitted up' and sent to prison for life.

I have also undertaken research into the name Roslyn that D'Onston adopted. I received the following letter from Sidney Foster, which included further information:

Looking at your diagram again what struck me was the Ripper's alias Dr. Roslyn D'Onston. It is an amazing coincidence, is it not Ivor, that you sent me the HISTORY etc. of ROSLYN CHAPEL!! I leave you to fathom that one out. Without breaking the oath I took when I was initiated into the CRAFT, I cannot tell you any more. For further thought about the VESICA PISCIS I enclose some information about the THIRD CIRCLE, which together with the other two of the V.P. forms a symbol especially significance to all HOLY ROYAL ARCH MASONS maybe this diagram could be found on your map of the streets of LONDON where the murders took place? I've written you a page referring to the CENTRE MAKERS of LONDON note the word centre. Ivor, I can do no more for you now, it is up to your good self to take the matter forward as you wish, but be warned, it may rebound to your detriment?? Be careful.

With best wishes Sidney.

This diagram is especially significant to all HOLY ROYAL ARCH MASONS, whose ritual is carried out by 3 PRINCIPALS, who have to work together.

The VESICA PISCIS is associated with curved rods whose exposed lengths are 3, 4, and 5, the width of the rod being the unit and the radius of curvature being 5. (As all HOLY ROYAL ARCH MASONS should know) 3, 4, and 5 is of course the PYTHAGORAS RIGHT L TRIANGLE.

See also the MASONS DIAMOND and the SWASTIKA, the oldest symbol in the world. (r/f Dr.Carr) Symbol of EL SHADDAI and the POLE STAR etc. See book No 15. by S.C. George Martin (Dundee).

In London there was an old GUILD of MASONS called the CENTRE MAKERS, who were also called BOW-MAKERS. Hence the names in LONDON – BOW, BOW STREET, BOW CHURCH, BOW BELLS.

Also Relevant to LONDON were the OPERATIVE MASONS and the following are some references that may be applicable to your researches, Ivor.

1632–1723

St Paul's – Sir C. Wren erected a cross on the top of the CUPOLA, in July 1708. Queen Anne died on 1 August 1714 after which King George entered the city on 20 September 1714. After the rebellion was over 1716, the few LONDON LODGES, neglected by WREN (who was GRAND MASTER) thought fit to cement under a GRAND MASTER as the centre of UNION and HARMONY the LODGES that met at:

1. THE GOOSE AND GRIDIRON ALE HOUSE in ST PAUL'S CHURCHYARD.

2. THE CROWN ALE HOUSE in PARKERS LANE, near DRURY LANE.

3. THE APPLE TREE TAVERN in CHARLES STREET, COVENT GARDEN.

4. THE RUMMER AND GRAPES TAVERN in CHANNEL ROW, WESTMINSTER.

In the APPLE TREE TAVERN some elderly brethren installed their oldest member in due form, thereby constituting a GRAND LODGE protempori. And accordingly on ST JOHN the BAPTIST'S DAY in the 3rd year of KING GEORGE I, 1717, the assembly and feast of free and accepted masons was held at the GOOSE AND GRIDIRON.

Having had a keen interest in architecture and archaeology since the age of thirteen, I knew that sacred geometry had been used in the building of such structures as the Great Pyramids, the temple at Jerusalem and Stonehenge. Sacred geometry was also used on a much larger scale for the purpose of town planning from ancient times through to the medieval period.

Architect Harries Thomas has carried out extensive work on the subject, two such examples being Caernarfon Castle and its environs and Stonehenge. Some scholars believe that sacred geometry was used on a far grander scale than previously thought, encompassing sites worldwide. Sacred geometry has many hidden meanings incorporated into the symbols utilised for either building or planning. It is such secret knowledge which has been jealously guarded down the ages.

During my research I sat observing a programme on astronomy and the cosmos which showed a new discovery made with a new and very powerful telescope. Astronomers had seen a Vesica Piscis shape never before seen. Running the length of the Vesica Piscis was a system, which may or may not have been the Milky Way.

The odd thing about this was that while the stars were to be seen inside the shape of Vesica Piscis nothing appeared outside it. In fact its layout looked very similar to my plan of the murders. Only site 2 remained outside of the Vesica Piscis. All other relevant sites and the killer's activity remained inside the shape.

This does indeed appear to be a yoni containing a foetus system waiting to be born.

I decided to contact astrologer Mr Terry Nevin in Hawaii with information including papers on sacred geometry, and the pyramids, etc. Terry Nevin has been working on astronomy and the pyramids for many years and has worked on very large telescopes. In fact, he has gone from one extreme to the other by working on the invention of the smallest microscope in the world. Terry Nevin was and became a great help to me. He stated that he was very exited by some of the information he had received from me and that he was thinking about writing a book based on it. He kindly sent me the following letter to include in my work:

This all started one day in 1979. I was at the 88-inch telescope on the summit of Mauna Kea in Hawaii. The observatory crew were in the lounge swapping stories about the various astronomers with whom they had worked. The stories had been mostly derogatory until somebody brought up Dr. Brent Tulley. I was surprised by the respect and admiration these blue-collar workers had for this astronomer. Somebody said cryptically, 'I think Brent is the one who is going to figure it all out.' When I asked, 'What would he figure out?' He answered simply, 'The universe.' He turned out to be correct.

I guess the easiest way to explain what was figured out is to talk about a possible past view. (The past view I'm making up to help you get the picture.) Imagine a dark universe (no stars, no galaxies) filled with bubbles. They are all spherical about 300 million light years in diameter, optically clear and none are touching. And then for some reason, either expansion or movement, the spherical bubbles intersected and the galaxies appeared.

What Brent, and other astronomers, see today are these intersecting bubbles. They observe that galaxies (in great long clusters) are only found along these lines of intersection. The galaxies are not ever seen inside any bubble. The bubbles today appear totally empty; they are clear and you can see right through them (that's why they were never noticed before). This summarises what we know about cosmology and what the astronomers call 'The Bubble Universe'.

I left astronomy in 1985 and shortly thereafter, for fun, I started researching the mathematics behind the Great Pyramid. Eventually, I published my research and the findings at my website (http://www.aloha.net/hawmtn/pyramid.htm). Because of this webpage, I was contacted by Ivor Edwards, who in the course of his investigation into Jack the Ripper, had acquired a lot of Pyramid material. He asked me to take a look at it.

One of Mr. Edwards' main interests was the ancient symbol called Vesica Piscis. It can be constructed by drawing a circle with a compass and then moving the point of the compass to the edge of this circle and drawing a second circle. The oblong shape in the centre definitely looks like a fish, hence the name piscis. For centuries it was the secret symbol Christians used to identify themselves.

What really startled me was just one sentence from one of the papers he sent me. It was 'The .. diagram is but a symbol of the cosmos, a representation in [two] dimension[s] of an organism that embraces many.' This meant if I wanted to see a symbol of the cosmos in the Vesica Piscis, I should not look at it as the intersection of two circles, but as the intersection of two spheres. Wonder of wonders, the Vesica Piscis can indeed be seen as the two dimensional symbol of 'The Bubble Universe'. There are only two possibilities. The first is that this is all just a coincidence. But then why would the Vesica Piscis be called a symbol of the cosmos and drawings of multiple Vesica Piscis be called a cosmogram. The second possibility has deep implications.

(From an upcoming book by Terrence G. Nevin.)

The deeper implications to which Terry Nevin refers relate to the question: How did certain sacred knowledge including Vesica Piscis and the cosmos become available to the ancients when such facts were only discovered quite recently by the invention and use of the most powerful telescopes in the world?

APPENDIX 4

The Origins of Occult Intimidation and Terror Tactics

Egypt was one of the earliest of the great civilisations which arose 5,000 years ago. The key theme of Egyptian history was laid down in ideals of centralised power, a cult of the dead and the royal rituals. These three themes intertwined to make Egypt the creator of the world's first unified state and establishing this involved a few manipulating and controlling the masses. This was achieved through the black arts, using subterfuge and depending on the guile of the populace.

The temple in Egypt believed that if the law, kingship, occult religion and ritual were kept to the same pattern then all would last for eternity. All civilisations since have sought validation for their power over the masses by creating great public symbols. One early Egyptian example was the Great Pyramid at Giza.

Hitler had the same idea about the German Reich. In the 20th century, Nazi Germany started on a massive building project which was the largest programme to be undertaken since the days of the Roman Empire. As with the pagan ancient Egyptians, Hitler and the Nazi party practised the occult. The symbol seen on the murder plan, the lightning bolt, was adopted by the SS.

The swastika was another ancient occult symbol adopted as the national symbol of Nazi Germany. Hitler tried to dominate the world with the aid of occult doctrine. Fear was implemented to achieve these aims. Haiti is a country which was taken over by those who practised Voodoo. The masses in Haiti were indoctrinated and controlled by its use.

Today almost all of us live in nations with some or all of those Egyptian symbols. Modern thinking is shaped by religious and social myth, especially the myth of the great ruler, king or God. It was in his name, in the Bronze Age, that the many surrendered power to the few to live in the conditions in which most people on the planet still live today.

The Egyptian pagan religion had two main themes:

No. 1

A dying and rising saviour god who could confer on believers the gift of immortality. This was first sought by the pharaohs and then by the masses.

No. 2

Post-mortem judgement in which the quality of the deceased's life would influence his ultimate fate.

Christian beliefs have identical tenets; believe in Jesus and you will be granted everlasting life, and you will be held to account on judgement day. So it would appear that the old pagan beliefs are very similar to Christian beliefs. Down through the ages many cults and religious groups have utilised the old Egyptian occult pagan beliefs and have put their own interpretations on them.

Freemasons base their society on the old Egyptian cult religion. The Golden Dawn, a Masonic offshoot, are involved in the old Egyptian religion. When a Mason takes his oath, a symbolic gesture and a verbal threat at throat cutting are made to make certain that his silence is ensured. The old order achieved control over the masses by simply preying on their ignorance and superstition.

That is how cults, secret societies and religious groups achieve their results. It would not do for the masses to know certain secrets, for if the masses were as wise as the few that manipulated them the power structure would be in jeopardy.

The old temple in Egypt had 30,000 people on its payroll (much later the figure was placed at between 80,000–100,000) and it was a booming business. Each year, thousands of people set out on a pilgrimage to middle Egypt to celebrate the resurrection of Osiris, King of the Dead. Millions of mummified animal deities have been unearthed which were sold by the priests to the pilgrims to make as offerings to the gods.

The priests used fear of the unknown and their knowledge of black magic to keep the masses in line. The sphinx was termed by the Arabs as Abu Al-Hawl, 'Father of Terror'. Magic text from Egypt includes incantations and charms to protect against dangerous creatures. An important category of epigraphs is constituted by curses, imprecations, and threats of divine vengeance against enemies, evildoers and tomb violators, in particular. Black magic, in all its shapes and forms, can be traced back to Egypt, for it was there that the state used it to obtain power and wealth.

Organised religions have always tried to dupe the masses in one form or another while playing for the number one position. Pieces of wood alleged to originate from the True Cross, glass phials containing the tears of Jesus, old bones alleged to be the remains of saints, the Shroud of Turin are some of the more famous examples of attempts to boost the income from pilgrims.

The Knights Templars started on the road to power by protecting pilgrims in the Holy Land. When they became powerful and a threat to the King of France they were purged and all their wealth was taken by the crown.

It is only a question of time before we leave behind the old superstitions and establishments that have lingered with us down through the ages. For they should be placed where they truly belong, in the past.

APPENDIX 5

Present Day Occult Ritual Murder

Occult ritual murder has travelled hand in hand with man throughout the ages and is unfortunately fact not fiction. A lack of understanding on the subject tends to make the ignorant sceptical of events and many ridicule the idea. It is partly due to ignorance that the Ripper's murders were never solved. Even the killer tried to educate the ignorant by writing to the police and newspapers on the subject.

People from all walks of life are involved in the practical side of occult rituals, some of which include diabolical acts of murder and mutilation of the dead. Grace Kelly, for example, paid a large sum of money in US dollars to become a high priestess in an occult group in Monaco. The group was headed by a very close friend of Prince Rainier of Monaco.

This particular group is under investigation today by the police and murder is just one aspect of the inquiry. They are being held responsible for an untold number of deaths. One female witness (under police investigation) and a member of this particular occult group, gave an interview for British television in relation to Grace Kelly's initial contact with this particular secret society. The witness stated that she personally gave Grace Kelly sexual stimulation which led to the latter having several orgasms.

The witness then went on to give details of Kelly's initiation ceremony into the group. On Thursday 5 April 2001, *The Times* published an article by their Rome correspondent Richard Owen entitled 'Net closes on Satanic High Priest'. The basics of the story are that eight double Satanic murders were carried out in Tuscany between 1968 and 1985. A farmhand labourer named Pietro Pacciani was believed by police to be the killer known as the Monster of Florence. He was found guilty of six of the murders in 1994 but his conviction was quashed on appeal.

When interviewed by Richard Owen in Mercatale, near Florence, Pacciani stated that he was not clever enough to be the killer. Under Italian law he was going to be retried but before justice could take its course he was murdered in 1998 and the case was closed.

He was found dead in very mysterious circumstances. All the doors and windows in the house had been opened. The victim's trousers were pulled down slightly and his vest tucked up as if he had been pulled along by his feet. Three years later police reopened the case because of new evidence.

While Pacciani carried out some of the murders it was found that the remaining murders were committed by someone else. It was concluded that the real masterminds behind the killings were a group of high society Satanists who carried out occult rituals that defied comprehension. The leader of the group is believed to be a very distinguished doctor.

The police believe that the mastermind who ordered the killings also instructed the killers (Pacciani and his accomplices, Mario Vanni and Giancarlo Lotti) which parts of the body to mutilate and which parts to take. This trio was known as the 'teatime companions' or 'Peeping Toms' and was known to hold macabre drunken picnics in the woods, often in the company of prostitutes.

During the trial Lotti said that a doctor whose name he did not know ordered the 'jobs'. It would appear that they were paid large sums of cash for their efforts. Pacciani's various bank accounts show that cash sums adding up to a staggering 300,000 pounds had been received by him over the years. The magistrate in the case, Paolo Canessa, stated that he has identified three suspects, including the doctor.

The female murder victims were found with their left breasts and genitals missing, which has puzzled police. There have also been six other mysterious deaths including that of Pacciani. It is believed that those who wanted the missing body parts have also been eliminating witnesses to cover their tracks.

Pacciani was a diabetic and suffered from heart complaints. He was found dead on 23 February 1998. He had stopped taking the prescribed medication from his own doctor. Someone had been prescribing medicine to Pacciani that killed him instead of curing him. Michele Giuttari, the head of the investigating police force stated that Pacciani had pointed out that some of the murders occurred while he was under arrest.

The killings of the victims who had become a liability because they knew too much started in 1981. The first to go was Renato Malatesta, Pacciani's close friend. He was found hanging in a stable with his feet resting on the ground. Renato's wife, Maria Sperduto, was having an affair with Pacciani. Some 12 years later, Malatesta's daughter, Milva, and her three-year-old son were found dead in a burned out Fiat Panda. Just a few days later the lover of Milva Malatesta, and a friend of Pucciani, Francesco Vinci (who was suspected of being the killer) was also found dead in a burned out car.

A year later a local prostitute named Anna Milva Mettei, who had an affair with Vinci's son, was also found murdered and burned. Carmelo Lavorino, Pacciani's defence lawyer during the trial, believes the mastermind behind the killings is a satanic high priest. They all took orders from one person who it was believed took part in the killings and the mutilations.

Lavorino and other investigators believe that the female body parts were taken for use in black masses held at night in remote farmhouses attended by those involved in the murders. Police are also anxious to trace an unnamed artist who Pacciani worked for as a gardener. The artist disappeared just days before the trial began. Police are convinced that black masses took place on his properties.

When police searched his premises they found accurate portraits of the murder victims and drawings of mutilated women. Police also found a special type of artist's paper, made in Germany, that Pacciani had stolen from two Germans, Horst Meyer and Uwe Rusch Sens. Both were found murdered in a woods near Galluzo in September 1983.

In another property owned by the painter, police found drawings by Pacciani. These showed female corpses and mythical beasts that were half female and half animal. The killing of a French couple which took place on 8 September 1985, at Scopeti, was near a farmhouse that since 1981 had been used as a meeting place by those involved in the murders.

It was owned by a magician who was known to have made potions from pubic hair and vaginal secretions. This magician died of cancer in 1986. Police stated that the Monster of Florence seemed to be two steps ahead of everybody during the enquiries. The mastermind behind the murders was not the rough peasant Pacciani but a very cultured man of great professional success – rich, esteemed, powerful and with hidden psychopathic impulses. Giuttari made the observation that it makes one wonder how many Jekylls and Hydes there were in civilised cities like Florence.

Speaking to an official from the Italian Embassy in London, I was informed that the police in Italy were still making ongoing enquiries and were investigating a private clinic which cared for the elderly. I was informed that the patients at the clinic were found to be very badly abused and that very bizarre things took place at the clinic. I was hoping to place further material about this case in my book and also include further information on occult ritual murder from the Durban Police Department in South Africa.

This department has had to set up a special murder squad to deal solely with occult ritual murder. The reason being that the instances of such murders are growing at an alarming rate. This work must now go to press so unfortunately such facts including further research will perhaps be added to a revised edition in the future.

On page 222, I explained briefly about occult ritual murder taking place on the west coast of Africa in present times. I added that it was not an uncommon occurrence for children in West Africa to become occult ritual murder victims. Since I made those comments, national newspapers, including the *Mail on Sunday,* and various television news programmes carried the following story during September 2001.

The torso of a five to six year old boy, of African origin, was spotted in the Thames, near Tower Bridge, by a passer-by on 21 September 200. A post-mortem examination found the boy had had his throat cut and may have been dumped in the river up to 10 days previously. At first, the press reported that the police believed that a paedophile gang was responsible for the boy's death, and that he had been dumped from a boat in the Thames.

When I first learned of this incident, I concluded that the young boy was an occult ritual murder victim. I contacted the police at Tower Bridge and informed them of my conclusions. I also informed the television programme, *Crimestoppers*, who had asked for information relating to the crime. I added that the police were quite wrong to conclude that the victim was murdered by a paedophile gang. I also contacted Scotland Yard concerning my conclusion, because of the negative attitude shown by several police officers I had spoken to about this matter.

A colonel in the African police force, who happened to be on holiday in London at the time, heard of the incident and also contacted the police to inform them that the boy found in the Thames had been the victim of a black magic occult ritual murder. Police then called in H J Scholtz – a South African expert on 'muti' occult killings – to carry out a new post-mortem. Muti occult ritual killers tend to remove the genitals, breasts and extremities of their victims. The police concluded that the young boy had been a victim of a black magic occult ritual murder.

The outcome of this conclusion was that a television company sent a crew to a village in Africa. They made a programme, highlighting black magic occult ritual murder, and in doing so, interviewed many West Africans in the village, who had either been victims of such attacks and had survived, or who had lost relatives or friends to such attacks. One young man who was interviewed had been abducted by a couple who then cut off his genitals while he was still alive.

Another man was walking with his girlfriend, along a riverbank near their village, when two men with guns appeared and scared off the young man. He ran to the village to obtain help, but when villagers arrived back at the scene, they found the girl dead. She had been very badly mutilated and certain parts of her body had been stolen.

White people are also invloved in such occult ritual murder. police arrested a woman in Scotland in connection with the murder of the young victim found in the Thames. If that body had not been found floating in the Thames, no one would have been any the wiser about occult ritual murder in this country. How many other cases would have gone undetected? How many others' bodies or body parts have been found, only to be attributed to some other incorrect motive? I have also recently learnt that two men have been arrested by Italian police in connection with the occult ritual murders in Florence, Itlay.